AMELIA EARHART LIVES

*A Trip through
Intrigue to Find America's
First Lady of Mystery*

by

JOE KLAAS

AN AUTHORS GUILD BACKINPRINT.COM EDITION

AN AUTHORS GUILD BACKINPRINT.COM EDITION

Published by iUniverse.com, Inc.

For information address:
iUniverse.com, Inc.
620 North 48th Street, Suite 201
Lincoln, NE 68504-3467
www.iuniverse.com

Originally published by McGraw-Hill Book Company

Design by Christine Aulicino

ISBN: 0-595-09038-9

Printed in the United States of America

To you,
Amelia Earhart,
wherever you are

CONTENTS

OPERATION EARHART

IN 1937 a twin-engined monoplane number NR-16020, piloted by Amelia Earhart and navigated by Fred Noonan, took off from New Guinea across the Pacific Ocean and vanished without a trace.

Twenty-four years later, in 1961, a plane bearing the same identifying number crashed into a California mountain, killing two U-2 pilots who had been making spy flights over Russia with Gary Powers.

What possible relationship could there be between the "first lady of aviation," declared drowned at sea in 1937, and the spy-in-the-sky agents a quarter of a century later in that tragically resurrected airplane?

And if she had not simply gotten lost and run out of gas at sea, what *had* happened to Amelia Earhart?

It was Major Joseph Gervais who first started Operation Earhart in 1960 with a loose coalition of Air Force officers interested in finding the answer to that question. He began it with Paul Briand, Jr., an assistant professor of English at the Air Force Academy, who while doing research for his book *Daughter of the Sky* had run across a woman, then living in California, who as a child on Saipan in 1937 remembered seeing Amelia Earhart alive. Others joined and abandoned Operation Earhart. Briand turned to another subject for his next book. And Bob Dinger, an Air Force officer and neighbor of Gervais at Okinawa in 1960, later tired of the investigation and asked me to take over as its historian. But Gervais became obsessed with the mystery and never abandoned it until he found answers. Operation Earhart became more than a mere puzzle to be solved. It became a time capsule buried in 1937 and not opened to reveal the history and intrigue it contained until now.

Operation Earhart had begun by looking for her crashed plane in the Pacific and finding it in California. We looked for her bones on Saipan and Truk and found no graves at all. Instead we found the spore there of a possibility almost beyond belief.

We found references to a white woman called Tokyo Rose. A Rose by the name of Earhart? A coincidence so obvious that it couldn't be anything but coincidence. Or could it?

We followed a trail around the world from her home, visited by White House confidants, in Toluca Lake, California, to the Imperial Palace in Tokyo.

We found not one Amelia Earhart round-the-world airplane, but two . . . or possibly three or four.

We discovered a man who said he had found Amelia Earhart and we followed him as he was shunted from one mental hospital to another for twenty-five years until he too disappeared. And we looked up the published address of this prisoner of mystery and found it to be the bottom of New York's East River.

We discovered the United States Navy had been operating on the extrasensory perception of Amelia Earhart's best friend in the biggest sea hunt for an individual in history, while the Imperial Navy of Japan apparently snatched the living prize in a most ingenious game.

And we learned of codes and surreptitious negotiations between heads of state and giants of industry in which the life of a woman may have been ransomed for that of an Emperor.

We exposed a secret so well kept it has remained shrouded in mystery until now.

We found a woman who looks like Amelia Earhart, talks like Amelia Earhart, walks like her and knows her well but won't talk.

What Joe Gervais and I found in Operation Earhart was the greatest operation since the wooden horse was gratefully dragged through the gates of Troy, and the most closely guarded secret since *The Man in the Iron Mask* was imprisoned in a castle of France.

I shall always be grateful to Lieut. Col. Robert S. Dinger, U.S. Air Force (Ret.), for relinquishing to me the opportunity to live the greatest adventure of my life. It has been like being Agent 007 or living in the middle of *The Man from U.N.C.L.E.*

CHAPTER ONE

THE BIRD

"Find Amelia Earhart's airplane and you'll learn what happened to Amelia," Joe Gervais recited to me in a sun-drenched room high in the tower of the Las Vegas Dunes Hotel one October afternoon in 1966. "You've heard that many times. Find the bird and you'll find Amelia."

Gervais, retired young as a command pilot from the United States Air Force, possessed a wild shock of gray hair and his dark eyes flashed like an eagle's beneath his bushy eyebrows. He waved an arm toward the chamois hills west of the valley of Las Vegas.

"The mountains of the world are littered with crashed airplanes," he said. "See that saddle in the mountains over there? That's where Carole Lombard crashed and died in 1942. I wonder how many bleary-eyed gamblers know their early-morning-to-bed view includes her death-place."

I reminded the often-decorated former Major that we were discussing the death-place of Amelia Earhart.

Gervais smiled. "How do you know Amelia Earhart is dead?"

I assumed she was dead, killed when her plane went down in the Pacific Ocean somewhere near Howland Island on

1

July 2, 1937, or executed by the Japanese at Saipan shortly thereafter, as many had theorized.

"The oceans of the world are also the graves of broken birds—especially the Pacific. I have examined hundreds of wrecked aircraft at Saipan and at Truk . . . looking for hers."

It was another Air Force officer, then Major Robert Dinger, who had told me about Joe Gervais. It was in 1966, while I was on reserve duty at Hamilton Air Force Base as deputy chief of information for the Sixth Air Force Reserve Region, that Dinger asked me if I would like to write a book on what happened to Amelia Earhart.

"You've got to be kidding," I laughed. "Someone has already written the story, and it's about to be published."

"Not this story," Dinger had said solemnly. "A friend of mine—Joe Gervais—and I started an investigation years ago when we were stationed on Okinawa. We decided to look for the remains of Amelia Earhart and her navigator, Fred Noonan. We called it 'Operation Earhart' and it got us into trouble with the Air Force. Finding Amelia Earhart's grave became an obsession with Gervais. I couldn't keep up with him, Joe. Perhaps you can."

Dinger had persuaded me at least to listen to Gervais, who was now saying, "I am a trained, scientific, aircraft-accident investigator. I examined the remains of every bird known to have crashed in those islands. Even the ones in the water. They are all still there, you know—all the Japanese planes and American planes that crashed there during and before the war . . . bulldozed out of the harbors of Truk and Saipan, or scattered along the beaches. I spent three days in a mangrove swamp at Truk before I found the last uninvestigated wreckage of a twin-engined aircraft that had piled in there. It turned out to be a Jap Betty bomber. Those twenty- to thirty-year-old wrecks out there are in a remarkable state of preservation, you know, both in and out of the water. Even the paint is intact."

"What about Saipan?"

"There's a shelf of coral reef just outside the harbor where the Japanese and our people shoved the wrecks to keep the harbor clear. I have skin-dived among them, examined them all. Another fellow waded in and fished up a generator which he claimed was Amelia Earhart's. It wasn't. The Bendix people identified it as a Japanese generator."

"Wasn't she seen at Saipan? After she disappeared?"

Gervais went on to tell me that he was the first to interview the natives who lived there under Japanese rule when Amelia Earhart disappeared on her round-the-world flight in 1937. He talked to witnesses who saw a twin-engined plane crash on the beach and who saw a man and a woman arrested. Many agreed that the "spy lady" had died and that the man with her had been executed.

"It was easy for me to believe that this was Amelia Earhart and that the man with her was the navigator, Fred Noonan," Gervais said. "It doesn't take any investigative training to jump to a conclusion like that. In fact, the less scientific you are about it, the more you are apt to believe that Amelia Earhart and Fred Noonan crashed at Saipan, were captured there, died there, and were buried there."

"Didn't the Marine Corps dig up their bodies in 1945 and ship them back to the States?"

"The Marine Corps says no. The Department of Defense says no. Every official source in Washington says no. We have asked. Others have asked. The answer is no."

"What do the Japanese say?"

"The Japanese say Amelia Earhart and Fred Noonan never fell into their hands."

"And the United States?"

"The United States conducted a four-and-a-half-million-dollar search with an aircraft carrier, a battleship, and four destroyers immediately after the disappearance in 1937 but did not find Noonan and Earhart . . . nor their Lockheed Electra 10E airplane."

"No body? No bones? No records? No airplane?"

"In other words, no corpus delecti. Amelia Earhart, one of the world's greatest pilots, and Fred Noonan, the most experienced aerial navigator on earth, took off from Lae, New Guinea, at 10 A.M. on July 2, 1937, bound for Howland Island where the U.S. Coast Guard cutter *Itasca* was standing by with radio direction-finding gear. And they vanished."

"Then they must be dead."

Gervais' eyes flashed. "My friend, she is not dead."

For years, he told me, he has been living with this thing; he has talked to her sister, her maid, her friends, read her letters and her poetry, studied her living habits and her flying habits.

Joe grinned self-consciously. "I know more about Amelia Earhart then anyone alive, and as far as I'm concerned, Amelia Earhart is not dead."

"But legally, she is dead."

"Her husband had her declared dead eighteen months after she vanished. Usually such a declaration without a body takes seven years. Her body was not found . . . and her plane was not found. Her body has not been found to this day."

"And her plane?"

Joe paced a little before answering. "I have found it. I have found Amelia Earhart's plane."

"In the Pacific?"

Joe shook his head. "No. Amelia Earhart and Fred Noonan vanished in the middle of the ocean in her Lockheed Electra 10E, Civil Aeronautics Authority registration number NR-16020, on July 2, 1937. A Lockheed Electra with the same registration number N-16020—the R for 'restricted use' had been removed from the number—this same airplane crashed into a moutain in California and exploded at 3 A.M. Pacific Standard Time on the morning of December 16, 1961."

Twenty-four years later?

"Here is a piece of it." Joe laid a manifold exhaust manufacturer's plate on the bed. It was dated 1937.

"And here are two photographs of the wreck."

He laid out two official Federal Aviation Agency (FAA) photographs. It was a twin-engined Lockheed Electra with a buckled wing and the forward part of the fuselage burned away. But back toward the twin-finned stabilizer, half the registration number remained on one side in the first photograph. "N-16" was painted on the port side of the fuselage. In the second photograph "020" remained painted on the starboard side. On each side the rest of the number was burned away.

"Put the two numbers together," suggested Joe. "N-16020. It was the number assigned to Amelia Earhart's aircraft. I checked it out with the Federal Aviation Agency. It was the same number—Amelia Earhart's—sure enough."

Joe leaned forward. "Now I ask you . . . if the airplane Amelia Earhart vanished in back in 1937 was still flying in California twenty-four years later, why should anyone assume Amelia Earhart is dead?"

"If she isn't . . . then what became of her?"

Joe nodded. "I think we are getting close to finding her. Find the bird, and you'll find Amelia. Well, we've found the bird. Now let's find Amelia Earhart."

CHAPTER TWO

THE TAKEOFF

When Amelia Earhart and her navigator took off from Lae, New Guinea, their destination, ostensibly, was a tiny strip of land called Howland Island, 2556 uninhabited miles eastward.

Amelia, a sensitive, artistic, and humane woman whose private life remained a mystery, was the most famous pilot since Lindbergh. Fred Noonan, a quiet man troubled by alcoholism, was a sailing-ship captain and chief plotter of overseas routes for Pan American World Airways.

Furnished with names of eyewitnesses of the takeoff from Lae by Inspector Frank Hoeter, Gervais wrote to several of them. One was Jane O'Dea, wife of T. O'Dea, of New South Wales, Australia, who was manager of the Stephens Aircraft Company at Lae.

"I shall always remember the takeoff," she wrote back to Gervais. "Every member of our tiny sun-scorched, rain-drenched settlement gathered. We stood silent and watched with bated breath as the Lockheed raced on and on down the runway. Would those wheels never leave the ground? At last, at long last, she was airborne—only just. A tiny tree at the end of the runway bent in a farewell salute as the Lockheed

AMELIA
EARHART
LIVES

Books by Joe Klaas

AMELIA EARHART LIVES

MAYBE I'M DEAD

skimmed by overhead. We watched on until she was lost in the haze that hung low over the sea . . . ."

In his tiny cubicle behind the special huge cylindrical gas tank, Fred Noonan was feeling the effects of a bad hangover as the renowned aviatrix nursed the overloaded aircraft perilously close to the ocean. Jim Collopy of Melbourne, Australia, the New Guinea district superintendent of Civil Aviation at the time, drank with Fred Noonan on a "fling" that lasted all through the night before takeoff. Collopy, who helped Noonan aboard Amelia's aircraft after less than an hour's sleep, also remembers the departure very well. He wrote:

> The takeoff was hair-raising, since the aircraft had not left the ground fifty yards from the end of the runway. When it did leave, it sank away but was by this time out over the sea. It continued to sink to about five or six feet above the water and had not climbed to more than one-hundred feet before it disappeared from sight.

Allan Board of Dolls Point, Australia, a wire-service reporter who was also there, recalls:

> Sid Marshall, who had been an aero-engineer with Guinea Airways, spent some time with Amelia Earhart and Noonan, showing them around and helping to service their Lockheed. He was standing near me at the time of the final, and near-fatal, takeoff with his movie camera, and nearly dropped it at the last minute when it looked as though the machine was not going to leave the ground.
> At the last possible moment, Amelia Earhart jumped the plane over a slightly raised road running across the seaward end of the drome, but we all had another sick feeling, and I really mean it, when it looked as though it was simply going to flop onto the sea about twenty feet

below the shore level. In fact, it went so close that the two slipstreams sent up wakes of salt spray for a considerable distance, and when disappearing from sight about twenty miles out it was just beginning to raise from sea level.

Harry Balfour, the Lae radio operator, now living in Cairns, Australia, remembers the Earhart-Noonan arrival:

I called the aircraft on 6540 kilocycles but received no reply at any time, but that was explained later . . . she had no knowledge that we were equipped for aeronautical communication. On arrival she was met by all the necessary "big shots" and plans were made to give them both a great social round-up. She acknowledged the welcome and was very nice to everybody and was photographed quite a lot by T. O'Dea.

Amelia Earhart and Fred eventually settled into the hotel at Lae and would not see anyone, but sent a message that she particularly wanted to see me.

I went down to the hotel and she wanted all the weather and private messages that had stacked up for her. I went over all these with her in detail and she asked me if I could come to the hotel each day and bring the weather reports and any other traffic for her. Fred trotted around quite a bit. I cannot remember everywhere we went, but Amelia Earhart was so enthusiastic over the flight that she did not want to go anywhere or be entertained by the local ladies, much to the displeasure of the local ladies.

She never even dressed like a woman while she was in Lae. She had her hair cut short like a man, and wore trousers and a checkered shirt, and from a short distance she looked like a slim freckle-faced youth. But to talk to, she was very charming and seemed to take in all that was said to her. She was an excellent pilot, and won the respect of our pilots for the way she handled that Lockheed.

Two days before her flight from Lae, she unloaded quite a lot of surplus weight such as books, papers, ammunition, and automatic pistol. I was to hold them and forward them to her when she requested them. The majority of the stuff I still have. I have not seen it now for some years, but it still exists.

Joe Gervais became curious about what Harry Balfour meant by Fred Noonan's "trotting around" in Lae. In a specially arranged interview at the Imperial Hotel in Tokyo, Gervais found the answer. The man who told him had been the radio operator at Bulolo, the mining village a few miles from Lae, at the time of the Earhart-Noonan layover there. His name is Alan Vagg.

"When Amelia Earhart and Fred Noonan arrived at Lae they were billeted in the local hotel. It was a rather rowdy place, with something of the wild frontier saloon atmosphere. Amelia Earhart did not like it, left, and stayed at the home of Eric Chater during her entire time at Lae. Fred stayed at this hotel and liked it. He struck up a warm friendship with Jim Collopy, who was also residing there. Jim and Fred hit it off from the first meeting and while there had one hell of a good time. While Amelia Earhart was concerning herself with arrangements, servicing, and final preparations, Noonan and Collopy were having a real fling."

Noonan complained that he had not had a drink of alcohol the entire two-thirds of the way around the world with Amelia. This was an unusual dry spell for him. His drinking habits had interfered with his career as chief navigator for Pan American, even though he had charted most of the overseas routes which the airline was then flying to South America and across the Pacific. Noonan looked upon the Earhart round-the-world flight as a second chance, and hoped to set up an aerial navigation school which would thrive as a result of the publicity. Vagg described Noonan's feelings up to the time of their arrival at Lae.

"Noonan told Collopy that the whole flight had been a real push-push program, with Amelia Earhart pushing Fred every minute since they had left Miami. Fred said he had 'had a belly full and was going to relax a little.'

"At 7:30 A.M. on the day of their takeoff from Lae, Jim and Fred had just returned to the local hotel after being out all night living it up. At 8:15 Amelia Earhart arrived at the hotel and knocked on Fred's door. Jim answered because Fred was asleep. Jim said Fred was getting dressed, for her not to wait, and he would bring Fred out to the airfield in a few minutes. Amelia Earhart was satisfied and departed for the airfield. Jim managed to get Fred ready and out to the airfield, where Fred and Amelia Earhart took off at 10 A.M."

Noonan had an absolute maximum of forty-five minutes to sleep off a night-long fling. An hour and a half after being abruptly awakened he was in the air as navigator on a virgin course. His responsibility was to hit an island 2½ miles by ½ mile some twenty-odd hours later and 2556 miles across the world's largest ocean.

They never arrived at Howland Island. The largest air-sea search in history failed to turn up any sign of them.

CHAPTER THREE

MISSION'S END

In June of 1936, a year before the last known flight of Amelia Earhart, the Army Air Corps awarded Lockheed a contract to build a modified Electra 10 capable of holding pressure in the cabin. The experimental craft was designated XC-35 and became the world's first successful pressurized substratospheric airplane.

Outwardly, the XC-35's appearance was much the same as that of the 10E Electra built for Amelia Earhart's round-the-world flight.

Inwardly, however, Lockheed engineers beefed up the XC-35 circular cross-section cabin with heavy doors and internal bracing. The XC-35 weighed 1486 pounds more than Amelia Earhart's similar-appearing Electra because it was designed to hold a 10-pounds-per-square-inch differential between inside and outside pressure.

The Electra allegedly flown by Amelia had a cruising speed of 165 miles per hour at 10,000 feet. Directly behind the cockpit, two large cabin tanks with a fuel capacity of 1000 gallons had been installed to provide extended range up to 4000 miles. The distance from Lae, New Guinea, to Howland Island was 2556 miles. Amelia's original Lockheed could be expected to make the distance in seventeen to eighteen hours with fuel to spare.

The XC-35, with the first supercharged engines ever installed on an airplane, had a cruising range of forty hours and a maximum speed of 200 miles per hour. At 20,000 feet with engine superchargers it would have a speed of approximately 230 miles per hour *and a considerably increased range.*

The XC-35 could cruise up to 80 miles each hour more than Amelia's original Electra. In eighteen hours the XC-35 could wander as many as 1440 miles off any course plotted for the slower, unmodified Electra 10E and arrive *at the same place at the same scheduled time.*

Unlike the 10E Electra, the XC-35 could have flown over Truk and Saipan at anywhere from 20,000 to 30,000 feet, photographed everything below much as its descendant the U-2 did twenty-three years later over the Soviet Union, and then continued nonstop all the way across the Pacific to California with plenty of fuel to spare.

Nicknamed "The Boiler," the XC-35 made its first flight on May 7, 1937.

Amelia Earhart took off from Oakland, California, for Miami, Florida, the starting point of her second round-the-world flight attempt, on May 22, 1937. Supposedly, her aircraft was the same model 10E Lockheed Electra in which she had crashed on March 20, 1937, while trying to take off from Hickam Field at Honolulu during her first round-the-world effort. This aircraft, registry number NR-16020, had been purchased for her by Purdue University for $80,000 as a "flying laboratory." The Honolulu crash occurred because the maximum gross weight limitation had been exceeded by 5000 pounds, which proved to be too much for the two 450-horsepower engines.

Motion-picture stunt pilot Paul Mantz, a close friend and advisor to Amelia Earhart, had accompanied her on the first leg of the flight from Oakland to meet his fiancee in Honolulu.

The crash occurred at dawn while Mantz was enjoying his honeymoon. Upon being notified of the takeoff crack-up, Mantz commented, "Well, I'm not surprised."

The Electra, constructed entirely of light alloys, suffered major damage in the crash. The Army Air Corps at Hickam Field dismantled and crated the machine and shipped it back to the Lockheed factory in Los Angeles.

There is no evidence of a fund-raising drive mentioned in the press. However, in less than sixty days newspapers reported that the aircraft had been completely rebuilt with "publicly contributed funds," and that the 450-horsepower engines had been replaced by 550-horsepower Pratt and Whitney model S3H1 engines.

In addition to the unpublicized fund raising, what else was happening between March 20 and May 22, 1937?

The world's first and secret, supercharged and pressurized, substratospheric photo reconnaissance plane, the XC-35, was test-flown over California's Mojave Desert. Amelia Earhart visited the White House. President Roosevelt's top dollar-a-year advisor and trouble-shooter, Bernard Baruch, visited Amelia Earhart. Japan was definitely building top-secret illegal naval bases on the Pacific islands of Truk and Saipan according to rumors drifting into the U.S. naval facilities at Guam.

And Corporal Joseph Pelligrini at Bolling Field, Washington, D.C., in the Army Air Corps First Photo Mapping Group, was participating in a sensitive project. Upon a map of some Pacific islands, Pelligrini was drawing the guidelines for cameras installed in a civilian aircraft to be flown by a woman pilot engaged in an intelligence flight.

Dinger and Gervais learned about Corporal Pelligrini by accident. Someone told them of a chance remark made by an Air Force sergeant at a party during the war, about how a Corporal Joe Pelligrini had worked on plans at Bolling Field in 1937 for a female pilot to take photographs in the Pacific.

By the time Gervais and Dinger located the former photo

corporal, he had been promoted all the way up to Lieut. Col. Joseph J. Pelligrini with his own office in the Pentagon.

Gervais asked the colonel if he ever installed cameras in civilian aircraft while he was an enlisted man in 1937 in the Army Air Corps and specifically at Bolling Field. The question seemed to make him uneasy. Pelligrini said he did not come to Bolling until 1939. He said that in 1936 and 1937 he was stationed at Hawaii and not doing photographic work. Pelligrini did state that in 1939 at Bolling Field, as a member of the First Photo Mapping Group, he participated in a sensitive project dealing with what he thought, as he best recalled, was an intelligence flight in the guise of searching for Amelia Earhart. He recalled he specifically drew up on a map the guidelines for the cameras installed in a civilian aircraft to be piloted by a woman flyer. He could not recall the woman flyer's name. This flight and the camera guidelines were drawn up for the Japanese base of Truk in the Caroline Islands.

The story seemed a little shaky, and yet Pelligrini denied that this could have happened in 1937 at Bolling Field. In fact, he denied having been at Bolling Field or in an aerial photography assignment in 1937.

Once out of Pelligrini's office, Dinger called a friend in the personnel records section of the Pentagon. "Can we get a look at the personnel records of Lieut. Col. Joseph J. Pelligrini?"

"You know better than that."

"Well, how about getting it out for me? I want to ask you one or two very impersonal questions."

"Well . . . O.K. Wait a minute." It didn't take long. "What do you want to know?"

"Was Pelligrini stationed in Hawaii in 1937?"

"No."

"Where was he stationed?"

"At Bolling Field in the First Photo Mapping Group."

The only recorded flight by an American woman pilot

during that decade which could have passed within a thousand miles of Truk was Amelia Earhart's.

The flight plan called for an estimated flight time of seventeen to eighteen hours at an average speed of 150 miles per hour.

Harry Balfour, the radio operator at Lae, New Guinea, was the unofficial radio link at the takeoff end of the flight. Commander Warner K. Thompson, captain of the U.S. Coast Guard cutter *Itasca,* was anchored with radio direction-finding equipment at Howland Island for the express purpose of guiding the Earhart-Noonan plane "home." He was the official radio link at the arrival end. A Navy seagoing tug, the U.S.S. *Ontario,* was hove to halfway along the Lae–Howland Island route. And eastward, beyond Howland Island, a third Navy vessel, the U.S.S. *Swan,* was anchored to assist in communications for the next lap of the round-the-world hop between Howland and Honolulu.

Balfour wrote to Joe Gervais and gave him a picture of the radio setup at Lae and described what took place before and after Amelia Earhart's takeoff.

The radio equipment was composed of two transmitters, one of 300 watts phone-fed into a dipole antenna cut to 3 megacycles. This transmitter at Lae was remote-controlled from an operating position in the cargo store on the airstrip and was normally operated by the cargo superintendent for the purpose of getting cargo information from Salamaua, Wau, and Bulolo on phone, usually on 6540 kilocycles. A separate receiving antenna was swung between the hangar and the cargo store.

The second radio transmitter was in the cargo store for the purpose of receiving early morning weather reports from inland and for communication with Rabaul and Salamaua coast stations, which sent and received all our commercial traffic. All Amelia Earhart's weather reports were received over this circuit from stations on her route, as well as weather forecasts and past weather from Howland. This transmitter was both phone and key and had one kilowatt of power.

I made arrangements to keep the station open for longer periods in the evening during her stay at Lae in case any extra traffic came in via Rabaul. She was very grateful for the extra service, but the man in charge, Eric Chater of Guinea Airways, did not like it. However, it was on my own time, and I felt that anything I could do was my business, and that the radio communication was going to be an important factor in the flight.

I was anxious to prove to Amelia Earhart that my transmitter could, under normal conditions, hold communication with her to the end of her flight. Modulation was always very clear on the phone. She seemed to be very happy and relieved to know this.

Now comes a very interesting part. During one of the conferences between Amelia, Fred, and myself at the hotel, I was explaining to them how they could make use of shipping along the route by my making it possible for them to communicate with ships in range.

It was then they both admitted that they could not read Morse Code and were only able to pick out an individual letter; an undeniable handicap, since it can be understood over far greater distances than the human voice.

Balfour, in making a test hop to try out the radio equipment, was the last man other than Noonan known to have flown with Amelia Earhart.

The night before the flight they were seriously thinking of making an offer to take me with them. She asked me if I would go along if they decided they could manage with the extra weight. She informed me-that they were going to arrive in the United States on the Fourth of July, if all went well, and that it would be a national holiday, and that if I had to lose my job by coming with them she would see that I got a job with Pan American Airways.

I said that I would consult my wife about it and let her know later on in the evening. My wife thought it would be all right. I told Amelia Earhart, and she decided later that I would be of more use to the flight by looking after her interests at this end of the radio station . . . .

Apart from the test flight which I made with her, I checked her direction-finder on the ground, but only two points were checked — 000 degrees and 090 degrees, with Salamaua radio station on 500 kilocycles.

090 was the quadrant point which generally paralleled the intended track of 072 degrees to Howland Island. But 000 was north on the compass rose in the general direction of the mandated and forbidden Caroline and Marianas Islands, and more particularly, the general direction of Truk, where the Imperial Navy of Japan was secretly and illegally constructing its biggest and most heavily fortified Pacific Ocean base specifically for use in a future war with the United States.

The original Earhart Electra was equipped with one of the first loop antennae. It was fixed atop the cabin. Unlike later versions, it could not be rotated to measure signal strength in order to determine the direction of a broadcast station. Instead of rotating the antenna, the entire plane had to be turned to make the direction-finder work.

"My own personal opinion about the flight," continued Balfour, "was that it was not particularly hazardous because she had a good machine, a good radio, a good navigator with radio assistance at both ends, plenty of fuel, and up-to-date weather reports that included an excellent forecast before takeoff."

Later, during the war years, Balfour flew with Qantas on many 30-hour, 3600-mile, nonstop trips in twin-engined Catalinas through Japanese-occupied territory from Perth to Ceylon.

"I would almost consider our conditions similar to hers . . . just a flying gas tank, but we had to put up with radio silence.

"I did remark to Amelia one day, looking inside the fuselage, that even if she had to ditch, that enormous cylindrical gas tank that she carried inside would keep them afloat. I doubted it would ever sink . . . that is, if it did not break up on landing."

Balfour kept a log and wrote a report about his participation in the Earhart affair. Those were handed over to Eric Chater, and it was shortly thereafter that Balfour had a big disagreement with the management and resigned. He criticized the company in his report for not allowing him more time in which to carry out further checks on Amelia Earhart's radio equipment, and for telling him to close the station after 8 P.M. on the day of her takeoff.

So after all the communications planning, the man in whose home Amelia Earhart had been living at Lae, Eric Chater, prevented Balfour from keeping his promise of "looking after her interests at this end of the radio station."

After the takeoff, Balfour remained in communication. But he had to surrender access to the radio shack halfway into the flight. He was therefore able to offer little aid when a search was eventually required.

Balfour said, "We had no means of taking any radio bearings at Lae, but I felt that if I had stayed on all night I might have been able to pick up something or QSO the *Itasca*.

My last schedule with her was at either 7:15 or 7:45 P.M. Lae time. At that time she reported everything O.K. and on course at 7500 feet and that she would change to 3105 kilocycles for the next schedule. In the meantime I rushed home and had something to eat and drove back to the strip as soon as possible. Without my log, I cannot remember whether it was at 7:15 or 7:45 that I last contacted her on 6200/6540 kilocycles, but she was loud and clear and I particularly asked her not to change to the 3105 frequency because there was no need to do that.

Communication up to that time was excellent, and during the day people working in the cargo store could hear her over the loud-speaker.

My opinion why she wanted to change frequency was to try and contact the *Itasca,* thinking that the night frequency was better. I did hear her voice through the static, but was unable to make any sense from the signal. In fact, I could not even say if it was her. The signal I received may have been from the *Itasca.*

It was a night of fairly heavy static for phone operation, but a radio operator using Morse Code could have got through.

When the broadcast capability of a disgruntled Harry Balfour was terminated at 8 P.M. by Eric Chater at Lae, there remained at the Howland Island end of the radio link an equally disgruntled Commander Warner K. Thompson on the *Itasca.* Commander Thompson's radio log aboard the *Itasca* was classified "Secret" for twenty-five years and released on July 2, 1962. It is a log of frustration.

When he sailed from San Pedro, California, under orders to proceed to Howland Island by way of Honolulu, nobody had bothered to tell Thompson what the mission of the *Itasca* was to be. Two days out of San Pedro, he guessed that it would be to assist Amelia Earhart and asked Division at San Francisco for her radio frequencies, schedules, and plans.

Next day Division replied that it did not know. The day after that, Division told Thompson that the Coast Guard radio station at Miami reported that "Miss Earhart had, while passing through Miami, let drop that she would come up on 6210 kilocycles at fifteen minutes before the hour and fifteen minutes after and use her receiver to take bearings." It wasn't much to go on as he steamed to Pearl Harbor.

The *Itasca* lay for two days in Pearl Harbor in continuing ignorance of the mission's details. The next information came on June 16 from Amelia Earhart's husband, George Palmer Putnam, in Los Angeles in answer to a request by the Commandant of the Coast Guard. Putnam's message was relayed to Thompson aboard the *Itasca:*

"Miss Earhart plans to reach Lae, her takeoff point for Howland, June 23."

Richard Black, an official of the Interior Department who later became a rear admiral in the Navy, boarded the *Itasca.* He and an Army Lieutenant Cooper brought aboard a Navy high-frequency "emergency direction-finder."

Commander Thompson did not care for this at all. He thought "the gear was untried, erratic." He already had a solid, dependable, low-frequency direction-finder aboard the *Itasca.* But he agreed to carry the new gear to Howland Island.

Putnam appointed Black the Earhart representative aboard, and also messaged the Chief of Naval Operations that "*Itasca* will never make it to Howland on time. Please send the U.S.S. *Ontario.*"

However, on June 18, the *Itasca* boiled out of Pearl Harbor at flank speed to try and reach Howland Island by June 23 in order to "chase birds off the landing strip for the Earhart landing on June 24."

On June 20, Putnam sent a message by wireless directly to the *Itasca* saying that "when Miss Earhart reaches Darwin, Australia, I will let *Itasca* know, and will then divulge her radio plans and needs."

On June 21, the same promise of information came to Black aboard the *Itasca* from a "Hampton" at the Department of the Interior in Washington, who also suggested weather communication with Amelia Earhart via Samoa. The commander of the *Itasca* referred to Hampton, who was apparently Black's superior, as "Mrs. Hampton" in the log, where he also registered his general discontent.

"We now have the following persons endeavoring to control the Earhart flight communications: Mr. Putnam; Mrs. Hampton in Washington; San Francisco Division; and Mr. Black on *Itasca.*"

On June 22, Thompson asked Division to please get Miss Earhart to give *Itasca* twelve hours notice of her hop. On the same day, Black sent a message to James Kamakaiwi on Howland Island:

"Please burn large fire your camp site starting at dusk. Remove as many large birds as possible from runways. Catch enough lobsters for ship."

The bonfire was duly burned the night before the *Itasca* arrived at Howland Island for a lobster feed on June 23. Apparently Black believed the Earhart-Noonan plane might arrive early.

On June 24, Thompson received a message that Amelia Earhart was in Batavia and would be there three days for repairs. The *Itasca* relaxed and made an excursion trip to Baker Island, southeast of Howland.

On June 26, Division told the *Itasca* in what purported to be a definitive message from Amelia Earhart that her "homing device covers range from 200 to 1500 kilocycles and from 2400 to 4800 kilocycles. Suggest try 333 or 545. For voice use 3105."

The same day, June 26, in her one and only preflight message to the *Itasca*, Amelia Earhart said she wanted these three things:

1. U.S.S. *Ontario* (then standing halfway from Lae, New Guinea, to Howland Island) to broadcast by key the letter N on 400 kilocycles.

2. The Navy's coal burner, U.S.S. *Swan* (halfway from Howland to Hawaii), to transmit by voice on 99 kilocycles.

3. The U.S.S. *Itasca* at Howland to transmit letter A on 7.5 megacycles.

"I will give a long call in voice 3105 kilocycles quarter after hour, possibly quarter to hour," she added.

7.5 megacycles is 7500 kilocycles—2700 kilocycles higher than the limit fixed by Amelia Earhart on her direction-finding loop in the message relayed through Division. In consternation, Commander Thompson immediately asked Division to free him from all previously arranged broadcast schedules and give him complete independence of communications, using Navy relays. The request was granted.

On June 27, Putnam messaged the *Itasca* and asked Thompson to "remind Miss Earhart to have lots of publicity pictures taken to bring home with both stills and movies."

On the same day, an informational copy of an Amelia Earhart message to another station for weather reports indicated she thought there was a meteorologist aboard the *Itasca*. There wasn't.

By way of the Navy on June 28, Thompson sent his only message to Amelia Earhart in an effort to clear up the radio picture: "*Itasca* transmitters calibrated to 7500, 6210, 3105, 500, 425. *Itasca* direction-finder frequency range 550 to 570 kilocycles."

The message referred only to the low-frequency-range direction-finder which was permanent equipment aboard the *Itasca*. No reference was made to the direction-finder brought aboard at Pearl Harbor by Black, although this high-frequency emergency Navy direction-finder had already been set up ashore on Howland Island.

On June 29, Amelia Earhart was reported by Division to be en route from Darwin, Australia, to Lae and planning a July 1 takeoff. The same day, Putnam messaged his globe-circling wife news of a "nice, fat radio contract back home." And Amelia Earhart sent a message to Black aboard the *Itasca*:

"Understand *Itasca* to transmit long continuous signal on 3105."

In a June 30 entry in the log, Commander Thompson reflected on the fact that "*Itasca* doesn't know just what Earhart's plans are." In Thompson's words, "Entire day of July 1 was devoted to trying to ascertain whether Earhart had hopped."

It was July 1 aboard the *Itasca* at Howland and July 2 at

Lae, New Guinea, when the Earhart plane took off, scheduled to arrive at Howland Island the next morning but on the same date, July 2, having gained a day on the calendar by crossing the international date line.

The world received word of the takeoff when Jim Collopy sent a wireless to Amalgamated Wireless, Limited, in Sydney, Australia: EARHART LEFT LAE TEN AM SECOND DELAYED LAE AWAITING WEATHER REPORTS — COLLOPY.

The message was dated 9 A.M., July 2, 1937, at Lae.

Late in the day, first via San Francisco Division, then by the press, then by message to Black signed "Vacuum," the *Itasca* received word she had started the 2560-mile flight.

The Coast Guard cutter settled down for a long night vigil. Commander Thompson figured she would land about 8 o'clock next morning, refuel, and be off toward Honolulu. Boat parties were organized in the event she landed nearby at sea. The Navy's new high-frequency direction-finder was manned ashore by *Itasca* radiomen. The runways were cleared of birds. The cutter's searchlights were set to go on after midnight. The ship's boilers would "make smoke like mad" with the breaking dawn. There was nothing now but to wait . . . and listen.

By midnight things began to get tense. Fifteen minutes before each hour and fifteen minutes after—the times scheduled for her to broadcast—all ears in the radio shack aboard the *Itasca* strained toward the ship's receivers. There was no sound except static.

Officers, radio operators, and newspapermen waited through the night in the little shack. It was a July night right on the equator and there was no air conditioning.

A quarter to one came and a quarter after. There was still no word, although she should have been well within radio range by then.

A quarter to two . . . a quarter after. Still nothing.

But at a quarter to three a voice burst through the static.

It was unintelligible, but newspapermen identified the voice as Amelia Earhart's. Only the words "cloudy and overcast" could be understood.

On the dot of 3:45 A M. a clear message came through at last.

"*Itasca* from Earhart. *Itasca* from Earhart. Overcast. Will listen on the hour and on the half-hour."

The *Itasca* had been calling the Earhart plane on 3105 kilocycles all night.

Nothing was heard at the next scheduled broadcast time of 4:15 A.M., nor at 4:45. At 4:55 A.M., according to the log, "Earhart broke in on phone unreadable."

The *Itasca* kept calling. At 5:15 A.M. nothing. Nothing at 5:45. The *Itasca* called and called and received no reply. From 6 A.M. on, the log entries give only the gist of what was heard or said:

"0615: Earhart wants bearing on 3105 KC on the hour and will whistle in mike.

"0615: About 200 miles out approximately; whistling."

Commander Thompson used his radio to call the Navy's direction-finder ashore on Howland Island. He asked his crew there if they had gotten a bearing on Amelia Earhart's whistling transmission. They replied that she hadn't whistled long enough on the air for the Navy direction-finder to get a minimum signal necessary to take a bearing.

"0645: KHAQQ [Earhart] said please take bearing on us and report in half an hour. About 100 miles out."

Radiomen estimate the strength of voice signals on a scale of from 1 for weak signals through 5 for a strong signal. The *Itasca* log duly noted a rating for Amelia Earhart's 6:45 A M. voice broadcast: "Signal strength a strong four; but she still wasn't up long enough for Howland DF to get a cut . . . nor on a frequency from which *Itasca* could even try to get one." The lament refers to the fact that the standard-equipment direction-finder aboard the Coast Guard cutter was a low-frequency receiver with a range of from 270 to 550 kilocycles.

Amelia Earhart was transmitting on 3105 kilocycles. The Navy direction-finder ashore was the only one that could have measured her bearing from Howland Island.

The log continues. "Nothing from KHAQQ at 7:15. At 0718 *Itasca* said by radiophone to Earhart 'can't take bearing so good on 3105. Send on 500.'"

There was no acknowledgment, and indeed there had been no reply to any *Itasca* message all night long. But then Amelia Earhart came on again.

"0742 from KHAQQ: 'We must be on you but we cannot see you. Gas is running low. Been unable to reach you by radio. Flying at 1000 feet. Only half-hour's gas left.'"

The next message came four minutes later.

"We are circling but cannot hear you. Go ahead on 7500 either now or on the scheduled time on half-hour."

The *Itasca* radio log noted that the reception strength of that message was "maximum 5," or loud and clear. Commander Thompson attempted to call on 7500 kilocycles.

A reply from Amelia Earhart came for three minutes beginning at 8 A.M., according to the *Itasca* radio log. "KHAQQ calling *Itasca*. We received your signals but unable to get a minimum. Please take bearing on us and answer on 3105 with voice." The Earhart transmitter then broadcast a series of long dashes for five seconds on 3105 kilocycles.

The log notes that the Navy direction-finder on Howland Island again failed to get a minimum signal necessary to take a bearing on the aircraft. The *Itasca*'s 550-kilocycle direction-finder was incapable of picking up the 3105-kilocycle transmission at all.

The log records the last official message from Amelia Earhart at "0844–46: We are in line of position 157-337. Will repeat this message. We will repeat this message on 6210 KC. Wait listening on 6210. We are running north and south."

The signal strength was still tops at "maximum 5." Throughout the message there was a definite rising note of anxiety in her voice.

Itasca waited.

But that was all.

In her last message Amelia Earhart had directed those aboard the *Itasca* to "Wait listening on 6210."

Fourteen minutes of waiting convinced Commander Thompson that Amelia Earhart and Fred Noonan were down at sea. He assumed her "line of position 157-337" to be a northwest-southeast line through Howland Island from 157 degrees on the compass rose to 337 degrees. The Commander had to make a quick decision whether to race his cutter to the rescue on a course 157 degrees southeast from Howland Island or 337 degrees northwest.

Considering the stength of her radio signals, Thompson assumed she must have come very close to Howland Island. He quickly reasoned that to the south she would have seen either nearby Baker Island or the ten-mile wall of smoke laid down by the *Itasca*, which was blowing to the southeast. It seemed more likely Amelia Earhart had near-missed to the unlandmarked northwest than to the easily identifiable southeast.

The *Itasca* sped forty miles along a 337-degree northwesterly course from Howland Island and proceeded to cover a quadrant of ocean. The plane had buoyancy from its great empty gas tanks and could be expected to float for a long time if it had been ditched in the sea.

Word flashed around the world that Amelia Earhart was down at sea.

CHAPTER FOUR

THE SEARCH
IN THE PACIFIC

The premise upon which Commander Thompson based his search northwest of Howland was that "line of position 157–337" as broadcast by the missing woman flyer had indicated a line of position bearing directly on Howland Island.

Joe Gervais, who has flown the Pacific before and during his investigation into the Earhart-Noonan disappearance, asked a very logical question.

If Amelia Earhart and Fred Noonan were unable to get a bearing on Howland Island—indeed, did not even know in which direction Howland Island lay—then how could they give a "line of position" based on Howland Island at all?

It seems to follow, then, that their "line of position 157–337" was on something other than Howland Island, for which they were desperately searching.

A San Francisco radio announcer, Fred Goerner, who wrote a best-selling book, *The Search for Amelia Earhart*, theorized that "Fred [Noonan] succeeded in shooting a sun line—157–337 degrees—and in desperation Amelia radioed that to *Itasca*. They had no reference point with which to place themselves along the sun line, but at least it was something."

A sun line 157–337 degrees at the equator at 8 A.M. in July would have been something, all right. It would have meant the earth was off its axis. If Noonan were looking at the sun through his sextant, as a lost navigator would be apt to do, and they were within five or six hundred miles of Howland Island, the instrument would have revealed them to be reasonably somewhere between the equator and 5 or 6 degrees north or south latitude and 165 to 175 degrees west longitude.

At 8 A.M., in the near vicinity of the equator, the sun could not have been climbing above the horizon at 157 degrees, which is south-by-southeast, nor could it have been anywhere in the sky at 337 degrees, which is north-by-northwest. No matter in which direction the plane was flying (and Amelia Earhart in the same message said they were "running north and south"), the sun would still have been shining from the east at roughly 60 degrees.

The disappearance and ensuing search for Amelia Earhart has been rated by journalists as one of the ten biggest stories of the century. Involvement of the shocked public in the search was staggering. Millions of radio listeners remained by their sets waiting for word of the fallen heroine.

Amateur radio "ham" operators throughout the world began hearing messages from the fallen flyers, although the Navy and Coast Guard reported hearing nothing. After forty-eight hours some of these operators in Los Angeles reported the flyers had signaled they were "down and alive" southeast of Howland Island. Commander Thompson diverted the search of the U.S.S. *Itasca* to that area as a result of reports from the amateur short-wave set owners. He later characterized most of these reports as "deliberate fabrications," and believed they had confused him with "critically false transmissions."

A States-side radio network program, *The March of Time,* dramatized the entire flight, disappearance, and search. The program itself was heard by dozens of "ham" operators who immediately flashed that they had indeed heard Amelia Earhart and Fred Noonan. Amateurs hearing the U.S.S. *Itasca* broadcasts calling out the Earhart plane's call letters KHAQQ mistakenly reported they were picking up the signals from Amelia Earhart herself.

The Lockheed Aircraft Corporation sent a message to the *Itasca* that parts of the Electra, which they had built, were so situated that the radio transmitter "positively could not broadcast if the plane was in the water."

Amelia Earhart's husband, in California, figured he knew exactly what had happened and messaged Commander Thompson where and how to search.

Black and Thompson, on board ship, didn't see eye to eye about what to do. The Commander ignored Black, along with some other Interior Department civilians.

A finishing touch to the confusion came from the fact that Howland Island lies near the 180-degrees-longitude international date line. The practice of using Greenwich mean time for communications had not yet been established. So the *Itasca* and those talking to her were often using different names for the same day or the same name for different days.

The night following the disappearance, a Navy patrol plane took off from Hawaii and approached within 420 miles of Howland Island. It then turned back to Honolulu after running into snow and sleet squalls in the vicinity of the equator.

President Roosevelt ordered the 33,000-ton battleship U.S.S. *Colorado,* stationed at Pearl Harbor, to steam flank speed for the search area southeast of Howland Island in the Phoenix Group. The United States' mightiest aircraft carrier, the U.S.S. *Lexington,* was dispatched along with four destroyers from San Diego to comb the islands of the Pacific for signs of survival.

The Navy's U.S.S. *Ontario* arrived at Howland Island on July 7, and her skipper, being senior to Thompson, relieved him of responsibility.

When Joe Gervais was allowed to look at the *Itasca* radio log after it had been classified for twenty-five years, he learned someone else had gotten there ahead of him. Hollywood stunt pilot Paul Mantz turned up in the investigation again. The former advisor to Amelia Earhart had been given special permission to look at the log.

There were some pencil marks in the margins with the word "include" written several times. At one place the word "omit" was penciled, and there was evidence that every one of the log pages had been photographed with the "Confidential" label covered.

The sentence marked for omission was: "The Navy direction-finder on Howland was powered by *Itasca*'s gun batteries, *which ran down during the night.*"

This, then, explained why the high-frequency Navy direction-finder ashore never got a bearing on any of Amelia Earhart's transmissions. Never once had she broadcast on frequencies below 500 kilocycles, which could have been picked up by the *Itasca*'s low-frequency direction-finder. And the high-frequency direction-finder she might have been depending upon was out of order because of run-down batteries.

The U.S.S. *Itasca* steamed 337 degrees northwest and thus began the greatest peacetime sea hunt for an individual in history.

The first published hint in the United States that it might have been something else as well appeared in the November, 1942 issue of *Skyways* magazine in an article entitled "The War's First Casualty? Amelia Earhart."

To find Amelia Earhart, the U.S. Navy launched the most wide-flung search in the history of aviation. For sixteen days, American and Japanese ships and planes literally combed the waters of the Southwest Pacific. The then-strange names of islands and island groups flared momentarily in public consciousness and were quickly forgotten—the Solomon Islands . . . the Marshall Islands . . . the Gilbert Islands—names which have been indelibly etched in the memory of all Americans—and Japanese—since the fateful Sunday in December, 1941.

The article asked a question which is still being asked today:

Were these two flyers the first victims in the present war between the United States and Japan? Did an alert U.S. Navy, already aware in 1937 that America sooner or later would be locked in conflict with the small yellow "Aryans" of Nippon, grasp an opportunity to observe secret war preparations in the closely guarded Japanese-mandated islands—strategic stepping-stones between Hawaii and the heart of Japan? . . .

If we assume, then, that the greatest rescue expedition in the history of flying was actually predicated upon an extraordinary opportunity to pry beneath the lid of secrecy covering Japanese activities in the South Pacific in 1937, the Navy deserves an accolade for a piece of smart thinking and execution which may prove to have supplied a turning point in the present struggle.

While the press of the United States may have been more naïve than our government in such matters by not mentioning for years what now appears to be obvious, this was not true of the foreign press. *Pacific Islands Monthly,* published in Australia on August 25, 1937, less than a month after the naval search was called off, regarded the entire affair with sophisticated amusement in a story datelined:

HONOLULU, July 14. Japan pulled an interesting bit of Yankee bluff during the search for the missing American aviators, Mrs. Earhart Putnam and Mr. Fred Noonan, in the vicinity of the Phoenix and Gilbert Islands.

For long Japan has been intrigued by the American activities on Jarvis, Baker and Howland, the newly colonized equatorial islands, and by British activities south-east of Japan's mandated islands.

Instantly the American aviators were missing, the Japanese Government through Washington offered every facility for the search. Japan wasted no time. The U.S. Navy soon reported that a Japanese aircraft carrier, convoyed by a navy survey ship and several warships, was steaming toward Howland, which the U.S. army and navy have converted into a modern airport, suitable for the longest-ranged military aircraft.

Politely Japanese Ambassador Hiroshi Saito in Washington informed U.S. Secretary for State Cordell Hull that the Japanese war vessels simply wanted to be of service!

So, by using Japanese Marshall Islands as operating bases, the Japanese have inspected the Gilbert, Ellice and Phoenix Groups, and gone further eastward to Howland and Baker, and, it is possible, northward towards the Hawaiian Islands to Johnston (midway between Hawaii and Howland) where America is creating a new and permanent patrol airboat operating base.

The Japanese have tackled the search with the same enthusiasm as the American navy and coast guard ships have inspected the three groups which are British-owned. The American press has not mentioned that, of course. And, off the record in private to reporters, U.S. navy officials boast that the long-range planes from the aircraft carrier *Lexington* will take more than a peep at the Marshall Islands (Japanese Mandate)!

It is most likely that the U.S. Government will not permit any more long-distance flights to be undertaken by American aviators. The Government stopped the proposed New York–Paris air race, in celebration of the 10th anniversary of Lindbergh's solo flight, from starting from American soil, and Mrs. Putnam's ill-fated flight was okayed only because she was a close friend of the President's wife. The newspapers did not hesitate to ask of what use was the flight, what did it contribute to the science of aviation that already was not known?

The article continued with details of the flight and then regarded with wry objectivity some Yankee behavior and reactions.

The following week proved a tremendous strain for everybody involved in the search and this included dozens of amateur radio operators, who remained at their sets almost without sleep. The strain was climaxed when Mr. George Palmer Putnam, husband of the missing aviatrix, requested the U.S. navy to fly him from Hawaii down to Howland Island so that there he might set up a broadcast series and play up the search commercially on American national networks.

In very plain language, Rear Admiral Orin G. Murfin, in charge of the search, turned down the extraordinary request.

Bitter criticism of the navy's hunt for the aviators with costly battleships and aircraft carriers rang out in the U.S. Congress. Representative Charles I. Faddis, of Pennsylvania, said what was in millions of people's minds:

"Do you suppose the navy would spend 250,000 dollars a day to hunt for some poor fisherman, perhaps the father of a family, if he were lost in the Pacific?"

Added Representative Byron N. Scott, of California: "It is time someone in authority announced that henceforth the navy would not be used to search for 'publicity-stunt' aviators."

During sixteen days' search, this veritable task force—a battleship with three catapult planes aboard, an aircraft carrier with sixty-three planes, four destroyers, a cruiser, two Coast Guard cutters, and a minesweeper—covered 250,000 square miles of ocean, and the aircraft involved scoured a radius of 150,000 square miles.

That the Japanese Imperial Navy also had a task force in those waters escaped the attention of the American press, but was duly noted in Australia's *Pacific Islands Monthly.* The diplomatic charm and etiquette involved in bringing this second and alien task force into the operation was discovered by Joe Gervais in the National Archives in a "Memorandum by Mr. Joseph W. Ballantine of the Division of Far Eastern Affairs of a Conversation with the Second Secretary of the Japanese Embassy (Hayama)."

(Washington) July 5, 1937

Mr. Hayama informed Mr. Ballantine over the telephone that the Japanese Embassy had received an urgent telegram from Tokyo asking that inquiry be made of this Government whether the Japanese Government could be of assistance in connection with the search for Amelia Earhart, in view of the fact that Japan had radio stations and warships in the Marshall Islands. Mr. Ballantine expressed his appreciation of the kind offer of the Japanese Government and said that he would refer it at once to the authorities of the American Government.

It was a diplomatic trap. Just as the emotional climate of a watching world would make it too embarrassing for Japan to object to a U.S. fleet's search of forbidden waters for a famous lost woman flier, it would be impossible for the United States to object too strenuously to any Japanese warships in the vicinity looking among the islands which might contain our own secret interests.

Ballantine quickly got into touch with Stanley K. Hornbeck, chief of the Division of Far Eastern Affairs for the State Department. Hornbeck talked to Admiral Leahy and Ballantine got back on the phone to the Japanese Embassy.

"Mr. Ballantine told Mr. Hayama that the Navy had received a faint message which offered a clue that Miss Earhart's plane might be down at a spot about 200 miles north of Howland Island, that the U.S.S. *Lexington* was now on its way to the spot from the Pacific Coast, and the *Colorado* from Honolulu, but that as the spot in question was some days' sailing distant, if the Japanese Government had any vessels which could reach the spot earlier any assistance they could give would be appreciated."

At that moment, the U.S.S. *Colorado,* which would arrive on the scene days ahead of the U.S.S. *Lexington,* was heading not for a point 200 miles north of Howland Island, as the Japanese had been told, but boiling along at flank speed directly for the Phoenix Group of islands more than 400 miles southeast of Howland Island. There were no U.S. installations north of Howland, but on Canton Island in the Phoenix Group there was an airstrip with a 6000-foot runway capable of landing any airplane in the air . . . then or now.

The next day, July 6, 1937, Ballantine received a phone call from the Japanese Ambassador's second secretary.

"Mr. Hayama telephoned that the Naval Attaché of the Japanese Embassy had been informed that the Japanese Navy Department had instructed the survey ship *Koshu,* 2500 tons, which is now somewhere in the South Seas, to take part in the search for the airplane of Miss Earhart and to get into touch with Japanese vessels near the place where Miss Earhart's airplane is reported to have been lost."

The U.S.S. *Colorado* with its three catapult planes was still a day away from joining force with the *Itasca.* And it was three days away from a point from which it could catapult the planes to have a look at the Phoenix Group, toward which it had been actually ordered. The U.S.S. *Swan* was heading toward Canton Island in the Phoenix Group to put ashore a landing party to see if the landing strip there had been used by the fallen flyers.

Now an entirely different kind of message than the "faint message which offered a clue that Miss Earhart's plane might be down at a spot about 200 miles north of Howland Island" was used in an effort to shift any potential Japanese naval assistance farther westward toward the British-held Gilbert Islands. As bizarre as it may seem, the new information to be fed to the volunteering Japanese was ESP—extrasensory perception.

Reportedly, Amelia Earhart's husband, George Palmer Putnam, had called upon a close family friend and number-two-rated woman flyer, Jacqueline Cochran. "Jackie," who was married to Floyd Odlum, one of the big financial contributors to the Earhart round-the-world attempt, claimed to be able to locate crashed airplanes by occult vision. The story given out at the time was that she and Amelia had often discussed and believed in extrasensory perception. Once when a plane had disappeared on a flight between Los Angeles and Salt Lake City, Amelia Earhart had actually looked three days for the crash at a location which Jackie used her strange and wonderful powers to describe, including details of landscape and roads at the site. The downed plane in that instance was not found from the air by Amelia because snow covered it; but it was found there the following spring after the snows had melted. It was reported that on another occasion, Jacqueline Cochran was able to use her second sight to locate a missing airliner that had crashed on a mountainside exactly as she had described it, with its "nose pointed downward." Paul Mantz was in on these ESP demonstrations of locating downed airplanes.

According to Putnam, Amelia and Jackie had agreed that if she should ever turn up missing on a flight, Jackie would tell the searchers where to look for her. Jackie applied her extrasensory perception and "saw" where the plane had gone down in the Pacific, that it had ditched in the ocean, that Amelia was alive but Fred Noonan had fractured his head against the bulkhead, and that the plane was floating on the water. Although she had never heard the name of the Coast Guard cutter assigned to Howland Island, she "saw" and named the *Itasca,* according to the report.

Not satisfied that the 2500-ton survey ship *Koshu* was the full complement of Japanese naval forces in the area, Secretary of State Cordell Hull used Jacqueline Cochran's extrasensory information in a message on July 10 to the Japanese government through our Ambassador Grew in Tokyo. The message was designed, if followed, to suck the Japanese Navy even further away from the American islands toward the British Gilbert Islands in the west.

Washington, July 10, 1937 — 2 P.M.

The authorities of the Navy Department and the relatives of Miss Earhart express the opinion that if Miss Earhart's plane was forced down on the ocean it may have drifted, because of the prevailing currents, in the general direction of the Gilbert Islands.

In view of the urgency of the time element involved, please endeavor to advise the appropriate authorities of the Japanese Government immediately of these facts and state to them that because of the generous offer of assistance tendered by the Japanese Government and because of the continuing interest which the Japanese Government has taken in the search for Miss Earhart's plane, your Government suggests that if any suitable vessels or airplanes of the Japanese Government are located in or near the Gilbert Islands they may be asked to be on the lookout for Miss Earhart's plane.

Please telegraph such reply as may be made to you by the Japanese Government.

Hull

Meanwhile, according to the captain's report of the U.S.S. *Colorado*, a flight of three catapult planes was launched on July 9.

The purpose of the flight in the afternoon was to search the water ahead of the ship to locate Hull Island and to search the island and the water in the vicinity for any signs of the Earhart plane.

The U.S.S. *Swan* was looking over Canton Island with its 6000-foot runway at one end of the Phoenix Group, and planes from the U.S.S. *Colorado* were looking for Hull Island at the other end of the Phoenix Group. The report continues:

As the planes approached Hull Island, natives were seen running out of their huts and waving clothes at the plane. Lieutenant John O. Lambrecht, the senior aviator and in charge of the flight, landed for the purpose of asking if the inhabitants had seen or heard of the Earhart plane. A European Resident Manager of the natives came out in a canoe to meet the plane. He and his natives were astonished and excited in seeing the three planes. The Resident Manager asked where the planes were from and, when informed Honolulu, nearly upset the canoe in his excitement. It was necessary to explain to him that the planes had not come direct but had arrived by the battleship *Colorado*, which was relatively close by. The Resident Manager said that there was a radio on the island, however, he knew nothing of the Earhart flight and created doubt of his having ever heard of Miss Earhart herself. Neither he nor his natives had seen or heard a plane. The planes returned to the ship . . . .

During the night the ship steamed north and then east . . . .

The *Swan* had been directed . . . to proceed to rendezvous with the *Colorado* . . . and to search in the vicinity of Canton Island en route. The planes were launched [again] at 0700 and proceeded to Sydney,

Phoenix, Enderbury and Birnie Islands in the order named . . . .

At 11 A.M. the next day, July 11, Ambassador Grew telegraphed the reply to Secretary of State Hull's request for Japanese aircraft and naval vessels to assist in the search near the Gilbert Islands.

Contents of Department's telegram under reference communicated immediately to Senior Aide to the Navy Minister who stated that no Japanese aircraft in the area but survey ship *Koshu* has proceeded toward Marshall Islands and should now be there. Japanese radio stations have been ordered to be on continuous watch for Earhart signals and many Japanese fishing craft in and to east of Marshall Islands have been instructed to be on lookout. The Senior Aide expressed greatest willingness to cooperate.

Grew

So far the announced Japanese participation in the U.S. naval maneuvers during the search consisted of one insignificant ship *Koshu*, steaming toward Japan's protectorate, the Marshall Islands, more than 600 miles north of Howland Island.

But on the next day, July 12, 1937, a letter which had been in transit by slow boat and finally train since June 25 arrived to reveal the actual strength of the Japanese Imperial Navy in the area. The letter, which was sent by regular mail from the United States Consul at Yokohama to the Secretary of State, revealed not only Japanese naval strength, but also Japanese sensitivity and behavior in the interest of keeping her Pacific secrets.

Yokohama, June 25, 1937
[Received July 12]
SIR: I have the honor to report, as of possible interest to the Department, that an officer of this Consulate has

had several interviews with Captain Alfred Parker, who was an applicant at this office for a Section 3 (2) Non-immigration Visa, concerning his experiences and observations while stranded in the Japanese Mandated Islands.

Captain Parker, a Norwegian subject, was the captain of the M.S. *Fijian,* a motorship under Panamanian registry and owned by Flood Brothers, 444 Market Street, San Francisco, California, which sank after an explosion, on March 25, 1937, near the island of Majuro. The captain and crew, consisting of Norwegian and Chinese nationals, were rescued by the Japanese vessel, *Shinko Maru.* They were taken by this vessel to the island of Ahrno.

After staying at Ahrno for 36 hours, the *Shinko Maru* proceeded to the island of Jaluit. [Jaluit is roughly 650 miles northwest of Howland Island.]

At Jaluit the captain and crew of the *Fijian* disembarked under police supervision. They remained on this island from March 28 to April 24, on which date they sailed on the *Kasagi Maru* for Yokohama. En route to Yokohama, the vessel made brief stops at the islands of Kusaie, Ponape, Truk and Saipan.

According to Captain Parker he was questioned by the police on 21 different occasions during his stay at Jaluit. He believes that the police regarded him as a spy of some foreign nation and for that reason greatly restricted his freedom of action on Jaluit and refused to allow him or the members of the crew to land at any of the islands visited en route to Yokohama.

Captain Parker stated that Jaluit has an excellent harbor which can only be entered by vessels under the guidance of pilots familiar with the reef formations in the channel. *There were three Japanese naval destroyers and one airplane carrier stationed in Jaluit harbor.* The captain saw no indications of fortifications on the island.

While on Jaluit Captain Parker became acquainted with Mr. Carl Heine, a missionary representative of the American Foreign Board of Missions, who has been on the islands for 48 years. Mr. Heine travels throughout the Mandated Islands in his work and is acquainted with a number of Japanese naval officers. Mr. Heine stated that these officers had told him that their naval plans provided for the immediate capture of Guam in case of war between Japan and the United States. Captain Parker also stated that Mr. Heine did not believe that the Japanese would allow him to leave the islands.

Captain Parker observed from the vessel on the voyage to Yokohama that a large airport was being constructed on the island of Kusaie. He stated that of the islands visited radio stations were located on Jaluit, Truk and Saipan.

The Consulate has no way of verifying Captain Parker's statements.

Very respectfully yours,

Richard F. Boyce

So long before the U.S.S. *Colorado* had its three catapult planes flying over the Phoenix Group on the ninth of July, and before the U.S.S. *Lexington* arrived to put sixty of its planes into the air on July 13, the Japanese had their own task force on hand—three destroyers and an aircraft carrier from nearby Jaluit in the Marshall Islands. That air-and-sea force of Japan had been waiting there for four months . . . ever since Amelia Earhart had started her first round-the-world flight attempt from Oakland in March of 1937. And also, the Japanese carrier, the *Akagi*, carried low-winged metal combat planes, far superior to the biplanes aboard the U.S.S. *Lexington*.

During the month of April, while the Japanese interceptor force lay anchored at Jaluit, Bernard Baruch and Brigadier General Oscar Westover visited Amelia Earhart on three separate occasions in her home at Toluca Lake, while her Electra which had crashed in Hawaii on March 19 during her first west-east attempt was being "repaired" at the nearby Lockheed plant. Joe Gervais learned this from the Earhart maid, Margot DeCarie, now living in Los Angeles. The Lockheed XC-35 was being test-flown over nearby Mojave Desert. And Corporal Joseph Pelligrini was drawing his guidelines on a map of the Pacific.

And in Jaluit harbor, a Japanese aircraft carrier with a full complement of the latest-type combat planes aboard and an escort of three destroyers patiently waited.

"If Earhart and Noonan wanted to refuel in the middle of the Pacific Ocean," Gervais asked, "why did they pick that flyspeck of an island at Howland with its bird-ridden runway? Why not that great big long runway that had already been used by Pan American Airways at Canton Island in the Phoenix Group, with six other islands around it for easy landmarks?"

And if the lost plane was aiming for Howland, then why was Canton Island the first place headed for by the U.S.S. *Swan,* and a searching party put ashore? And the first place headed for by the U.S.S. *Colorado* was also in the Phoenix Group, where one of its planes landed in the lagoon at the other end of the cluster at Hull Island.

By prearrangement with Bernard Baruch and General Westover, could Amelia Earhart have flown the Army's pressurized XC-35 on a photographic mission to Truk? Then, with the increased range and speed of the XC-35's supercharged engines, could she have flown a long beeline for Canton Island, breaking radio silence only after intercepting her announced course a couple of hundred miles west of Howland Island so that the direction-finders, if they had worked, would finally pick her up in the right direction?

On this course, from Truk to Canton Island, she could easily have picked up more valuable photographs while passing over the Japanese airfields at Ponape, Kusaie, and Tarawa—all on course from Truk to Canton.

And then could she have continued on, intending to disappear for a couple of weeks at Canton, to give the United States Navy time to sweep the rest of Japan's secret fortifications in the Pacific under guise of looking for a missing famous woman flyer?

According to her last few transmissions she was lost—until something suddenly happened which caused her to reveal she was not lost at all, but knew exactly where she was all the time. But she had the presence not to reveal totally her then-secret position.

"We are in line of position 157-337," she said hastily, her voice rising in pitch with anxiety. "We are running north and south," she added on second thought, indicating she was now flying from north to south of the equator on a bearing of 157 degrees from Howland Island.

Four hundred and twenty miles along a direct bearing of 157 degrees, she would have been within sight and forced-landing glide distance of the lagoon and beach at Hull Island, which was the only land on the 157 degree bearing anywhere near Canton Island.

"Wait listening on 6210 kilocycles," the *Itasca* radio log indicates were the last words of Amelia Earhart, assumed to be a request for the *Itasca* to "wait listening" to that frequency. But the author of the log was perhaps scribbling rather carelessly at that time to get the gist of the messages down and left out a punctuation mark.

"Wait, listening . . ." or "Wait. Listening . . ." or "Wait! Listening on 6210 kilocycles. We are running north and south" could have meant on a line which ran from her last known location 157-337 degrees northwest right through Howland Island where she knew it was all the time.

Commander Thompson aboard the *Itasca* was not in on any secret mission. Figuring the flyers would see Baker Island or his own billowing smoke along the 157-degree course, he logically headed the *Itasca* 337 degrees northwest and searched in the wrong direction. It was, without the knowl-

edge that Amelia Earhart had never been heading for Howland Island in the first place, a perfectly reasonable and
sound decision by Commander Thompson.

But what happened to interrupt the Earhart flight before
it had reached the hiding place at Canton Island?

What had made Amelia Earhart cry out, "Wait"?

Could low-winged metal monoplanes have swooped down
out of the morning sun and shot the XC-35 down? Could the
Japanese carrier, lurking nearby, have made its interception?

For if part of the game were that Amelia Earhart was
actually flying the first highly sophisticated U-1 mission
for the United States prior to World War II, then the other
part of the game surely was that the Japanese aircraft carrier's mission was to intercept.

The beach at Hull Island is not big enough to accommodate
a wheels-down landing of either a twin-engined Electra or
of a Japanese fighter plane.

The first seaplane to enter the story was the Navy patrol
plane from Honolulu which on the evening of Amelia Earhart's disappearance radioed from a position 420 miles from
Howland Island that it was turning back because of snow
and sleet. Four hundred and twenty miles is the exact distance from Howland to Hull Island.

One week later, on July 9, Lieutenant John O. Lambrecht
landed a catapult seaplane from the U.S.S. *Colorado* in the
lagoon at Hull Island. Only one plane made the landing at
Hull Island, while two others circled above.

Did the first patrol plane from Honolulu on July 2 secretly
determine that Amelia Earhart and Fred Noonan had survived a crash-landing at Hull Island? And did the second
Navy seaplane land there one week later only to discover
that they had been picked up by the Japanese? Would the
United States at that time have admitted to being caught
red-handed in an espionage trap set by the Japanese? And
would the Japanese have boasted of shooting down a female
spy who happened to be the idol of millions of enthusiastic

admirers throughout the world? Or would they have used her to blackmail the United States in some fashion?

These were the questions Joe Gervais and I asked over and over. These were the theories, among others, that we sought to prove or disprove while collecting a filing case full of evidence as to what happened to Amelia Earhart and Fred Noonan.

On July 19, 1937, the Navy called off its search.

On July 20, Ambassador Grew in Tokyo routinely informed the Japanese Navy Ministry that our own "Navy Department proposes that the U.S.S. *Gold Star* make informal visits to Palau August 30 to September 1, Truk September 6 to 8 and Saipan September 11 to 13."

The Japanese Navy Ministry informed Grew that "visits of *Gold Star* to Palau, Saipan and Truk would not be agreeable but visits to Yokohama, Kobe and Miike would be agreeable."

Things were back to normal in the Pacific. But the course of history had been altered. And the quest for Amelia Earhart had barely begun.

CHAPTER FIVE

THE CALIFORNIA CRASH

Amelia Earhart's "last flight" was not the last recorded flight of a Lockheed 10E Electra bearing the registration number NR-16020. While making a routine title search on that particular airplane at the FAA Records Center in Oklahoma City, Joe Gervais discovered a startling discrepancy. It has always been regulation practice for the United States government to issue an individual registration number to each aircraft it licenses. The aircraft may be rebuilt, as reportedly the Earhart plane was after her Honolulu crash of March 20, 1937, and still retain the same registration number. But it has never been the practice of our government to issue the same registration number to two different airplanes.

When Gervais looked into the official aircraft registry folder on N-16020 he discovered the registration number of NR-16020 had apparently been assigned to two Lockheed Electras. One was Amelia Earhart's Electra model 10E, which had a manufacturing number of 1055. The other was allegedly a modified version of the same kind of Electra called the 12A, which, it was indicated, had a manufacturing number of 1243. The R in NR-16020 indicated that the airplane was *restricted* to fly for a specific purpose . . . such as the round-the-world flight.

If these two Electras numbered NR-16020 and N-16020 were not indeed the same aircraft, it is the only case on record in which two different airplanes were given the same registration number.

Gervais' hands trembled as he dug through the file folder for the history of the "second" NR-16020 Electra. In all further entries, the NR- had been changed to N-16020, indicating the plane was no longer restricted to its original purpose; and NR-16020, the 10E, had become as one with Electra N-16020, the 12A.

No transfers of ownership of Electra number N-16020 from the manufacturer, Lockheed Aircraft Corporation, were recorded between 1937 and 1940.

But then, inexplicably, a New York firm, Charles H. Babb Company, purchased Electra N-16020 from the Canadian government's Department of National Defense at Ottawa, Ontario, on June 16, 1940. The missing Electra apparently re-entered the United States when Babb obtained it from Canada and then insured the legality of its title by also having ownership transferred from the original manufacturer, Lockheed Aircraft. This double transaction bypassed Amelia Earhart, Purdue University, and any others who may have possessed the plane from July 2, 1937, to June 16, 1940. Then Babb purchased the same Electra N-16020 from Lockheed Aircraft eight days later, June 24. These transactions were recorded respectively on Federal Aviation Agency documents #24834 and #24833 on June 26, 1940. Apparently Babb sold the plane, because the Canadian government, through its War Assets Corporation in Montreal again sold Electra N-16020, this time to Algoma Air Transport Company, Ltd., of Ontario on January 24, 1946.

The next day, January 25, 1946, Edward Ahr of Timmins, Ontario, bought Electra N-16020 from Algoma Air Transport.

Paul Mantz, Amelia Earhart's close friend and advisor for the round-the-world flight in which she had supposedly died in Electra N-16020, re-entered the mystery at this point in the FAA files.

Operating an aviation museum and motion picture flying business at Lockheed Air Terminal in Burbank, California, later to be moved to Santa Ana, California, Mantz had on January 21, 1946, already closed the deal to buy the 12A Electra bearing Amelia Earhart's number N-16020 from Mr. Ahr.

All three of these transactions are recorded at Oklahoma City on Federal Aviation Agency documents #180931, #180 932, and #180933 and dated March 11, 1946, three months after the title transfers actually occurred.

Further entries, as required by FAA regulations, showed that Paul Mantz remained the owner of Electra N-16020 in September, 1956, under the corporate name of Paul Mantz Air Services, and in August, 1961, under the name Mantz Air, Inc.

Although Mantz maintained an aviation museum at Santa Ana which displayed many original historic airplanes, such as the single-engine Lockheed Vega monoplane in which Amelia Earhart had made the first Honolulu-to-Oakland flight in 1932, the Electra which bore her original number and which the records indicate he owned free and clear was never displayed.

The last sale and transfer of Electra N-16020 was on August 9, 1961, when Mantz sold the twenty-four-year-old mystery plane to California Aircraft Investors at Palmdale, California. The record showed this to be a three-man company headed by Charles Allan Kitchens, a Lockheed Aircraft Corporation test pilot who lived in Palmdale. Kitchens was thirty-nine-years-old and engaged in top-secret flying activities at the Air Force Flight Test Center at nearby Edwards Air Force Base.

Twenty-four years is a long life for any airplane. And thirty-nine years is a long life for a test pilot. Charles Allan Kitchens was only fifteen years old when his final employer, Lockheed Aircraft Corporation, built Electra number N-16020. His widow told Joe Gervais that Kitchens was also employed as a secret U-2 pilot and had made clandestine photographic flights over the Soviet Union. In fact, she said, Kitchens was actually along in a second Lockheed U-2 the day Gary Powers was shot down and captured by the U.S.S.R.

When cautioned by Lockheed's security chief that perhaps she ought not to speak of such things, Gervais remembers what she said: "My husband gave his life to them. I'm not going to keep my mouth shut."

Starting with cocktails at six in the evening of December 15, 1961, a group of civilian pilots and Air Force officers gathered at the Palmdale Country Club for the annual Lockheed pilots' party. It was a happy celebration for some of the nation's bravest flyers—a once-a-year occasion for men engaged in a serious and dangerous business to let off steam.

Around midnight, the pilots were rightfully boasting of their abilities and daring one another to do something spectacular. Eight pilots, all drinking, went out to nearby Quartz Hill Airport, where one of them "owned an airplane," to watch Lockheed test pilots Charles Allan Kitchens and Braxton William Harrell, Jr., take off on a spur-of-the-moment flight to Las Vegas.

According to FAA Form 2400 covering the incident, Kitchens as pilot and Harrell as co-pilot took off in the twenty-four-year-old Electra N-16020 for destination Las Vegas at approximately 2 A.M. Pacific Standard Time on December 16, 1961. The report continues as follows:

At 0245 PST Daggett Radio...heard a May Day [distress call] from the Lockheed requesting a radar steer. The aircraft was answered by...Daggett radio and (radio) contact was established. Contact was lost before its last known position could be established... [by radar].

At approximately 3 A.M. the aircraft was observed by an Army enlisted man to fly over the desert Bicycle Lake Army Air Base on a westerly heading and then make a circle to the left as in an attempt to land on Runway 22, which was lighted.

At approximately 0301 PST the aircraft was observed to explode and burn when it ran into the mountains due east of the Air Base. The aircraft crashed into the mountains at an elevation of 2700 feet, killing both pilots. The mountains are estimated to be 5000 feet in elevation. Preliminary investigation indicates the left engine failed. The Lockheed 12 did not have feathering propellers.

The commanding general of Edwards Air Force Base, and Courtlandt Gross, vice-president of Lockheed, broke the tragic news to Kitchens' widow in the dark hours of early morning. Mrs. Kitchens remembered hearing Gross ask a strange question.

"Who gave him permission to take that plane up?"

"What do you mean . . . permission?" she demanded in her grief. "My husband was the owner of that airplane, wasn't he?"

Gross seemed caught short by the logical question. "Yes, of course," she remembered Gross stammering. "Everyone is pretty upset. It's just something that I shouldn't have asked."

Mt. Tierfort, where the Electra crashed, lies within Fort Irwin, the largest military reservation in the United States. From its commander Gervais learned that in December, after the Civil Aeronautics Board investigation was concluded, both wings, the engines, and tail section of the Electra had been hauled down the mountainside by persons unknown and removed by an unidentified commercial van.

Gervais obtained permission from the commander of Fort Irwin to climb the mountain. At the crash scene, overlooking the vast Mojave Desert, he found pieces of cowling, a landing-gear strut, bits of scattered aluminum, parts of the propellers, including the blades, and scorched earth. The identification plates had obviously been removed from the strut. He looked at the rear side of the propellers for identification stampings he knew should be there and protected from the forward thrust of the crash. The stampings had been hammered away.

Someone had made an effort to remove every identification mark from every piece of debris.

Gervais' years of experience as a crash investigator for the Air Force told him that other parts of the plane might be scattered some distance from the impact point, so he began to prowl the mountainside.

A hundred yards beyond and below the impact point, in the bottom of a ravine among scattered rock crevasses, he came upon three sections of exhaust manifold which were a part of both engines. The outward appearance of the manifold sections presented nothing visual in the way of identification markings, but Joe knew about manifolds.

With a hammer and chisel, he cut through the cowlings to the main manifolds. Their manufacturing identification plates had not been tampered with. The plates revealed the following information:

"Exhaust Manifold manufactured by Solar Aircraft Corp., Lindbergh Field, San Diego, California. Model 12A. *Delivery Date May 13, 1937 . . . ."*

This date of delivery was two weeks before Amelia Earhart left Burbank for Miami to start her second and last round-the-world flight attempt.

The Civil Aeronautics Board report reveals that this crashed Electra did not have featherable propellers. Neither did Amelia Earhart's, since the full-feathering, constant-speed propeller appeared for the first time on Lockheed aircraft in September, 1937, and has long been standard equipment.

Gervais learned from the CAB in Washington that their investigation of the crash indicated number-one engine to have serial number 24605. The records he obtained from the FAA in Oklahoma City, however, indicated that engine number 24605 had been removed from the Electra and replaced in 1955. In fact, the FAA records showed the aircraft had seven engine changes between 1955 and its final crash in 1961.

The FAA records through September, 1961 also indicated the airplane had logged a total flying time of 5137 hours, and yet Electra N-16020 crashed after twenty-four years still equipped with exhaust manifolds installed in 1937. (Certainly the National Aeronautics and Space Administration could use the secret of any manifold metal which could outlast 5000 hours of operational heat.)

Gervais talked to a mechanic who had worked on maintenance of the Electra while it was stored at Quartz Hill Airport before the crash. This mechanic had never seen N-16020 taken out of the hangar, but he remembered it well.

"This was the most beautiful Electra I had ever seen. Not a scratch or a dent on it. It appeared to have not more than 500 hours total time. It had seen a lot of storage in its day." This ancient bird, with Amelia Earhart's number N-16020 clearly visible in two official Civil Aeronautics Board photographs of the crash, appeared to the last mechanic to have worked on it to be in "mint condition."

Paul Mantz, who test-flew Amelia Earhart's Electra and advised her throughout the preparations for her last known flight, did not want to talk about the crashed plane, although he was its registered owner from 1946 until just before its flaming end in 1961.

"I know more about the Amelia Earhart story than all the rest of the people combined," Mantz growled to Gervais one sunny afternoon at his Santa Ana Air Museum. "When the last chapter is written about Earhart, I'll write it."

But Paul Mantz hadn't written a single word when he died in the 1965 crash of a freak airplane he was stunt-flying for the filming of *The Flight of the Phoenix*.

CHAPTER SIX

THE NEW YORK "HOAX"

The United States Navy, "assisted" by the Imperial Japanese Navy, reportedly spent more than four million dollars in a vast and intensive search for the two missing flyers.

Spiritualists from all over the world communicated with Amelia Earhart's husband and mother. Some described Amelia's body as recognizable only by Gordon Selfridge's watch still clasped around her wrist. Others described an emaciated, slightly crazed woman calling for help from a tiny coral reef.

Not having "found" Amelia Earhart by means of her extrasensory perception was a great disappointment to Jacqueline Cochran. After lighting candles for her dear friend and colleague, she reportedly never attempted to use her rare gifts again. However, she did afterwards employ a mentalist, Mrs. Maude Bronson, to "try to establish extrasensory contact with Amelia, either in this world or the next."

There was also a $2000 reward offered by Amelia's husband, George Putnam, for information leading to the rescue of Amelia Earhart and Fred Noonan.

While "Jackie" Cochran and others searched the spirit world, and while the navies of two nations searched the central Pacific, someone tried to collect the $2000 Putnam reward.

The name of the man who claimed to have found Amelia Earhart alive was given as Wilbur Rothar.

On August 4, 1937, George Putnam issued a newspaper release through the Pan Pacific Press Bureau. The story appeared in the August 5, 1937, edition of *The New York Times*.

JANITOR IS SEIZED FOR EARHART HOAX
Scarf he obtained 3 years ago inspired
a story of "Rescue," Police say he admits
$2000 asked of Putnam.
Father of 8 Accused of Trying to Extort,
Says Flier was Found by Cutthroat Crew.

Three years ago Wilbur Rothar, who lived with his wife and eight children . . . in the Bronx, journeyed to Roosevelt Field, L.I., in the hope of seeing Amelia Earhart make a routine landing in her plane.

He was then only one man in a crowd of autograph seekers, but after Miss Earhart landed, and as she was about to step from her plane, a wind blew her brown and white scarf into his hands.

For a reason he could not explain at the time, Rothar did not or could not return the scarf. He took it back with him that night to the Bronx apartment house, where he was a janitor, and until last Monday kept it as a souvenir.

Last Monday, however, he appeared with the scarf in the office of George Palmer Putnam . . . and offered it to the publisher as proof that his wife, Miss Earhart, still was alive, and that she had been rescued by an arms-running vessel from an island near New Guinea. The little janitor, who once had been a sailor, demanded $2000.00 for the safe return of Miss Earhart.

As a result of his demand he was a prisoner last night in the Elizabeth St. police station, where he was locked up on Mr. Putnam's complaint to Harold W. Hastings, acting District Attorney, on a charge of attempted extortion. In Mr. Hastings' possession was a signed confession obtained from Rothar by Rhea Whitley, agent in charge of the Federal Bureau of Investigation, that he had invented the rescue story to extort $2000.00 from Mr. Putnam and that his possession of the Earhart scarf inspired the idea.

Last Saturday Mr. Putnam received a note which had been left for him at the Hotel Barclay, written on the stationery of the hotel. It said, "We have your wife on the ship. I will call Sunday at 2 o'clock."

At about 10 P.M. the same day, Mr. Putnam received a telephone call at the hotel. The voice of a man told him that if he would arrange a meeting on Sunday, Mr. Putnam would receive important information about Miss Earhart. The meeting was arranged for 2 P.M. Sunday at the hotel.

TELLS STORY OF RESCUE

Rothar, who introduced himself as Johnson, arrived at the appointed hour and told Mr. Putnam the following story: he had been employed, he said, as a seaman on a vessel that was running arms to Spain. The ship, he declared, was on her way to Panama from New Guinea in the southern Pacific in the latter part of June. A few days out of New Guinea the skipper anchored off a small island to take on fresh water. In a cove on this island, Rothar said, a wrecked airplane was discovered. The body of a man was lying on a wing of the plane. On the rocky shore a woman was standing in nothing but a pair of athletic shorts. The sharks, he said, had eaten away the lower part of the man's body. The ship's crew buried the man at sea, and took aboard the woman, who was out of her mind, and badly injured.

A Chinese doctor on board the vessel treated the woman for the rest of the voyage. It had been necessary, Rothar said, to give her blood transfusions. No one knew at the time who the woman was, Rothar said, but upon arriving at Panama they recognized her from newspaper photographs as Amelia Earhart. Members of the crew, Rothar explained, became panic-stricken because they were afraid that their gun-running activity would be discovered if Miss Earhart were put ashore.

"We came to New York," he said, "and I was elected by the crew to see you to see if we can't get her off our hands. The boat has a lot of cutthroats aboard and they talked about dumping your wife into the sea."

Rothar explained that Miss Earhart was so ill she would have to be taken ashore soon to a hospital. The men on his vessel, he said, expected to be paid for the rescue before they would surrender her.

"Can you bring me a lock of her hair," Mr. Putnam asked, "or something to assure me that you have her aboard?" Rothar said he could and that he would call the following day at Mr. Putnam's office with his proof.

SCARF IS IDENTIFIED

The Bronx janitor called last Monday at Mr. Putnam's office, where the publisher introduced him to "my confidential secretary," one of Mr. Whitley's agents. He exhibited the brown and white scarf, and Mr. Putnam did not recognize it, but his stenographer identified it as one Miss Earhart had worn several years ago.

Rothar explained that the crew had decided not to release Miss Earhart unless $2000.00 was paid by Mr. Putnam. The publisher said he would pay that amount gladly and invited Rothar to return the following day to collect it. Rothar did. He accepted $1000 cash and was on his way to the bank to get a check for the remainder when Mr. Putnam's "secretary," who accompanied him, placed him under arrest.

While all the negotiations were going on, Federal agents had made a check on Rothar. They found out that he lived at the Bronx address under the name of Goodenough. He is 42 years old. He was born on City Island. Before he became a janitor, he was a woodworker. He will be arraigned in Felony Court this morning pending action by a New York County grand jury.

The foregoing press release, edited by *The New York Times*, effectively removed Wilbur Rothar from the case so far as the public was concerned. But not to the satisfaction of Joe Gervais, who had come to suspect all apparent "facts" surrounding the Earhart disappearance after he had found the crashed remnants of a plane bearing her registration number on a California mountainside.

"I thought it odd," said Gervais, "that Rothar was able to produce her scarf after Putnam had asked for evidence, but had apparently not started right out by offering the scarf as proof that Amelia was alive."

Amelia Earhart's sister, Mrs. Muriel Morrissey, told a slightly different story about Rothar in her 1963 book *Courage Is the Price.*

> GP was subjected to a cruel extortion hoax .... An ex-seaman had found one of Amelia's bright scarfs left in the hangar at Wheeler Field in Hawaii, probably at the time of the Electra's ill-fated [first] crash. Using the scarf, which GP recognized as belonging to Amelia, as a token of the authenticity of his information, the man demanded five thousand dollars for disclosing the name of the island in the Caroline cluster where Amelia was marooned and held prisoner by smugglers. Under the astute questioning of Mr. Black, who had observed the Navy's prodigious search efforts from the cutter *Itasca*, the fake informer was caught in such a maze of contradictions that he soon admitted he had no information to sell, but was looking for "easy money." Mr. Black urged George Putnam to have the man indicted for extortion, but he refused.
>
> "No, I'll not press charges. I know Amelia would not want it that way. Why, I remember she wouldn't even let me fire the houseman whose negligence was responsible for the fire at our Rye home, because she said anybody could be forgetful once in a while." Then, turning to the shamefaced and frightened young man, he said, "No, I won't have you jailed. You must be pretty hard

up to have tried such a low-down trick as this. Here is fifty dollars for my wife's scarf. Now, get out of my sight, but try going straight for Amelia's sake!"

In Muriel Morrissey's version, the scarf had been found in a hangar at Hawaii, probably in March, 1937. In the original press release, the scarf had blown into Rothar's hands at Roosevelt Field, Long Island, sometime in 1934. The little forty-two-year-old janitor and father of eight children of the *Times* story had changed to a "shamefaced and frightened young man" in the Morrissey version. The $2000 reward had changed to a $5000 demand; and Mr. Black, who accompanied the emergency direction-finder aboard the U.S.S. *Itasca*, was back in the story.

And Rothar, to be sentimentally released without charge by Putnam with "fifty dollars for my wife's scarf," began a terrifying journey which turned out to be a vital ingredient in solving the mystery of Amelia Earhart.

For Rothar was *not* turned loose. More drastic measures were taken, apparently recommended by the mysteriously present Interior Department official, Mr. Black. According to *The New York Times*, Wilbur Rothar, alias Wilbur Goodenough, alias Wilbur Johnson, was indicted on August 5, 1937, for extortion. The *Times* reporter observed that in court the prisoner "shook very nervously and pleaded not guilty."

On August 13, Rothar was sent to Bellevue Hospital in New York City for "10 days of sanity tests."

Two months later, on October 13, 1937, a General Sessions Court committed Rothar to the Matteawan State Hospital for the Criminally Insane for treatment prior to standing trial on the extortion charge. At the commitment hearing Rothar was legally represented by voluntary defender Edward T. Tighe.

Twenty-nine years later in 1966, Tighe, practicing law in New York City, refused to answer any correspondence from Gervais regarding his former client, Wilbur Rothar.

Appearing with Putnam against Rothar at the commitment proceedings was FBI Special Agent Thomas J. Donegan.

Two days later on October 15, 1937, Donegan was promoted to head up all FBI operations in the state of New Jersey. This was the first of many promotions for Donegan. *Who's Who 1969* reveals Donegan to have been a special assistant to the U.S. Attorney General from 1947 to 1957. From 1953 to 1954 Donegan served as Chairman of Internal Security on the National Security Council in Washington, D.C. From 1955 to 1957 he served as the FBI representative assigned to the Executive Office of the President of the United States in the White House. In that capacity Donegan was head of the Subversive Control Board, which in 1956 became the Internal Security Division of the Department of Justice.

On January 7, 1955, Donegan was authorized by Cabinet action to "advise department heads on difficult security cases requiring coordination . . . inimical to the public welfare by reason of his or her conduct, sympathies, or utterances, or because of other reasons growing out of war." He was also placed in charge of the passport security program "necessary to deter travel abroad by subversives bent on missions detrimental to the U.S." Gervais found all this information, about the man who testified against Rothar, in a 1965 government security report.

The same report showed Donegan to be serving as a member of the Subversive Activities Control Board, 811 Vermont Avenue, Washington, D.C., a membership which he shared with another person prominent in the mystery of Amelia Earhart, Jacqueline Cochran.

Who's Who 1969 also indicates that Donegan served for two years as "administrative assistant to J. Edgar Hoover," chief of the FBI, and that from 1937, the year that Amelia Earhart and Fred Noonan disappeared and Wilbur Rothar was committed to a hospital for the criminally insane, until 1940, Donegan was commissioned a lieutenant in the U.S. Naval Reserve.

In 1966, Donegan, a professional keeper of our nation's most vital secrets, refused to answer any of the letters Gervais wrote to him inquiring about Wilbur Rothar, Fred Noonan, or Amelia Earhart.

While for thirty years Donegan was achieving sufficient success in the cloak-and-dagger field to be listed in *Who's Who*, another kind of life was being led by the "shamefaced and frightened young man," the forty-two-year-old "little janitor" known variously as Wilbur Rothar, Wilbur Goodenough, and Wilbur Johnson.

Under New York State law, a prisoner who is under indictment and is committed before a trial to a hospital for the criminally insane may not be transferred nor dismissed without being returned to the original court to stand trial.

A thorough search of New York City court records revealed that the patient had never been returned to stand trial. Therefore, Rothar should either have still been a patient at Matteawan when Gervais began looking for him in 1965, or he must have died while an inmate. Gervais wrote to the superintendent of Matteawan State Hospital on May 31, 1965.

Dear Dr. McNeil:
During the month of October, 1937, a Mr. Wilbur Rothar, formerly of 316 E. 155th Street, New York City, was committed to your hospital after examination by the Bellview [sic] Hospital and by order of Judge Frechi of the New York General Sessions Court. Mr. Rothar at that time was age 42, married, the father of eight children, and charged with extortion against a publisher, G. P. Putnam.

Can you advise if Mr. Rothar is still confined to your hospital and his present state of health? Also, if he has been released, can you furnish the date he was discharged, to whose custody, and last forwarding address?

My interest in Mr. Rothar concerns a historical research project and I would like to interview him if he

is still alive. If not, I would like to be able to make contact with a member of his immediate family.

> Very truly yours,
> J. Gervais

While awaiting a reply, Gervais tried to find the wife or
any of the eight children in New York. Looking in new and
old telephone books and city directories, he called everyone
with the name of Goodenough and none said he was in any
way related. He also could find no one at all named Rothar,
the name given as the extortionist's legitimate name in the
court records.

A reply from Matteawan Hospital came on June 3, 1965.
The answer was unsigned and typed across the bottom of
Gervais' original letter of inquiry.

> This patient was known to us as Wilbur Rokar and
> transferred under this name to Harlem Valley State
> Hospital, Wingdale, Duchess County, New York on
> 4/19/60. We have had no further information concerning
> him. You might write to Harlem Valley State Hospital
> for the information you desire.

Apparently a charge of extortion which had never been
brought to trial had resulted in Rothar becoming confined
to a hospital for the criminally insane for twenty-three years
under another, slightly different name.

The envelope in which the letter of inquiry had been returned with its unsigned reply was incorrectly addressed,
not to J. Gervais, but to "J. Genair."

The patient, Rothar, now Rokar, had apparently been
transferred on April 19, 1960, without having been brought
to trial on his original charge.

As with the name, Rothar, no one named Rokar could be
found listed anywhere in New York City.

Gervais wrote to Harlem Valley State Hospital in Wing-
dale. The reply was dated June 17, 1965.

Re: ROKAR, Wilbur
Dear Sir:

In answer to your letter of recent date, we wish to advise you that the above-named was transferred to the Central Islip State Hospital on March 23, 1962, and you should direct your inquiry to Doctor Francis J. O'Neill, Director, Central Islip State Hospital, Central Islip, New York.

> Very truly yours,
> Lawrence P. Roberts, M.D.
> Director

After twenty-five years of consecutive commitment, the prisoner had again been transferred without standing trial on the original extortion charge.

With growing excitement, Gervais wrote to Dr. O'Neill at Central Islip State Hospital and received a reply dated July 6, 1965.

RE: ROKAR, Wilbur — #56655
Dear Sir:

In reply to your recent inquiry I wish to advise that the above-named was discharged from our records on October 25, 1963, at which time his whereabouts were unknown.

> Very truly yours,
> Francis J. O'Neill, M.D.
> Director

Because the state law prohibits the discharge from a state hospital of a prisoner who is under indictment without having stood trial, Gervais wrote next to the Police Department, County of Suffolk, to see if Rothar, alias Rokar, appeared in their records. He did, as indicated in a reply dated July 21, 1965.

Re: ROKAR, WILBUR
Dear Mr. Gervais:

This is to acknowledge receipt of your letter dated 16 July 1965 pertaining to the above-captioned.

Records of this Department indicate that the subject eloped* from Central Islip State Hospital on 17 October 1962 and on 29 October 1963 our teletype alarm was cancelled, as subject returned.

We do not have any information as to his present whereabouts, nor do we have any knowledge of existing relatives.

By direction of the Commissioner:

John P. Finnerty
Deputy Commissioner

Deputy Commissioner Finnerty's letter indicated that Rothar, now known as Rokar, escaped from Central Islip State Hospital on October 17, 1962, after twenty-five years of confinement for mental illness. And after a year of freedom, the prisoner returned to the hospital and the police search for him was cancelled on October 29, 1963. This was four days after Dr. O'Neill said Wilbur Rokar "was discharged from our records on October 25, 1963, at which time his whereabouts were unknown."

For awhile, Gervais gave up the search for Wilbur Rothar (alias Goodenough, Johnson, and Rokar). Then he decided to check the neighborhood surrounding 316 E. 155th Street, where, according to the *Times,* Rothar had lived with a wife and eight children twenty-eight years earlier.

Gervais remembers that his vision blurred and he felt shivers down his spine when he discovered that there is not and never has been a 316 E. 155th Street. If there were, it would be located somewhere in New York's East River.

It was enough to arouse suspicion of a massive subterfuge in the mind of any investigator. Gervais was no exception. He decided to try a little innocent subterfuge of his own. Giving himself the alias of Dr. Jurgens of Sunrise Hospital in Las Vegas, Gervais called Central Islip State Hospital at 7:30 P.M. on a holiday weekend, reasoning that no one in high authority would be on duty, and thus it might be possible for him to catch a lesser authority off guard.

* The word "eloped" is the legal word for escaped.

A night registration clerk on duty at Central Islip State Hospital told Gervais, in his guise as "Dr. Jurgens," that the patient was listed on the records as "Rakor, not Rokar." Gervais learned that Rakor had left the hospital "without permission," and never returned, that his age was uncertain but he was believed to be sixty-seven or sixty-eight years old, and that he was discharged from the hospital records on October 25, 1963.

Gervais tried an inquiry through official channels again and received another letter from Dr. O'Neill dated October 5, 1966.

> RE: ROKAR, Wilbur — #56655
> Dear Sir:
>   In reply to your inquiry of September 29, 1966, I wish to advise that the above-named was discharged from our records and jurisdiction on October 25, 1963, and we have no further contact with him.
>
> Very truly yours,
Francis J. O,Neill, M.D.
Director

It was similar to the reply of a year before, except that the words "and jurisdiction" had been added.

A man convicted for a first offense of extortion might be expected to serve two or three years at most in the penitentiary. The records show that the mysterious Rothar was imprisoned under a diagnosis of criminal insanity for twenty-five years.

For twenty-three of those years the record shows that Wilbur Rothar was confined in the Matteawan Hospital. Then on April 19, 1960, just five days before the publication date of *Daughter of the Sky* by Paul Briand, the first biography of Amelia Earhart to be published in twenty-three years, Rothar was quietly transferred, apparently under the name of Rokar, to another hospital. It was as if a step had been taken to remove Rothar from the possibility of being remembered and found by reporters.

Briand, an Air Force lieutenant colonel who taught English at the Air Force Academy, had been an associate of Gervais and Dinger in the early days of "Operation Earhart." His book, published when he was a captain, also posed the question: What happened to Amelia Earhart?

On October 19, 1937, six days after Rothar was originally committed to the hospital for the criminally insane, Amelia Earhart's widower, George Palmer Putnam, filed a petition in Superior Court in Los Angeles to be named trustee of his wife's estate. On November 3, 1937, the court made him the trustee. On November 14 of that year, five months after his wife's disappearance, Putnam published *Last Flight,* the only book prior to Briand's about Amelia Earhart. In it the reader was given no reason to assume she was not dead.

On June 26, 1938, a California court declared Fred Noonan "legally dead." There was no estate to probate. It was less than a year after he and Amelia Earhart had vanished—six years less than the usual time required for a legal declaration of death without a corpse.

Eighteen months after the "last flight" Amelia Earhart was declared "legally dead" on New Year's Day, 1939. Her estate, probated at $47,000, was inherited by Putnam.

The attorney for Putnam, who had also been Amelia Earhart's attorney, was Clyde Holly of Los Angeles. Holly, who had succeeded in having Amelia Earhart declared legally dead after only eighteen months, paid a surprise visit to the Gervais home in Las Vegas nearly twenty-four years later on October 14, 1962. The attorney demanded to know what Gervais had found out in his investigation into the death of Amelia Earhart.

"Who says she is dead?" Gervais answered with a question of his own.

Gervais remembers that Holly became extremely agitated at the suggestion that his former client might still be alive. Gervais revealed some of the "Operation Earhart" research up until that time.

"They'll never let you print that," said Holly.

"Who won't let me print it?" asked Gervais, surprised at the attorney's irritation.

"The government will prevent you from printing it," said Holly.

Holly asked a lot of questions, which Gervais answered to the best of his ability before asking some of his own. At that point, Holly refused to discuss the matter further and left as abruptly as he had come.

Three days later on October 17, 1962, the record shows that Rothar, now Rokar, "eloped" from Central Islip Hospital after twenty-five years of confinement for criminal insanity and was never heard from again.

"Can you imagine what it would be like for any mentally ill patient who had been confined behind walls for twenty-five years to suddenly walk out into the world of the sixties?" Gervais asked. "If you had been in a mental hospital from 1937 until 1962, how long do you think you would last on the outside with the police looking for you?" Gervais shook his head. "I simply don't believe it."

Joe Gervais embarked upon "Operation Earhart" with a great deal of admiration and fondness for the former "first lady of American aviation." Misgivings and forebodings about what he would find began to set in with his investigation into what had happened to Wilbur Rothar.

He had no doubt that Amelia Earhart was engaged in an espionage conspiracy in 1937 against our subsequent enemy, Japan. Nor did he question such activity as anything but a patriotic and totally justified operation against a potential enemy. But the evidence was mounting that Amelia Earhart's flight over the secret fortifications on the mandated Pacific islands of Japan in 1937 was only a small portion of a much greater activity which continues enshrouded in secrecy and protected by codes even today.

CHAPTER SEVEN

FIRST PACIFIC
INTERVIEWS

Joe Gervais was a B-29 Superfortress commander in the Pacific when he read a statement by Amelia Earhart's mother, Mrs. Amy Otis Earhart, on July 25, 1949, in *The New York Times.*

"Amelia told me many things," Mrs. Earhart said. "But there were some things she couldn't tell me. I am convinced she was on some sort of a government mission, probably on verbal orders."

Gervais again encountered Amelia Earhart in print in April, 1960. In *Stars and Stripes* he read a summary of a new book about Amelia Earhart, *Daughter of the Sky,* by Captain Paul L. Briand, Jr.

Briand had written of reports that Amelia Earhart and Fred Noonan "had flown over islands in the Japanese mandate which were being illegally fortified, the plane had been shot down by anti-aircraft guns, the pilot and navigator had been taken and held as spies."

Briand told how the story persisted after more than twenty years, largely because of an RKO film released in 1942 called *Flight to Freedom,* starring Rosalind Russell and Fred Mac-Murray, in which a fictionalized woman pilot named "Tonie Carter" and her navigator were asked to "get lost" during a round-the-world flight and "make it look good" so the U.S. Navy, under guise of a search, could look over the Japanese fortifications in the South Pacific.

This movie story, which also appeared as fiction in the January, 1943 issue of *Woman's Home Companion* magazine, was so obviously based on the Earhart-Noonan disappearance that George Palmer Putnam sued RKO because of a romance between the pilot and navigator in the film. RKO settled with Putnam out of court.

Briand also quoted Dr. M. L. Brittain, president of Georgia Tech, who was a passenger aboard the U.S.S. *Colorado* during the search for Amelia Earhart.

"We got the definite feeling," Dr. Brittain said, "that Miss Earhart had some sort of understanding with government officials that the last part of her voyage around the world would be over some Japanese islands, probably the Marshalls." Dr. Brittain, now dead, suggested as late as 1944 that Amelia was a prisoner of the Japanese and might soon be liberated by the advancing U.S. Marines.

Briand told the story of Ajima, a Japanese trader who said that an American woman pilot came down between Jaluit and Ailinglapalap Atolls in the southeastern Marshall Islands and was picked up by a Japanese fishing boat, imprisoned by Japanese authorities, and taken to Japan.

The book told of a photograph album containing pictures of Amelia Earhart found in a Japanese barracks by a Marine, who was later killed, during the 1944 invasion of Saipan. Later the album had also "disappeared."

Briand reported how Jacqueline Cochran at the end of World War II was sent to Tokyo by General Hap Arnold "to investigate the role played by Japanese women in aviation during the war." Miss Cochran was reported to have "found numerous files on Amelia Earhart in Imperial Air Force Headquarters." Since then, these files too have "disappeared."

It made exciting reading for Gervais, but the portion of

the book condensed in that issue of *Stars and Stripes* which triggered Gervais' great woman hunt reads as follows:

Josephine Blanco, now Mrs. Maximo Akiyama, and living in California with her husband and their young son, was witness to an incident which is as incredible as it is enlightening.

In the summer of 1937 Josephine was riding her bicycle toward Tanapag Harbor. She was taking lunch to her Japanese brother-in-law, J. Y. Matsumoto, and was hurrying along because it was nearly twelve o'clock.

Josephine had a special pass to the Japanese military area near the harbor. Not even Japanese civilians were admitted to the area unless they carried the proper credentials . . . .

On the way to meet her brother-in-law, Josephine heard an airplane flying overhead. She looked up and saw a silver two-engined plane. The plane seemed to be in trouble, for it came down low, headed out into the harbor, and belly-landed on the water.

It was not until she met her brother-in-law that Josephine discovered who it was that had crash-landed in the harbor.

"The American woman," everyone was saying, greatly excited. "Come and see the American woman." Josephine and her brother-in-law joined the knot of people who gathered to watch.

She saw the American woman standing next to a tall man wearing a short-sleeved sports shirt, and was surprised because the woman was not dressed as a woman usually dressed. Instead of a dress, the American woman wore a man's shirt and trousers; and instead of long hair, she wore her hair cut short, like a man. The faces of the man and woman were white and drawn, as if they were sick.

Then followed the first report of the "execution" of Amelia Earhart.

The American woman who looked like a man and the tall man with her were led away by the Japanese soldiers. The fliers were taken to a clearing in the woods. Shots rang out. The soldiers returned alone.

Mrs. Akiyama has affirmed, after identifying a photograph of Amelia Earhart and Fred Noonan taken on the world flight, that the couple was unquestionably the same man and woman . . . .

Briand concluded that "when they survived the crash-landing in Tanapag Harbor only to be taken into custody as spies, their joy must have turned to inexplicable bitterness: they had been saved not for life, but for death before a Japanese firing squad."

Something in Gervais' mind then clicked. He immediately went to the base exchange, purchased a copy of *Daughter of the Sky,* and read it.

Within the last sixteen pages of Briand's biography of Amelia Earhart were two theories of her disappearance that have persisted until this day. First, the Japanese fisherman's story that she had been picked up out of the water near Jaluit Atoll, 600 miles northwest of Howland Island, as later "proclaimed" by Fred Goerner in 1967. Second, that she had crash-landed at Saipan as reported by Josephine Akiyama. This latter theory was the one favored by Briand.

"The fact, as Briand maintained, that they had ended their flight 91 degrees off their publicized route and in the Japanese mandated islands created many sleepless nights for me," Gervais said. "I just couldn't convince myself that such an error could occur with the experienced pilot and navigator aboard this aircraft."

Relieved from temporary duty in Japan, Gervais returned to his permanent B-29 base in Okinawa on May 1, 1960.

"I thought for many hours about Amelia Earhart; and Captain Bob Dinger, a B-29 instructor pilot who lived next door to me in Okinawa, also became interested."

The two veteran Pacific flyers found themselves discussing Amelia Earhart every spare moment they were together.

"In the next two months we 'flew' on paper over sixty varied missions within the realm of Amelia Earhart's Lockheed Electra. We 'flew' her airplane in the best weather and the worst. With our experience of typhoon reconnaissance in the Pacific, we 'flew' her airplane in varied typhoon conditions. We intentionally 'flew' with head winds, tail winds, cross winds, and all possible weather variations. We simulated loss of power, testing one-engine and two-engine endurance along the intended track.

"We further postulated the loss of critical navigation instruments and radio communications difficulties. This gave us what the aircraft was capable of and what it could not do. It further defined a specific area in the Pacific for future operations on our part. Although the entire Pacific is vast, the area where we were to concentrate our investigation was well within our capabilities and resources.

"Our next step was to research everything we thought was relevant—American, Australian, and Japanese—for the period of 1936 and 1937. From here on in we would think, evaluate, and pursue every action as though we were living during that era and in those islands."

Gervais and Dinger sent the first of many letters exchanged between them and Briand.

"We told Briand his theory was very interesting; however, a theory is a lot like telling a story, and there is always someone who can tell a better one. His theory was supported by only one eye witness account. We told him that, since we were already in the Pacific, we would like to investigate further. We would pursue his theory with the intention of proving or disproving it."

Briand agreed to this, and there were now three Air Force officers investigating—two command pilots, one of whom was also a qualified aircraft accident investigator; and Briand, a professor of English at the Air Force Academy, who had been awarded a Ph.D. for his thesis on the life of Amelia Earhart. Gervais, Dinger, and Briand provided their own funds and investigated while on ordinary leaves from the service.

"Bob and I planned to depart together on leave for Saipan by way of Guam in June of 1960," Gervais said. "Bob was suddenly selected to take a B-29 and crew to Japan for three weeks. His leave was cancelled. It was decided that I would proceed to the Marianas alone and get our operational plan launched."

En route to Guam via the Philippine Islands, Gervais sat in the cargo compartment of a C-124 air transport plane for fourteen hours and reviewed his research on the Marianas from 1935 to 1938.

All of the Marianas Group of islands except Guam had been mandated to Japan by the League of Nations in 1920. Within ten years the islands had become an important source of sugar for Japan. By the time the war broke out in 1941, Japanese citizens outnumbered the island natives by more than two to one. Japan resented the American possession of Guam and captured it swiftly within two days of the attack on Pearl Harbor.

During its forty-three years of American rule Guam had been a good example of that "salutary neglect" which Edmund Burke regarded as the best colonial policy. The United States Navy Department had appointed a series of naval officers as governors. The Guamanian Chamorro natives were provided Yankee assistance in health, education, and welfare and no attempt was made to colonize the island or develop its resources. Although bigger than Japanese Saipan, American Guam produced much less.

A Guamanian of the thirties might sail over to a Japanese-held island such as Saipan to earn money as labor for illegal military construction, but he usually found Japanese rule irksome and returned home to Guam if he could get away.

The three principal Japanese-held islands of the Marianas were Rota, Tinian, and Saipan, which was the seat of the

Japanese South Seas Bureau with administrative headquarters located in the harbor town of Garapan.

There were several newspapers in the mandated territory, all published in Japanese. Regulations prohibited "secret associations." Japan in 1935 had established radio communications between the Caroline, Marshall, and Marianas Islands. The radio station at Saipan, call sign JRV, had constant communications throughout the network.

The territory after 1936 was jealously guarded against visits by Europeans. It was generally known that by 1938 the Japanese immigrant settlers outnumbered the native Chamorros and that, in defiance of the terms of the League of Nations mandate, Japan had built powerful naval and air bases at many points throughout the archipelagos.

The Asleto Airfield on the southern end of Saipan was constructed "for cultural purposes" and coincidentally became the most important airdrome between Japan and Truk.

What were the Americans doing in the Pacific during this same period? A presidential order placed Wake Island under jurisdiction of the Navy Department on December 29, 1934. On May 5, 1935, Pan American Airlines had built its facilities there. In August of 1935, the China Clipper Inaugural Flight with Captain Eddie Musick as pilot, Fred Noonan as navigator, and Bill Van Dusen along as public relations director landed on Wake Island. Regular clipper service from San Francisco to the Orient, with stops at Honolulu, Midway, Wake, Guam, Manila, and Hong Kong, was established in 1936.

A U.S. Navy officer served as governor of Guam in 1936 and 1937 with a detachment of 112 Marines. He was faced with a peculiar situation. Many of the Chamorro natives on Guam were leaving for the nearby local Japanese islands of Rota, Tinian, and Saipan. They were taking employment in various Japanese construction projects. These included coastal defenses, dock facilities, and airport runway clearing. Some stayed and some returned to Guam to recruit others. Although Europeans and other Caucasians were not permitted in these areas, the United States had reliable information as to what was taking place. No Guamanians were employed at Truk, where it was rumored massive naval installations were being built, so there were no eyewitness reports about Truk. There were no American airplanes or airfields on Guam at that time, and the China Clipper landed in the lagoon for refueling during trans-Pacific crossings.

A presidential order placed a colony of four people on Howland Island, which was Amelia Earhart's destination on her last flight. The U.S. colony was set up there in the spring of 1935. On May 13, 1936, President Roosevelt placed the island under the jurisdiction of the Secretary of the Interior. The construction of a runway to accommodate the Amelia Earhart flight was accomplished by the Public Works Administration, an anti-Depression agency commonly known as the PWA. Japanese air attacks on December 8, 1941, killed two of the colonists. The remaining two Howland Island colonists were evacuated on January 31, 1942, by a U.S. destroyer.

When Gervais arrived at Guam he proceeded directly to the island's police headquarters in the hope of being directed to some key individuals who had lived in the Marianas during 1936 and 1937.

"When I met the Chief of Police, Captain Quintanilla, he became very interested, but doubted very seriously that Amelia Earhart had crashed in or been captured in the Marianas."

"I don't see how anything as unusual as Amelia Earhart's being captured by the Japanese or held prisoner at Saipan could have happened without my having heard about it somewhere along the line," Quintanilla said. "But I would be very much interested in helping you track the story down if my superior will let me."

Gervais talked to Quintanilla's superior, retired Marine General J. S. Cook, director of public safety for Guam. General Cook agreed to allow Quintanilla to accompany Gervais to Saipan if the United States Navy would permit the trip.

"I then proceeded to the Guam Navy headquarters and talked to Commander Carey, who had formerly been the commander of Saipan. I specifically requested that Captain Quintanilla and I be authorized to go to Saipan and look at what I thought was the crash site area and interview some people who were residents of Saipan in 1937."

"Look," Commander Carey said, "during my four years as administrator of Saipan I knew the people very well, and the area you are interested in. I simply don't believe Earhart and Noonan could have ever been there. The Navy has investigated Tanapag Harbor operations during those years very extensively. If the people there knew anything about Earhart and Noonan it would have been uncovered by now."

Gervais persisted in his request to visit Saipan and offered to obtain his own Air Force transportation. Carey said it would be necessary to get permission back at Gervais' home base through official channels from the Commander in the Pacific at Honolulu. He then continued to raise one obstacle after another to the Saipan trip.

"Near the conclusion of our interview, Commander Carey referred me to Commander Voight of Navy Intelligence to present to him what I had on the matter. I cooperated to the point where it was quite evident that if I turned over everything I had acquired to the Navy, they would gladly take over the investigation. This I would not do."

As Gervais was about to leave, Commander Voight leaned forward. "Would you like to interview the mayor of Saipan, Mr. Benivente? Mayor Benivente just happens to be somewhere in the building." Of course Gervais said yes.

While waiting for the Navy to round up Saipan's mayor, Gervais received a phone call from Quintanilla.

"I have just talked to Joe Cruz," the Guam police chief related. "Cruz is a member of the Saipan legislature. Joe tells me that about a month ago the Naval administration through Mayor Benivente selected Mr. Elias Sablan, a former mayor of Saipan, to conduct an investigation among the Saipanese people regarding Amelia Earhart."

Gervais regarded the composed faces of Commanders Carey and Voight as he used their phone to converse with Quintanilla. "How did it turn out?"

"Negative," answered Quintanilla. "Jesus Guerrero, who was head of the police during the Japanese administration, spread the word around for the Saipanese people not to co-operate, and they are not cooperating. They don't understand the questionnaire that was circulated, and they still remember how they were interrogated by the Japanese and later by the Americans, who placed them in compounds after the invasion of Saipan."

"You mean they got nowhere at all?"

"Nowhere," replied Quintanilla. "And they will get nowhere with the amateur methods they are using with the Chamorro natives. Oh. And Joe Cruz also told me there is a Mr. Patten now on Guam working on the Earhart case."

"Who's he?" asked Gervais.

"Patten is a Naval Intelligence agent."

Gervais thanked the police chief and hung up as Mayor Benivente of Saipan was ushered into the office. The Mayor appeared very nervous and somewhat frightened.

"I don't know anything about Amelia Earhart ever being at Saipan," said the Mayor. "I am certain that if the incident you describe had ever happened at Saipan I would have heard of it. However, in 1937 I went away from Saipan to Yap Island in the Carolines, so if the incident occurred, it happened while I was away from Saipan."

Gervais then asked about J. Y. Matsumoto, the brother-in-law of Josephine Akiyama to whom she was supposed to be taking a lunch in 1937 when Amelia Earhart's twin-engined plane "crashed on the beach at Tanapag Harbor."

"Yes," answered Mayor Benivente. "I think Mr. Matsumoto has left for Japan on some business concerning a by-product of coconut oil."

"But isn't Matsumoto a motion picture operator and musician?" asked Gervais. "What's he got to do with coconut oil?"

Commander Voight interrupted. "Well, we'll have to terminate this interview, gentlemen. Mayor Benivente is falling behind schedule and today is a very busy day for him."

Gervais wondered if Matsumoto's sudden departure for Japan had anything to do with his being the only Saipanese resident mentioned in Josephine Akiyama's eyewitness account of the 1937 crash that had just been published in Briand's book *Daughter of the Sky*.

"By the way," Gervais asked as he rose to leave, "how is the Navy's questionnaire program on Amelia Earhart coming along at Saipan?"

The two Navy commanders showed surprise. "Where did you hear about that?" Voight asked.

Gervais grinned. "No comment."

Later, Captain Quintanilla smiled as if he had known in advance how the Navy interview with Mayor Benivente would turn out. "You know," he said to Gervais, "their refusal to let you go to Saipan right now may be a blessing in disguise. Some of the key people who were in Saipan in 1937 have moved back here to Guam since the end of the war."

Quintanilla said the Saipanese people had been through a lot in the past fifty years. They had been under the Spanish, the Germans, the Japanese, and now the Americans. There had been occupations, invasion, many changes of government, languages, and economics.

"If there is any loyalty left in the Saipanese it is to their origin, which is Chamorro, and not to the mixtures of later years. They are loyal to local police now, because they are in power. But their greatest loyalty is to their elders . . . the senior Chamorro citizens." He pounded his fist on his desk. "By God, the oldest living Chamorro native today is here on Guam. If the Amelia Earhart incident ever took place she would know about it, because if she didn't see it, she would have at least heard about it."

Quintanilla and Detective Sergeant E. M. Camacho took Gervais to see Mrs. Juana Aquiningo, age seventy-nine, at the home of her daughter, Mrs. Maria Taiyeron. Mrs. Aquiningo was very alert, coherent, of fine stature and respected by her people.

Quintanilla translated Gervais' questions into the Chamorro language. "Mrs. Aquiningo, do you recall any kind of aircraft crash on Saipan about four years before the war?"

The old lady nodded. "I remember the incident because it disturbed the Japanese so much at the time. From what I was told, the plane came in from the southerly direction of Laulu. It hit the tops of some trees in the coffee plantation area, and the owner of the plantation, a friend of mine, was very alarmed by the tops of the trees being broken by the aircraft. The aircraft went on for a short duration and crashed in the water at Sadog-Tasi (now known as Tanapag village) close to both the mouth of the river and the shore. This was very close to the Japanese security area around their naval base and seaplane ramps.

"The Japanese told the local natives to stay out of this area and particularly not to observe anything. When my friend heard it was an American aircraft and American people in it, she wanted to see them for curiosity reasons, but was not permitted into the area by the Japanese. The Japanese finally said later that it was one of their own aircraft that crashed in the area."

"Do you know anything about any American pilots or what happened to them?" she was asked.

"No," she replied. "That is all I remember of the incident as I heard it years ago."

"Did you ever hear of Amelia Earhart?"

"No."

"Do you know now who Amelia Earhart was?"

"I never heard of her."

Quintanilla next took Gervais to see Jose Ada, a former Saipan resident in his seventies who was bedridden from a stroke and living with his daughter. Recently, a second stroke had left the old man almost totally paralyzed.

"My father can hear you but cannot speak except for sounds that you cannot understand," the daughter told them. "His memory is vague, and he can move his head and his arms on a limited basis. Please don't question him too long."

At the old man's bedside, Quintanilla pointed at Gervais. "This is an American who is searching for some airplane information."

The man nodded and also pointed at Gervais.

"Did any kind of airplane crash on Saipan about four years before the war?" Quintanilla asked.

The old man nodded with surprising vigor. Before any more questions could be asked, he made a motion with his hand, first pointing again at Gervais; then, simulating the movement of an airplane with his hand, he brought it down on the bedclothes in pantomime of a crash. Once again he pointed at Gervais and held up two fingers. Then he appeared to relax.

As they were leaving, Gervais and Quintanilla thanked the daughter.

"No," she smiled. "Thank you. You made my father very happy by your visit. He has been bedridden for a long time and few people come to see him any more."

The next former Saipan residents interviewed were H. Tenorio and his wife. Four years before the war Tenorio had been employed by the Japanese South Seas Development Company. In 1954 they had moved to Guam, where he now operated a general store.

Tenorio did not remember anything about an airplane crash four years before the war, nor about two American pilots, or any American woman.

"I saw the story about Josephine Akiyama in the local Agana paper this year," he said. "I know her family—the Blanco family—and remember they lived at Garapan, where Josephine said the plane crashed. All I know about it is what I read in the paper."

Tenorio said he also knew Josephine Akiyama's brother-in-law, J. Y. Matsumoto, a musician at the Japanese Navy's Chico Base at Puntan Flores on Saipan. Mrs. Tenorio had a vague recollection of the incident.

"I remember an airplane crash about four years before the war," she volunteered, "but only through talk from my people at the time. I don't know where the incident occurred on Saipan, if it did occur."

"The Japanese were very strict with us about the base," Tenorio said. "It was the prime security area of the Japanese. You had to have a pass to get into it, but we were allowed to pass alongside of it on the way to the farm work areas at Sadog-Tasi. However, we had to hurry on by and make no observations. The Japanese were very suspicious of all Chamorros at that time."

The next interview was with a Mrs. Bora, age forty-eight, one of the ten Blanco children and eldest sister of Josephine Blanco Akiyama, the eyewitness to the crash now living in California.

"I don't think I should say anything," she answered when Gervais and Quintanilla began to question her. "I don't want to hurt my sister Josephine in California."

Mrs. Bora really appeared to be frightened, but Quintanilla persisted.

"Yes, I heard of the plane crash from Josephine at home," she finally admitted. "I was the eldest of ten Blanco children and had the responsibility of second mother."

"What did Josephine tell you about it at the time?" Quintanilla asked.

"She was only eleven then. I don't think I should say any more about it until my husband gets home."

Her husband was a barber who also ran a small general store. He soon arrived, and after he and Quintanilla reassured her with a lengthy explanation of the harmless purpose of the investigation, Mrs. Bora relaxed a bit.

"The husband of one of my sisters, Mr. Matsumoto, was

working at the Japanese military area as a musician. My younger sister Josephine had the duty and responsibility as errand girl of the family. She had a bicycle and traveled freely around the island. She took her brother-in-law Matsumoto his lunch at the military area on many occasions.

"I remember Josephine telling us one day something about a plane crash, but paid very little attention to it, because Josephine was only eleven and I was concerned with my duties in our home. I was also not interested because the Japanese military were very suspicious of persons who discussed or even knew about such things. All Chamorros were cautious not to imply at any time that we had any military information. We were all afraid of being accused as spies and being shot or having our head chopped off. We were all afraid of the secret police. People were being shot or getting heads chopped off during the entire Japanese occupation. So whatever Josephine told me, I told her to be quiet about it and pushed it out of my mind. I just barely remember her mentioning something, that's all."

Gervais and Quintanilla next questioned Mrs. Maria Flores, age forty-eight, who lived at the south end of Saipan at Chalan Kanoa in 1937.

"I never heard of it and know nothing of it now," said Mrs. Flores. "You could get your head cut off for knowing about a thing like that in those days. I made it a point never to hear or discuss anything of a military nature."

Antonio M. Cepada, a fifty-two-year-old employee of the Buick garage at Agana, remembered a lot more than that.

"One summer about two years after I got married, I saw an American girl who was referred to by some as the 'American spy woman.' She was quartered on the second floor of the Hotel Kobayashi Royokan in the summer of 1937. I don't remember any plane crash, but I saw the girl twice on two separate occasions outside the hotel over a period of two or three months."

With no prompting of any kind, Cepada described the girl he remembered having seen.

"I saw her while going to work outside the hotel, which is located in East Garapan village. She wore unusual clothes —a long raincoat belted in the center. The color was a faded khaki. She was average height American girl—not short, not extra tall—had thin build. Chest somewhat flat, not out like other American girl. Her hair appeared to be a reddish-brown color and cut short like man's hair, trimmed close in the back like man. She did not wear powder or lipstick as I see other American women wear now."

Gervais was astonished. "What else can you tell us?"

Cepada's accent grew more pronounced the more he relaxed. "I did not know how she was caught, but rumor was that she then took secret pictures with flying suit in front hidden camera, maybe."

"What happened to her?"

"I saw her only twice. Maybe she was deported to Japan. That's all I know."

"Can you describe her facial expression, or the way she appeared to you?"

Cepada reflected a moment. "The girl looked soft, very calm. Not expressive. No smile. Seemed to be thinking far away. She didn't notice her surroundings and the people much. Tokyo Rosa was maybe thirty-five years old.

"Everyone on Saipan then referred to her as Tokyo Rosa. Tokyo Rosa in 1937 meant American spy girl."

"You mean Tokyo Rose on the Japanese radio during the war? That Tokyo Rose?"

Cepada shook his head impatiently. "Not that one. Tokyo Rosa in 1937 meant American spy girl. That's all. Nothing else."

"That's right," offered Cepada's wife, who had been listening. "Tokyo Rosa always meant the same thing—American spy lady."

Gervais showed Cepada a photograph of Amelia Earhart. "Does this look like the girl you saw twice at Saipan?"

Cepada studied the photograph. "Looks just like the same girl."

"Did you ever hear of Amelia Earhart?"

"Who?"

"Amelia Earhart. Ever hear of her?"

Cepada and his wife looked at each other and shrugged. "Never heard of her."

"Do you know anyone else who might have seen the girl on Saipan?"

Cepada nodded. "Carlos Palacious. He was there. And Carlos lives here on Guam now."

Palacious, age forty-eight, was interviewed by Gervais, Quintanilla, and Sergeant Camacho immediately to make certain that Cepada could not possibly talk to Palacious before the interrogation. It was a cold call on Palacious with no notice of arrival.

Palacious started work in 1930 in Saipan as a salesman for the Ishi-Shoten, a merchandise store located near the Hotel Kobayashi-Royokan in East Garapan village.

"I saw her only twice in about a three-month period," Palacious said. "It was while I was going to and from the store where I worked. The first time I saw her was at a window on the second floor of the hotel. The window was open, and she had on what looked to me like a man's white shirt with short sleeves . . . open collar. The girl had short dark reddish-brown hair, cut like a man's hair in back, too."

"Was she wearing make-up?"

"I couldn't see any make-up or lipstick.

"The second time I saw the girl standing at the entrance to the hotel. She wore the same white shirt and dark skirt, and an American-type woman's shoes. She was the same girl I had seen before on the second floor. Same girl, hair cut short, no make-up, a slim girl . . . not fat . . . not big in the chest."

"Had there been a crash? Is that how they caught her?"

"I don't know where the girl was caught," Palacious answered. "I never heard anything about a crash . . . only that

Tokyo Rosa was an American spy girl and she had taken secret pictures."

"Why do you call her Tokyo Rosa?"

"Tokyo Rosa was my people's expression for American spy girl."

"Could the girl come and go freely from the hotel? Did you see any guards near her?"

Palacious shrugged. "Maybe she could come and go when I didn't see her. I don't think guards were necessary. No one was free to come and go from Saipan without Japanese knowledge and permission. If anyone tried it, they got killed. The Japanese knew everything about everyone."

"How old did the girl look to you?"

"Maybe thirty-four to thirty-six. Hard to tell; I only saw her twice."

"What do you think happened to her?"

"Probaby deported to Japan."

The picture of Amelia Earhart was then shown to Palacious. He nodded. "Face and haircut look like same girl in picture."

"Are you sure?"

"I only know what I saw, and what I have told you is true."

"Have you ever heard of Amelia Earhart?"

"No."

Gervais and the two Guamanian policemen next turned up an eyewitness to the crash. He was forty-five-year-old Thomas Blas, also known locally as "Buko." Blas had a badly mangled left arm, the result of a hand grenade being thrown into a cave in which his family was hiding from the Japanese and Americans during the invasion of Saipan in 1944. His arm had healed without medical aid and hung limply at his side.

Blas related the two most important incidents in his lifetime with great enthusiasm and detail. They were the grenade incident in 1944 and the airplane crash which he said he saw in 1937.

In 1937 Blas was foreman of a construction crew for Sagami-Sakuroda, a company doing cement work on new barracks buildings at Chico Naval Base. He and two other construction workers, Antonio V. Castro and Juan M. Camorotto, now living in Saipan, had just begun eating their lunch in the work area shortly after noon.

"I remember the time pretty well because I started work for this company in 1935, and this was in the summer two years later in June or July, as best I can recall. All three of us were facing toward Sadog-Tasi at the time. That is, we were facing west in the direction of the harbor. All three of us heard an airplane behind us coming from the direction of the coffee plantation. Just as we turned around, it passed over us. In descending we saw it hit the tops of the iron trees in the Sadog-Tasi area on the edge of the beach. It crash-landed on the beach about 2000 to 3000 feet from the main Japanese Chico Naval Base. It was a nice day with clear skies, no rain. The three of us were standing from 100 to 150 feet from where the airplane came to a full stop."

Gervais interrupted. "Were the airplane's motors running before it crash-landed?"

Blas nodded. "Both airplane motors were running with the propellers turning as it passed overhead until it hit the iron trees near the beach. The airplane was two-motored and aluminum-colored and had no Japanese marking or insignia on it. At the time there were Kiogan (Japanese Navy personnel) and other construction workers to the left of the crash. It was so close to the base and all construction that many people started to gather to watch. I got as close as about 100 feet and was not permitted to get any closer."

Blas described what he was able to see from his vantage point.

"The airplane was pretty well intact on the beach. Only at high tide was part of the left wing in the water. The rest of the time, the plane was not in the water at all. Before all the people gathered I saw one pilot on the ground lying face down and not moving. The other climbed out of the airplane and approached the pilot who seemed injured . . . but I could not be certain. I assumed the person on the ground was injured because he did not move. The airplane was not damaged much. The wings were not broken off, the motors were still on the wings, but the propellers were bent back. The fuselage and tail appeared to be intact. The front of the airplane was pushed in and had damage of bent and torn metal.

"When Navy Kiogan officers arrived, Japanese officers . . . some with swords . . . and some soldiers shortly thereafter pushed all native construction workers away and told them to stay away. They went back some distance but still tried to watch and see.

"The military surrounded the pilot standing up and pushed him back away from the other person on the ground. The standing pilot tried to resist being pushed, and was knocked down by a soldier with a gun that had a bayonet on the end. While the pilot was on his back, the soldier stood over him with a bayonet close to his chest so he could not get up. From where I was I could see that these were two Americano men pilots and not Japanese pilots. Both wore flight suits for pilots in khaki color that looked like it had been washed many times. They did not have black hair on their heads like Japanese, but a lighter color like Americano people have.

"The Japanese took all the clothes off both Americano pilots and then found out one pilot was an American girl. The Japanese were very disturbed over this. They said that the poor Americans have no more men pilots now, and use women pilots for military planes.

"The Japanese took many pictures of the crash. The Americano woman in flying clothes had her hair cut short just like the other pilot. She wore a long-sleeved black shirt under her flying suit which they took off. My impression was the woman flew the two-motor fighter-type airplane. I had never seen this kind before.

"The Japanese were so disturbed over this crash close to the base that they allowed all construction workers to go home immediately. The entire area was secured then, tighter than ever before. The perimeter road the native people were permitted to travel on was closed and the people were re-routed through another area further away where they could not see this area. My friends and I were taken off the job we were doing there and continued construction work in another area far away from the crash place."

Gervais showed Blas a photograph of Amelia Earhart's famous Electra.

Blas nodded. "The one I saw was the same kind."

"Are you sure?"

Blas was slightly insulted. "I tell only the truth and what I saw, and my friends who are still in Saipan will tell you the truth too. I will go with you to Saipan if you like."

Gervais then asked if the photo of Amelia Earhart looked like the girl Blas saw on the beach.

"It looks like the girl . . . same haircut. But I did not see her face close up."

"Do you know what happened to the airplane after that?"

"It was three months later before I returned to that area, and when I did, the plane had been removed. I do not know where, nor how."

"What about the pilots?"

"I don't know. I assumed they were deported to Japan."

The next person interviewed, fifty-two-year-old Antonio Tenorio, was employed from 1932 to 1936 as a member of the Japanese Saipan Insular Police Force.

"I was in Japan most of 1937 studying the Japanese language," Tenorio said nervously. "When I got back in late 1937 or early 1938 I headed a local Japanese boys' movement on Saipan . . . something like the Boy Scouts. I heard nothing about any plane crash or captured Americans . . . nothing at all. The Japanese were very strict then about anything of military importance. My wife's father was beheaded on Saipan before the war for suspicion as a spy. We've been through too much hell to remember anything."

Tenorio was now a civilian employee of the U.S. Navy on Guam. Gervais got the impression that Tenorio and his wife, both of whom were very nervous and remembered nothing, had learned how to survive under one government after another by keeping their mouths shut. Tenorio did furnish the names of two former police officials still alive on Saipan who might know something about the incident.

Mrs. Maria Cepeda Castro Cruz, age forty-seven, was next interviewed at her home. In 1937 she had been married to one of the Saipan insular policemen named Castro.

"I heard of the plane crash that summer from a friend," she said. "It happened at Puntan Flores near the Japanese naval base."

"Were the flyers who crashed American or Japanese?" she was asked.

"American maybe. I don't know. I asked my husband about it and he told me to keep my mouth shut. I never mentioned it again."

Mrs. Cruz provided the names of three men who were Saipan prison guards at the time. Two still lived on Saipan. The third lived in Guam.

Pedro M. Cepeda, age forty-six, was located where he was confined to bed in the Guam Memorial Hospital with a swelling in his neck, shoulders, and face. He sat up and spoke quite clearly.

"I was a carpenter on the housing construction at the Chico Base on Flores Point then," Cepeda remembered. "That afternoon I was playing ball not far from the seaplane ramp when I saw Jesus Guerrero, the number-one insular police detective, and other Japanese escorting an American woman to the main base. She looked like a man wearing pants, a black shirt and scarf, and a leather jacket. I don't remember if she was wearing or carrying the jacket. She had a man's type haircut and appeared to be about thirty years of age. She was thin, about average height. I didn't know she was a woman at first . . . not until Guerrero told me she was an American spy woman who took pictures in flying clothes up front. Guerrero said she would go to Japan soon. That's all I know."

Gervais and Camacho next called upon Ben Salas, age forty-three, a former carpenter at the Chico Navy Base in 1937, now employed in a lumberyard in Agana, Guam. Coincidentally, Joaquin Seman, age forty-eight, who had been employed in the sugar mill on Saipan in 1937, was visiting Salas when Gervais and Camacho dropped in on them. The Guamanian detective had to assure both of them at great length that no punishment would result from anything they said.

Both stated they remembered two Americans on Saipan in 1937 and one of them was the American spy woman.

"The executions did not take place at the prison," Salas said.

"Executions?" Gervais asked excitedly. "They were executed?"

"Yes, but not at the prison. They were executed at the main Chico Base."

Seman agreed.

"Jesus Guerrero knows all about it," said Seman. "They were buried after the execution, and we can take you to the cemetery if you like."

"Are you sure they were the same Americans?" asked Gervais, for some reason not wishing to accept the finality of their report.

"There were only two Americans killed on Saipan before the war by the Japanese," Salas said. "An American man and American woman."

"Where were they buried?"

"The cemetery is located in Liang on Saipan next to the quarry and is next to a lumberyard," Salas said. "It's about a mile south of the main prison that the Japanese built before the war."

"Are the graves still there?"

"I don't know why not," answered Salas.

"Sure," agreed Seman.

"The cemetery wasn't touched by the war. Many cemeteries on Saipan were blasted during the invasion in 1944, but not that one. It's one of the few that survived the bombings by the Americans in June of 1944."

"How can we locate the graves?" Gervais asked.

"Through the main Church on Saipan," Seman suggested. "All persons in the cemetery are accounted for."

Gervais thought for a moment. "It's a Catholic cemetery?"

Both men nodded.

"Why were they buried in a Catholic cemetery?"

Salas answered. "The Japanese thought at that time that the Americans were Catholic people and should be put there. The Japanese did not bury any Japanese in Saipan cemeteries before the war. They cremated their bodies and sent the remains home to Japan."

The former guard at the Saipan prison who was now living on Guam was called upon next by Gervais and Quintanilla. He was forty-one-year-old Ramon Cabrera. He remembered two American prisoners in the late summer of 1937.

"Two American pilots, blindfolded and bound, were brought to the prison," Cabrera recalled. "They both wore khaki-colored flying suits, and one had much whiskers. The other was a strange-looking American man with no whiskers and a smooth face . . . smaller in height and thin body. The one without whiskers had lighter skin, but both dressed the same and both had short haircuts.

"They were kept in separate cells at night but were permitted to exercise out in the main prison yard for short times during the day.

"There were about two hundred prisoners in the prison at the time, and until the war came.

"For first three or four days they could not seem to eat their prison food. It was very bad and I wouldn't eat it myself unless forced to. If I remember correctly, on or about the fourth day they began to eat even though they didn't like breadfruit and other bits thrown in. We fed all prisoners three times a day, but only one-third a regular meal-size portion — meaning you got one full meal a day."

Gervais interrupted. "Was one of the two American pilots a girl?"

Cabrera looked at them blankly. "Girl? What girl?"

"Was there a girl?"

"I don't understand. There were two American pilots."

"What happened to them?"

Cabrera sighed. "I don't know. Maybe deported or executed. I would not know in my job. They were taken away."

Cabrera gave Gervais pictures of himself standing with the Chief of the Japanese Military Police and of a Japanese officer standing with his wife.

"This officer was educated in U.S.A.," said Cabrera. "Fine man. He was the one who questioned the two American pilots. We still write. He lives in Japan now."

Gervais obtained the Japanese interrogator's address, as well as the names of other prisoners and guards who were in the prison at that time. The first of these to be interviewed was a former prisoner, Waks Mull, a Caroline native who lived on Saipan in 1937.

"But I didn't go to jail until 1939," he protested. "I know nothing of any Americans of any kind before the war, in jail or otherwise. In early '44 while I was in prison they brought in seven American men flyers in the nude. They stayed in prison a short time. They were given prison clothing. These Americans crashed in an airplane somewhere near Saipan and were picked up by the Japanese in their life rafts. They were taken from prison and we never saw them again. I think they were deported to Japan. Those are the only Americans I heard about up until the invasion."

Guam cab driver Mateo Ooka, age forty-one, who had been employed by the Japanese on Saipan as an apprentice mechanic during the summer of 1937 was interviewed next.

"All I can remember," Ooka said, "was that one Americano pilot was held in the home of D. Reyes. That house is located a short distance from the hotel."

"Was it a man or a woman?" Gervais asked.

Ooka rubbed the back of his head. "It was so long ago I can't remember if it was a man or woman . . . only American. That's all."

"Did you see the person?"

"No. I'm just telling something that was common knowledge of many that an American was being kept in this house by the Japanese."

After interviewing forty-one persons on Guam in two weeks, only the fifteen interviews just related seemed to have any bearing on the incident. Throughout the investigation, Gervais and the two Guamanian police officers used all the tricks of interrogation. They gave no advance notice of their arrival to anyone and made certain the last person interviewed made no contact with the next to be questioned. They furnished no prior details or photos of Amelia Earhart until the interview had been completed and offered no compensation for information. Everything they learned was volunteered by the individual. Sometimes they walked in on people during meals, sometimes while they were at work. Others were routed out of bed as late as 3 A.M.

After the interviews were completed, Gervais briefed General Cook on his progress to date. Cook then reminded him that President Eisenhower was about to visit Japan and suggested that he should use discretion in talking about any discoveries so as to avoid political embarrassment.

Gervais understood what General Cook was driving at and decided to pursue Operation Earhart no further at least until President Eisenhower reached Hawaii on his way back from the Far East.

"Don't worry," Gervais said to Captain Quintanilla at the airport, "you and I will get to Saipan if we have to go all the way to Washington and get permission."

They shook hands warmly, and the veteran island policeman smiled and said, "Don't take too long. The trail is already twenty-three years old."

The fact that Saipan is a great place to keep a secret was even then being demonstrated by the United States. The real reason why Gervais had been prevented from going to Saipan in June of 1960 was that our own Central Intelligence Agency was operating a top-secret spy school there for Orientals in the service of America.

CHAPTER EIGHT

THE RUNAROUND

Prevented by U.S. naval authorities at Guam from going to Saipan to continue his investigation, Gervais left Guam on June 18, 1960, to return to Okinawa.

On June 17, the day before Gervais' trip was cut short by Navy red tape, Rear Admiral Waldemar Wendt, the Guam commander, and his information officer, Commander George York, were hosts to San Francisco radio announcer Fred Goerner and Maxim Akiyama, the husband of the original eyewitness quoted in Briand's book, *Daughter of the Sky*. They were flying that same day "with permission" arranged by the Columbia Broadcasting System to Saipan to check out Josephine Akiyama's story and look for Amelia Earhart's crashed airplane.

On June 5, 1960, Goerner had seen an item in the San Francisco newspapers stating that Dinger and Gervais were headed for Saipan to investigate the story. He persuaded his employers at KCBS that it would make a good feature for his radio program if he could get there first. So the day before Gervais left Guam for Okinawa, Goerner took off for Saipan assured by Admiral Wendt that Gervais and Dinger would not be making the same trip.

"They wanted to, but I didn't grant them permission," the admiral told Goerner, as quoted in his subsequent book.

Back on Okinawa the night of June 18, Gervais and Dinger conferred unaware that there was now a CBS man seeking a "scoop" on Saipan.

"We both decided that even though what we had uncovered on Guam was done at our own expense and on leave, as Air Force officers it was our duty to submit our material to the Air Force for an Intelligence evaluation. Although the President did not get to Japan because of the rioting taking place at that time, public release of what we had uncovered would not have promoted the best American-Japanese relations."

They presented the eyewitness statements Gervais had transcribed at Guam to the highest Air Force level on Okinawa.

The purpose of the presentation was twofold, to get official Air Force sanction to continue the investigation, and to obtain approval to visit Saipan. Commanders to whom they talked on Okinawa responded enthusiastically to the request. On the evening of the Fourth of July Gervais and Dinger arrived at 5th Air Force Headquarters in Japan on classified orders.

The next morning they presented their findings to the 5th Air Force Chief of Staff and the Deputy Chief of Intelligence. All were in agreement that the Amelia Earhart matter should be reopened.

They then spent the entire afternoon going over every detail with the Deputy Chief of Staff for Intelligence. He was very much interested from both an Intelligence and human-interest point of view and congratulated them both on the way they had conducted the investigation. It looked very much like they would be on their way to Washington within a day or so.

Dinger and Gervais relaxed at their hotel the night of July

5, unaware that, while they were dutifully going through official channels for permission to pursue their investigation further, their unsuspected competitor, Fred Goerner, had already grabbed headlines in San Francisco with what the press described as "an obituary for Amelia Earhart."

Returning from Saipan, Goerner called a press conference for newspapers, radio, and television on July 1.

An eight-column banner headline across the top of the *Chronicle*'s front page proclaimed:

EARHART CLUE FOUND

... and the story was similarly treated throughout the United States.

"Earhart Plane Reported Found—'Execution' Told" read the July 2 headlines of the San Francisco *Chronicle.*

> Twenty-three years after she disappeared over the Pacific, a press-radio news team wrote an obituary yesterday for Amelia Earhart.
>
> They said the famed aviatrix and her navigator, Fred Noonan, crash-landed in Saipan Bay in July, 1937, and were executed by the Japanese.
>
> Fred Goerner of KCBS radio returned from Saipan Thursday with the rusty parts of a pre-war plane and recorded conversations with natives who, he said, "remember seeing the American lady" crash.
>
> Chief piece of evidence was a coral-coated generator skindivers hauled up from the depths of Saipan Bay.

In producing the generator, Goerner led the press, radio, and television reporters assembled to believe it came from Lockheed Electra N-16020. In this he was corroborated by one of Amelia Earhart's associates.

> Paul Mantz, Santa Ana air service operator who outfitted Miss Earhart's plane for the round-the-world

flight, said the generator "appears to be" the special one he installed.

Blinded by red tape in Okinawa and Tokyo, Dinger and Gervais had not seen the story, but Paul Briand, Jr., at the Air Force Academy had. Seeing his own witness, Josephine Akiyama, and her husband Maxim Akiyama, "taken over" by a San Francisco radio announcer without giving credit to Briand's newly published book was a low blow. So Briand called a press conference on July 5 in Los Angeles, where he had rushed to talk to Paul Mantz.

EARHART DEATH PHOTOS TOLD a four-column headline proclaimed in the San Francisco *Chronicle* of July 6, 1960.

> Japanese photographs and the affidavits of 72 witnesses prove that Amelia Earhart and her navigator, Fred Noonan, were executed on Japanese-held Saipan island in 1937, an Air Force officer said yesterday.
> Captain Paul L. Briand, Jr. assistant professor of English at the Air Force Academy in Colorado, told interviewers in Los Angeles that even the undisturbed burial site of the vanished flyers has been located.
> The proof, he said, is in the possession of Captain Gervais, a troop-carrier pilot stationed on Okinawa, who wrote Briand:
> "The Amelia Earhart incident is fantastic, it is true, and it is tragic . . . ."

The same story contained the first denial of the executions.

> In Tokyo, a former Japanese Imperial Navy captain in charge of executions denied flatly that Miss Earhart had been executed on Saipan. "No such execution could have taken place without my knowledge and approval," former Captain Zenshiro Hoshina asserted.

The governor—I forget his name—wouldn't have dared do anything like executing Americans without authorization from Tokyo," he added.

While that story was breaking, Dinger and Gervais were naïvely busy in the Intelligence division of Air Force Headquarters in Tokyo helping to draft a message to the Pentagon requesting that they take their findings to Washington for evaluation.

"By lunchtime the message was in a rough draft and ready for final typing," Gervais remembered. "It was a beautiful three-page endorsement of our project with recommended courses of action that we couldn't have improved on if we had written it ourselves. In the meantime the press had contacted Okinawa and learned that we were in Tokyo."

The message was signed by the commanding general, but not yet delivered to Gervais and Dinger when the workday ended.

"That night all hell broke loose in Tokyo," Gervais recalled. "AP and UPI had obtained interviews from Japanese officials denying the entire program and were calling 5th Air Force officials all night trying to get a statement from Dinger and me. They called the information officer. They called us at our rooms. They called the chief of staff. They called the BOQ, and they may have even called the commanding general. The Office of Information was ordered to set up a press conference for the specific purpose of denying that we had any concrete evidence and of generally discrediting the entire project.

"We held a two-hour press conference the next day and the information officer directed the whole show in a manner calculated to make us look like idiots and get the press off the back of the 5th Air Force."

Gervais and Dinger had been sitting on top of the world on July 6, 1960, ready to dive full-throttle into the investigation of Amelia Earhart. After the controlled press conference in Tokyo on July 7, they were ordered to return immediately to Okinawa.

In San Francisco, where Fred Goerner had made headlines with his presentation of "the Bendix generator from Amelia Earhart's plane crash at Saipan," the *Chronicle* now reported:

AF CAPTAIN BACKS DOWN
The Earhart "Proof"
Is Falling Apart

An Air Force officer backed down yesterday on his reported contention that Amelia Earhart, American flyer who vanished in the Pacific 23 years ago, had been executed by the Japanese on Saipan.

The officer, Captain Joseph Gervais, 36, now stationed on Okinawa, said yesterday he had never actually visited Saipan island—and he conceded that photographs he possessed were not really proof of Miss Earhart's execution.

Gervais also told a news conference in Tokyo yesterday that the 72 affidavits he held—described earlier as sworn statements by eyewitnesses to Miss Earhart's execution—did not actually describe any executions.

"They were," he explained, merely "72 names of people living today on Saipan and Guam who have information on the subject."

Associated Press also reported from Tokyo—without quoting any source—that "the Air Force confirmed it had ordered Gervais to halt his investigation."

"This was not completely true," Gervais said, "although we had been ridiculed before the world and in front of friends, relatives, and the Air Force officials who had helped us reach this pinnacle. Actually, we were ordered back to Okinawa to await action quietly on a much-toned-down message to Washington. It was now suggested that only one of us might go to the Pentagon to seek permission to conduct an official investigation based on the interviews I had obtained at Guam."

During the next three months on Okinawa, Gervais and Dinger contemplated the irony of their situation. They had in effect been disowned in their investigation because Paul Briand, Jr., in Los Angeles had broken confidence about the Guam interviews, after having been nudged into such action by Goerner's delivery in San Francisco of "the generator from Amelia Earhart's crashed airplane." And on July 9, the day after the embarrassed "Operation Earhart" duo had been exiled back to Okinawa, the world learned that Goerner's generator was not from the Earhart plane at all.

Reported the San Francisco *Chronicle:*

> The barnacle-encrusted generator found at Saipan and believed to be part of Amelia Earhart's vanished airplane was disowned yesterday by the Bendix Aviation Corp.
>
> Charles Smith, for the Eclipse Pioneer Division of Bendix, said in New York that a bearing from the generator had been traced to a firm in Osaka, Japan. . . .
>
> The Bendix generator on Miss Earhart's plane, when it disappeared on a flight from New Guinea to Honolulu in 1937, contained no Japan-made bearings, Smith said.

In fact, Goerner's first find in the Pacific was a generator taken from the World War II wreckage of a Japanese Betty bomber, which resembles a Lockheed 10 Electra only in that it has two engines, two wings, and was built by man for the purpose of flying through the air.

"We had been shot down at the start of our investigation," Gervais recalled, "only because the Navy at Guam refused to let me go to Saipan as an officer trained in aircraft accident investigation, and with a top-secret security clearance, while at the same time granting permission for a civilian CBS team from San Francisco to go there in search of a scoop. I could have told the difference between a Betty and an Electra even with barnacles on it."

"We weren't looking for a scoop," Dinger added. "All we were looking for was the truth, and the baloney about the generator only buried the truth deeper. We were going crazy on Okinawa waiting for an official invitation to Washington. We could have waited forever."

While waiting, Gervais received an encouraging letter from Viola Gentry, an aviatrix of the 1920s, famous among other things for flying under the Brooklyn Bridge, and for serving in the early 1930s with Amelia Earhart on the committee which organized the Bendix Trophy air races.

The correspondence between Gervais and Viola Gentry was a happenstance thing which started in the summer of 1960. Gervais' aunt, Eva Swift, who had at one time paid for his first airplane ride when he was a boy, was working in Miami as a maid in the Belleview-Biltmore, one of several resort hotels around the nation which seasonally employed Viola Gentry. Miss Gentry wrote to encourage Gervais in his quest for her missing friend, Amelia Earhart:

> We are so pleased to hear of your project to locate Amelia and Noonan. We hope with all of our hearts and prayers that you accomplish your visions . . . .
> You know that when anyone started on a flight, all of us were interested and did our bit to help . . . we had nautical charts of the Pacific that were made in May, 1932, from the Navy, and the winds were of 3 feathers cross on the nose (ten-mile head winds and cross winds). We had pilots that had been to the South Pole with Byrd, one from BOAC as well as Sir Hubert Wilkins, check gasoline mileage. And in our estimates of where she would be south of her course, we thought she would pass Nui, the most northern island of the Ellice Group en route. We knew Amelia would not take

off or start on that last uncharted leg with a faulty compass. At least she always told us not to start a flight unless instruments were as perfect as we could have them . . . .

The last time we heard Amelia speak, she said she had about a half-hour's worth of fuel, overcast a thousand feet, and position doubtful. All of us heard her over the Solomon Islands. So in her position, we feel sure that if a coral reef went past, we would try and land near it. There are many that believe flying south and north she would be sure to find a reef.

So our sincere prayers are that you will be able to find the truth in your search.

After three months of stewing in Okinawa, Dinger and Gervais took a thirty-day leave and headed for Washington at their own expense.

Their purpose was to try again to get authorization, facilities, and resources for an official Air Force investigation into the disappearance of Amelia Earhart in which they would participate using all the facilities and resources available in Washington and ending up with conclusive evidence of Amelia Earhart's fate. Shortly after their arrival at Headquarters USAF in the Pentagon, they gave a briefing on what they had uncovered to date to a general and a few colonels who were representatives of various departments. The Air Force was interested, but the answer was still no.

A letter was prepared, signed by a general, and handed to them. It read:

Concerning the evidence reported to have been found in the Far East indicating the cause of death of American Aviatrix Amelia Earhart, as this Office has previously indicated, the Air Force considers such evidence, found under the stated circumstances, to be the personal property of the finders. Therefore, you are free to dispose of this information in any way you see fit. This, of course, means that the Air Force is not officially concerned in this instance and, therefore, can not endorse your findings for factual accuracy or opinion. I trust this letter makes the Air Force's position completely clear in regard to this subject.

However, the Air Force in a semiofficial capacity arranged for a memo to be sent to Admiral Frost of Naval Intelligence requesting permission for Gervais and Dinger to visit Saipan.

While in Washington, Gervais received another letter from Viola Gentry. The letter read:

No doubt you remember Clyde Pangborn and Hugh Herendon, that were arrested in Japan for having a Kodak camera in their plane, a Bellanca, on their round-the-world flight. They were jailed three months. Took some work for our American counselor to get them out; as long as Pang lived he would never talk about his stay in Japan. There was talk that AE was doing something for the government, was denied, yet she was a frequent visitor at the White House. In 1949 in Berkeley, California, AE's mother was to see the Japanese counselor by an appointment; when the day arrived no one was there that had ever heard of AE. A chap, whose name I have forgotten, came to see mother Earhart telling her that he had also talked to people in the Marshall Islands that were sure they had seen them forced to land on the beach; we found out later that the whole staff of the embassy had been changed suddenly!!!

A quick check of the National Archives revealed that there was an Amelia Earhart file that Dinger and Gervais could not look into because it was classified, originally by the War Department. Through the Air Force they made a request to the Department of Defense for the file to be declassified . . . one more thing to wait for.

"What," asked Gervais, "is there about the file on the disappearance of a civilian aircraft that caused it to be classified by the War Department?"

Operation Earhart had not gone unnoticed in Washington.

"You know, at the time of your unfortunate press conference in Tokyo, things were really busting loose over at the State Department," a friend in the Pentagon confided to Gervais and Dinger.

"In the State Department?"

"Yes. Wires were flowing in from our Ambassador in Japan."

"Douglas MacArthur?"

"Yes. Ambassador MacArthur apparently was all worked up over what you had disclosed. And so was a Mr. Feldman here—a member of the Japanese-American relations section of the State Department. Feldman was about to confiscate every bit of evidence you had turned up."

"Why didn't he?"

"It was pointed out to Mr. Feldman that if he did seize your files and the press ever queried you about where the Earhart material was, you would probably say that Mr. Feldman had it. He didn't choose to be in that position, and that's why you were left alone for the time being. But I'd be wary of State if I were you."

At this point they decided to return to the Pacific, where they could continue their investigation in peace.

They had been in Washington for three weeks. At the beginning of their journey it had taken them thirty hours to cross the Pacific, with island stops all the way to Los Angeles. But the Air Force helped them get out of Washington in a hurry. They were put aboard a Special Air Mission VC-137 jet which flew nonstop to Tokyo. Also aboard were Senators Mike Mansfield and William Fulbright en route to an Intra-Parliamentary Conference in Tokyo.

Dinger and Gervais enjoyed conversing with the distinguished senators, but the subject of Amelia Earhart's mysterious disappearance was never brought up. If "Operation Earhart" had learned anything in Washington, it was the immeasurable value of silence. And from that point on, what had started out as one of the most publicized private investigations ever conducted—became one of the most secret.

CHAPTER NINE

THE POEM

Among the "Operation Earhart" papers spread out on the kitchen table in Joe Gervais' Okinawa house was a poem given to him and Bob Dinger by a middle-aged secretary as they were leaving the Pentagon.

"Here," she said. "I think you should have this."

It was a poem typewritten on a piece of white paper. Across the top of the sheet of bond was typed: "Written by Marcia Short on July 3, 1937." That would be one day after the disappearance of Amelia Earhart and Fred Noonan.

Slowly, and with growing interest, Gervais read from the poem.

> How brief a time ago you left us, winging
> Toward the rising sun, your engines singing!
> Pathfinder's courage yours, and high hopes burning!
> A breathless world awaited your returning!

His eyes searched the "Tribute to Amelia Earhart, Aviatrix" which followed, pausing at a passage which seemed almost prophetic.

> What lonely, lovely isle, with palm trees bending,
> Hides, in its coral reefs, your argosy's ending?

What dusky, strange-tongued tribes have found the
   twisted,
Torn scraps of wreckage that the waves resisted?

Gervais stared at the paper. Outside, the distant roar of a
B-29 engine came to a sudden halt. From the darkness came
the soft whir of wings as birds, disturbed by the startling
silence, shifted from tree to tree.

Who was Marcia Short? Gervais walked to a bookshelf
in the small living room and riffled through the pages of
Soaring Wings, George Putnam's biography of his missing
wife published in 1939.

"At one time and another," Putnam wrote, "AE wrote
many fragments of verse, for she found deep pleasure in
building little images with words. That aspect was very
private—almost secret."

Gervais read the poem of hers that followed. The first part
of it struck him deeply.

Courage is the price that life exacts for
   granting peace.
The soul that knows it not, knows no release
From little things;

Knows not the livid loneliness of fear
Nor mountain heights, where bitter joy can hear
The sound of wings.

The most famous woman in the world, idolized by millions,
sought after by the rich, exploited by the commercial, followed everywhere by the press, had a secret belief that
courage was the price of peace.

Gervais read again from the text of a letter Amelia Earhart
had written to Putnam setting forth the terms under which
she would agree to their marriage, in penciled longhand:

In our life together, I shall not hold you to any medieval
code of faithfulness to me, nor shall I consider myself

bound to you similarly. If we can be honest I think the difficulties which arise may best be avoided . . . .

Please let us not interfere with the other's work or play, nor let the world see our private joys or disagreements. In this connection I may have to keep some place where I can go to be myself now and then, for I cannot guarantee to endure at all times the confinements of even an attractive cage.

I must exact a cruel promise, and that is you will let me go in a year if we find no happiness together.

Her signature at the end of the remarkable letter had been a simple "AE."

"You know," she had in confidence told newsman C. B. Allen just before takeoff on her final round-the-world attempt, "I am not coming back from this flight."

"Nonsense," he had replied, agreeing to keep her remark "off the record."

Gervais thumbed back to the poem by Amelia Earhart.

How can life grant us boon of living, compensate
For dull gray ugliness and pregnant hate
Unless we dare
The soul's dominion? Each time we make a choice,
    we pay
With courage to behold resistless day
And count it fair.

There was little peace or privacy on the ground for the first lady of the air during her six years of marriage to George Palmer Putnam. In addition to being her husband under her own unconventional terms, Putnam was also her business manager, a job in which he excelled. Books, Amelia Earhart products, the Pan Pacific Press Bureau operated expressly to publicize her name—all these were the result of Putnam's labor. She refused to star in a movie for Carl Laemmle, to the disappointment of Putnam. His last message, never delivered to her, was news of a "big, fat radio contract" waiting for her upon her return. And when she disappeared, Putnam immediately attempted to arrange the sale, to the American Broadcasting Company, of exclusive broadcast rights of the Navy search for her.

"How can life grant us boon of living, compensate for dull gray ugliness and pregnant hate unless we dare the soul's dominion?"

Late in the Okinawa night, Gervais compared the vehemence of that verse of hers with another that was quoted in the Putnam book.

> To touch your hand or see your face, today,
> Is joy. Your casual presence in a room
> Recalls the stars that watched us as we lay.
> I mark you in the moving crowd
> And see again those stars
> A warm night lent us long ago.
> We loved so then — we love so now.

Gervais brought the book back with him to the kitchen and once again picked up the poem by Marcia Short.

> . . . maybe, in some paradise unknown,
> Some wild, uncharted island, lost, alone,
> You wander in primeval jungles, waiting
> Amid its dreamlike, glorious beauty . . . .

Gervais sat there until dawn comparing the poetry of Amelia Earhart with the poem by the unknown Marcia Short.

CHAPTER TEN

THE AMERICAN SPIES

While awaiting official permission to make the long-delayed trip to Saipan, Gervais and Dinger, in addition to flying their regularly scheduled Air Force missions, kept up the investigation of Amelia Earhart. The photograph of Nobuo Tanaka which they had been given at Guam interested them.

Tanaka, the Japanese police interpreter who supposedly had assisted in the interrogation of the two mysterious American flyers on Saipan in 1937, appeared in the photo with his wife. She wore a traditional Japanese kimono, as was the custom of Japanese wives in the thirties. She also wore a gold wedding band on the third finger of her left hand, which was not the Japanese custom. Gervais and Dinger wondered if the wedding ring could have been taken from Amelia Earhart.

In the lower left-hand portion of the photograph, a framed painting unaccountably was leaning against the porch of the Japanese couple's house. A blow-up of that portion of the photograph by the photo lab at Naha Air Force Base, Okinawa, revealed the painting to be a head-on shot of what appeared to be a crash-landed, twin-engined, low-winged monoplane.

The back of the photograph was stamped with an embossed Japanese seal similar to a notary seal. The official Air Force interpreter at the Naha Base translated the raised Japanese printing to read: "Passed inspection, Saipan Photo Shop, Saipan Island, South Sea Islands." Japanese script on the back of the photo said: "When Police Sergeant Tanaka was a policeman."

Gervais and Dinger wrote a letter to the FBI in San Francisco for possible information on Tanaka and received a reply from the Department of Justice Immigration Service.

> *Re* Nobuo Tanaka or Nobura Tanaka, an exhaustive search has been made from our Chicago office to locate any other files with the same name, but without success. File A3526314, to which you make reference, related to one Nobuo Tanaka who first arrived at the Port of Seattle, Washington, on September 6, 1918, on the "Chicago Maru" at which time he gave his age as 14 years; born in Tomiyama Mura, Chibaken, Japan (date of birth not shown on manifest); occupation, student; destination to Portland, Oregon. The next action in the case indicates he married Masuko Tanaka in 1922.

On September 4, 1960, "Operation Earhart" ran an ad in the *Chugoku*, Japanese newspaper in western Japan, trying to locate Tanaka. The ad brought no response.

Gervais and Dinger also interviewed Okinawa attorney Shigio Ikehara, who formerly had been a member of the Japanese police force on Saipan from 1934 to 1944. The interview took place in Gervais' home with an Air Force interpreter, as Ikehara insisted he spoke no English. Ikehara also demanded that a Mr. Oshira, age sixty-two, an Okinawa resident who had been a member of the Japanese administration at Saipan during the same period, be present throughout the interview.

"A foreign aircraft, not a Japanese aircraft, crashed on Saipan in 1937 or 1938," Ikehara said.

"No. No. No such thing ever happened," interrupted Oshira.

"Would you describe the aircraft?" Dinger asked.

"No."

"There was no such airplane crash," insisted Oshira.

"Who was on board and what became of them?"

Ikehara shook his head.

"No. No. No. No foreigners were in Saipan in 1937," insisted Oshira. "There was no airplane."

Ikehara shrugged and would say no more. Gervais drove them back to Naha City. As they approached the office of the Japanese attorney who claimed to neither speak nor understand English, Ikehara leaned forward from the rear seat and tapped Gervais on the shoulder.

"Would you stop here, please?" he asked in perfect English, and left smiling.

Gervais wrote many letters to off-chance sources of information throughout the Pacific islands. One of them located Brother Gregorio on Yap Island in the Carolines. He was the natural brother of Father Tardio, the Catholic priest at Saipan. Both had been there in 1937.

Brother Gregorio replied to Gervais' request for information:

I am writing this letter in Spanish rather than in English, because I feel I can express my reply more understandably for you.

I recall a little over 20 years ago before war was declared—during the Summer holidays for the children, when they came to the vestry to tell me of the two American spies who were apprehended on Saipan near Garapan. They mentioned one was an American woman who wore long pants like a man and had a haircut like a man. The Japanese police held these two Americans as spies. The woman's companion's face is very suntanned like Spanish people's faces. The Japanese took them away to ask questions. The children were Jesus Rios, Juan Sanches, Jose Sanches, Jose Gereyo, and the Americans were seen coming from the direction of Lisand near Garapan.

Kumoi spoke to me a few days later about these two American Intelligence Spies and said he would show them everything if they gave him a lot of money.

After the invasion of Saipan I went to the Intelligence Officer there on Saipan, whose name I can't recall, and asked him if they wanted any information about the two Americans, the man and the woman, who came to Saipan from Hawaii in an airplane to spy for American Intelligence before the invasion. He was not interested and I left.

I do not know if this will be of help. I don't know what became of these two Americans since the vestry was located far away from where they were apprehended.

Five months, and five miles of red tape, after Gervais and Dinger first applied for official permission to visit Saipan, they finally received a wire at Okinawa direct from Headquarters USAF in Washington: PASS TO CAPTAIN GERVAIS, DEPARTMENT OF NAVY HAS CLEARED YOUR VISIT TO SAIPAN WITH ALL AGENCIES CONCERNED, ADVISE DATES SOONEST. After another short delay to clear Dinger and Captain Quintanilla from Guam, they arrived in Saipan in mid-December, 1960. Captain Paul Bridwell, the naval commander of Saipan, met their plane and invited them to his office to offer assistance.

Bridwell participated in the first search for Amelia Earhart back in 1937. At that time he was a yeoman on the flagship *Colorado,* and he was also beachmaster for the invasion of Saipan in 1944. In various tours of duty he had lived a total of more than eight years on Saipan.

"Do you think Amelia Earhart and Fred Noonan were here at Saipan?" asked Dinger.

"From what the natives here have told me, I would say they were, but they didn't crash here."

"How do you know?"

"There is a lot of native talk of an American man and woman being at Saipan about 1937, but there is absolutely no real evidence that I have heard of that a plane ever crashed here with them in it."

"You mean you think they were brought here from somewhere else?"

The Navy captain shrugged. "Who knows? I think they may have been here all right, but I don't think they crashed here, nor is there any evidence that they were executed here. I gather from what the natives have told me that a man and woman who could have been Amelia Earhart and Fred Noonan crashed somewhere else in the Pacific. Then they were apprehended and taken by ship to Saipan. I have no reliable reports on what happened after that."

"Tell me this, Captain Bridwell," Dinger said. "We know only what the public was told in the newspapers about where the Navy searched for Earhart and Noonan in 1937. Did you search anyplace other than what was released in the papers?"

"I can't answer that," said Bridwell. "That whole matter was classified and I have never heard that it isn't still a classified matter. I'm sorry, but I don't feel I should talk about that."

The Navy provided Gervais, Dinger, and Quintanilla with quarters in a quonset hut and loaned them a pickup truck to get around the island in. Quintanilla recruited the assistance of Saipan's Sheriff Manuel Sablan, and between them they possessed fluency in four languages.

The population of Saipan in 1960 was about 7,800 Chamorro and Caroline natives, 4,000 cattle, and about a thousand jeeps which the U.S. government sold to the natives for $1 each following World War II. These had been kept in running order ever since.

Before interrogating anyone, they took the pickup for a tour of the island.

Sheriff Sablan pointed along the quiet beach. "Mr. Goerner

came down here expecting to find the Earhart plane crashed on the beach. I think he thought he would simply walk up to it, identify it, and go home with the news. But it wasn't here, so he took a boy across the harbor to where the wrecks of Japanese planes were bulldozed out of the bay, and had the boy fish up some parts of a Jap Betty bomber. He took that and left with it."

Dinger chuckled. "Yeah. We know."

They discussed the Goerner investigation and the Navy investigation and decided that neither had turned up anything worth following up on.

The first person they talked to was J. Y. Matsumoto, the brother-in-law of Josephine Blanco Akiyama and the person to whom she had been taking lunch when she witnessed the plane crash at Garapan.

"I remember the fuss," Matsumoto said. "I was working in the Japanese naval base doing excavation. I didn't see anything. I just heard about the crash, but I didn't see it."

"Your sister-in-law, Josephine Akiyama, said you saw the crash when she did."

"You know Josephine?"

"Yes," Gervais nodded. "Josephine says that when she was eleven years old she used to take you lunch, and that one day you both saw a plane crash on the beach and there were two people in it. An American man and woman."

"How about it?" prodded Sheriff Sablan.

Matsumoto appeared agitated. "Yes," he admitted. "I saw the crash. Two Americans were imprisoned."

"Two men?"

"No. One of them was a woman. How long are you going to stay in Saipan?

"Until we get the truth," said Gervais. "Were the man and woman executed?"

"Why don't you talk to the oldest Blanco sister? Go to Guam and talk to her."

"Were they executed?" repeated Sablan.

"I don't know of any execution. Why don't you go back to Guam and talk to the other Blanco woman?"

"We have already talked to the Blanco sister on Guam," said Gervais.

"I don't know anything more," said Matsumoto. He seemed unduly agitated that Dinger and Gervais might stay for some time on Saipan.

They next interviewed Mrs. Blanco, the mother of Josephine Akiyama.

"I remember my little girl telling me about it," she said. "I told her to be quiet about it. I didn't want to know. It wasn't safe to know such things in those days. But she told me about the plane crash and the man and woman in it. It was seven or eight years before the invasion of Saipan, just like Josephine said. We lived a ways from where it happened, so I didn't see it myself. But I believed my daughter at the time."

The investigators moved on to the Saipan Church and talked to its dean and pastor, Father Arnold Bendowski.

"I was not here in those days," Father Arnold said. "My first experience with the Japanese was in early 1942 when Father Felix Leye, who now operates the Catholic orphanage on Okinawa, and I were young priests."

"We are looking for the graves of Amelia Earhart and Fred Noonan," Gervais announced solemnly. "Are there records of the graves among the Church records here?"

Father Arnold nodded and opened a filing drawer. "You know Saipan was literally devastated during the invasion of 1944 and many records were either burned or destroyed." He produced an old ledger book and spread it out before them. "However, the Church records of 1924 through 1943 were hidden from the Japanese throughout the years of occupation. These are the records for those years, including all recorded burials on the island."

For hours they pored through the records beginning with July, 1937. There were no entries to indicate any Americans

Portrait of a Lady Flier! Amelia Earhart, circa 1930, in classic leather boots, mid-length flight coat, leather helmet and goggles.

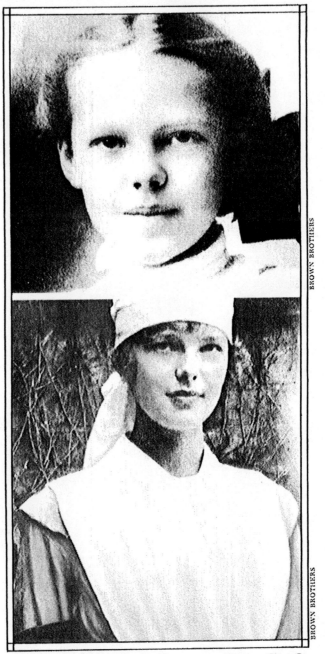

(Top) Amelia's childhood was spent in Kansas City, St. Paul, Des Moines, and finally Chicago, where she graduated from Hyde Park High in 1916. *(Bottom)* Amelia as a nurse's aide in a Toronto Military Hospital, 1917, caring for World War I wounded.

(Top) AE in her leather flying coat with that "against the gods" look. *(Middle)* The Lockheed Vega in which Amelia Earhart made her solo transatlantic flight. *(Bottom)* Her mother's favorite photo, taken when Amelia was learning to fly.

Amelia Earhart being accorded a London welcome as the first woman passenger to fly the Atlantic, 1928. *(Inset)* The National Geographic Society Medal presented to Amelia Earhart as the first woman to make a solo flight across the Atlantic, May 21, 1932.

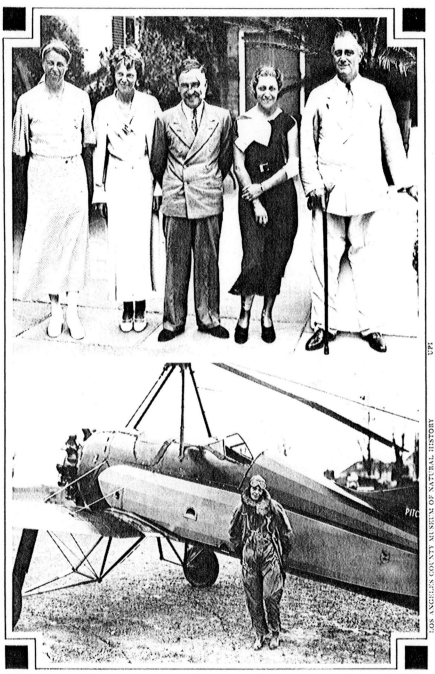

(*Top, left to right*) A 1933 visit to Hyde Park: Eleanor Roosevelt, Amelia Earhart, Jim and Amy Mollison (battered from their Atlantic crossing attempt), and President Franklin D. Roosevelt. (*Bottom*) AE was the first woman to fly an auto-gyro. She eventually cracked up in this one.

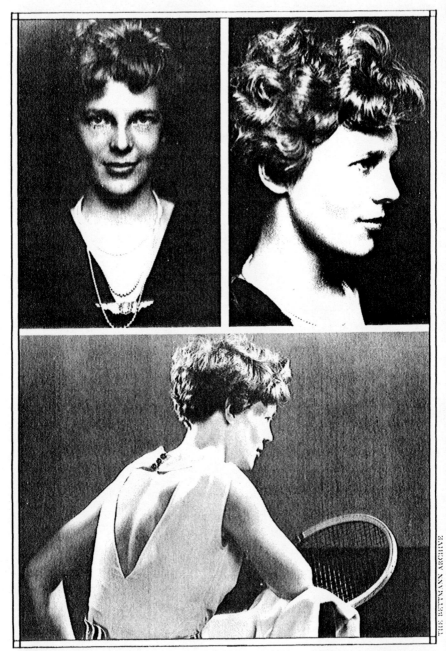

(*Top*) Amelia wearing silver Air Force wings awarded her when commissioned honorary major in 349th "Golden Gate" Air Force Reserve Wing at Hamilton Air Force Base, California. (*Bottom*) Amelia in tennis costume for *Vanity Fair*.

(*Top*) Out of her flying clothes and onto the fashion pages—Amelia Earhart sits for a 1928 studio portrait. (*Bottom*) Circa 1931, Amelia in a height-of-fashion white ensemble. Her fashion sense graced many pages of *Vanity Fair, Town and Country*, and newspaper rotogravure sections of the day.

A charcoal sketch of Amelia Earhart by James Montgomery Flagg. The profile is done much in the style of Charles Dana Gibson.

James Montgomery Flagg's romantic portrait of Amelia Earhart, showing open-necked blouse and ever-present wafting silk scarf.

Publisher George Palmer Putnam and Aviatrix Amelia Earhart.

(Above, left) AE and navigator Noonan on second round-the-world flight—note clear glass window in door and no crossbar. *(Above, right)* Amelia on her ranch getting a "barbecue" trim. *(Below)* A day at Santa Monica Beach—*(left to right)* Putnam, AE, and "The Flying Mollisons," Amy and Jim.

(Clockwise) An earlier Amelia looking jaunty on a "day off"—probably flying an auto-gyro or a biplane; AE and George Putnam going over engine modifications on the Electra at Lockheed's Burbank plant prior to the second round-the-world attempt; on another day—Amelia and Putnam back at the ranch.

One of the last photos of missing aviatrix Amelia Earhart, taken in front of the starboard engine of the Lockheed Electra, June 8, 1937.

(Left to right) George Putnam, Amelia Earhart, navigator Harry Manning, and mechanic Bo McKneely posed in front of the Lockheed at Los Angeles, February 24, 1937.

(Top) George and Amelia Earhart Putnam talking to reporters after crash at Hickam Field, Hawaii. (Bottom) AE at the controls of the Electra while it was being remodeled for larger fuel capacity.

(Top) Crack-up at Hickam Field, Hawaii, March 20, 1937, on the first round-the-world-try. *(Middle)* Another view of the crash. The site had become a crash laboratory by this time. *(Bottom)* The XC-35, a modified Lockheed Model 10 Electra, was the world's first successful pressurized airplane. Its first flight, May 7, 1937, was just two weeks before Earhart and Noonan's final departure from California.

(*Top*) Technical Advisor Paul Mantz, AE, and navigators Harry Manning and Fred Noonan at Oakland Airport prior to first flight. (*Middle*) Amelia and un-identified man in front of the Electra. Note navigation bubble in place of loop antennae and set-back navigation lights. Other photos show protruding navigation lights. (*Bottom*) This plane has underwing NR designation instead of R, as in above photo.

(*Top*) Amelia, a Cord 810 convertible, and the spanking-new Lockheed Electra 10. Note that trademark star of R-16020 is outlined with company name inside. Also, the door is solid and the four windows are equally spaced. (*Middle*) Takeoff from Oakland Airport on one of the world flights. Note that wing-tip lights do not protrude. (*Bottom*) Fred Noonan and Amelia boarding for takeoff from San Juan, Puerto Rico, on last flight.

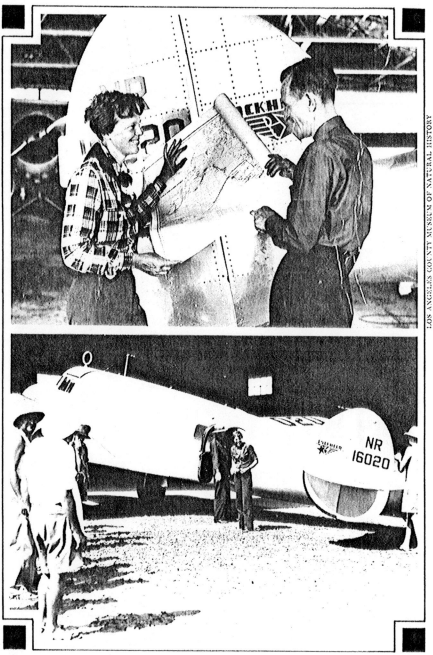

(Top) In hangar, Earhart and Noonan pose with map of the Pacific showing route of last flight. (Bottom) The Lockheed Electra at an unidentified airport on final flight.

(Top) The last known photo of Amelia Earhart and Fred Noonan, Lae, New Guinea, July 2, 1937. Note the clear glass window on cabin door. (Bottom) Just before takeoff Noonan and Earhart do some last-minute checking on the Electra. Note the four identical cabin window covers, divided two and two by a larger center window cover.

Amelia Floating, Radio Sputters

WASHINGTON, July 5 (AP).--A message to Coast Guard headquarters today said interception of "ragged" radio signals "indicated possibility Earhart plane still afloat 281 miles, north of Howland Island."

Sent from the Coast Guard Cutter Itasca at 1:10 p. m. (E.S.T.) the message said bearings taken with a Coast Guard radio direction finder on Howland confirmed the approximate position of the Earhart plane, indicated by the garbled radio signals, which were received earlier by the naval station at Honolulu.

"We will arrive at the indicated position this afternoon about 1700 plus 11,5 (11:30 p. m. Eastern Standard)." the message said.

AMELIA EARHART.
Smiling through official information indicates she is down off Howland Island.

Navy Speeds to Rescue

A brood of planes flying away the mother ship, U. S. S. Lexington, the huge plane carrier now rushing toward the vicinity of Howland Island, in the Pacific, to join the search for the disappearing Amelia Earhart and Fred Noonan.

Minnesota Weather

Today's Editorials
Violence as a Right
The Memorial Day Riot
The Siege of Vicksburg
Perpetuating the Spoils System
A New Art Foundation

St. Paul Pioneer Press

NO. 184. ST. PAUL, MINN., SATURDAY, JULY 8, 1937. PRICE THREE CENTS IN ST. PAUL.

AMELIA OUT OF GAS; FEARED DOWN IN SEA

Solons Agree On Income Tax

Adjournment by Next Saturday Forecast as House and Senate Conferees Reach Accord.

How The New Income Rates Affect You

The following tables show the items tax which a single person, a married person with two dependents and a corporation would pay under the rates agreed to Friday by Senate and House conferees as compared to the taxes paid now.

3-DAY FOURTH WILL LURE CITY INTO THE OPEN

Thousands to Take to Roads; Big Municipal Celebration Planned for Monday at Phalen.

Be Careful!

Russians Yield To Japan's Demand By Agreeing To Withdraw Troops

HUNTED BY COAST GUARDSMEN

BELIEVED ONLY 100 MILES OFF GOAL ON ISLAND

Coast Guard Speeds to Rescue; Flier and Her Navigator Equipped With Rubber Boat and Flares.

MARTIN CAIDIN AND EDWARD HYMOFF

(Top) Admiral Black, third from left, dedicating the Amelia Earhart Light at Howland Island, 1938. Black was the Putnam "family representative" aboard the Coast Guard cutter *Itasca,* and was present at the hearing on New Year's Day, 1939, in Superior Court, Los Angeles, which declared Amelia Earhart legally dead. *(Bottom)* Lockheed 12, NC-16022, used to transport then Navy Commander Lyndon Johnson around Australia in 1942 to prepare a friendly reception for American Negro troops. The airliner had the same markings as the Union Airways of New Zealand plane.

Form 9654
TREASURY DEPARTMENT
U. S. Coast Guard
July 1955

U. S. COAST GUARD
OFFICIAL DISPATCH

UNIT	DATE

INCOMING HEADING

Z HUNT V NRUI Q QUAX P HUNT   NITE QUAX   GR 136

TEXT

8002 YOUR 1003 0044   RECEIVED INCOMPLETE MESSAGES ON A GREED SCHEDULES

FROM 0248 TO 0855 TWO JULY PERIOD EARHART ONLY ACKNOWLEDGED RECEIVING ITASCA ONCE AND DID NOT ANSWER QUESTIONS AS TO POSITION COURSE SPEED ON EXPECTED TIME ARRIVAL PERIOD REPORTED AT 0615 TWO HUNDRED MILES OUT AT 0646 REPORTED 100 MILES OUT AT 0855 SHE GAVE ITASCA A LINE OF POSITION 157 337 BELIEVED TO BE RADIO BEARING AND STATED SHE WAS RUNNING NORTH AND SOUTH PERIOD LAE NEW GUINEA REPORTS LAST CONTACT WITH EARHART PLANE BY LEA RADIO WAS AT 1720   FRIDAY VAGE POSITION AS FOUR POINT THREE THREE SOUTH ONE FIFTYNINE POINT SIX EAST WHICH IS ABOUT 795 MILES DIRECTLY ON HER ROUTE TO HOWLAND PERIOD KRRN RECEIVED REPORT CIVILIAN HEARING POSITION REPORT FROM EARHART AS QUOTE ONE POINT SIX ONE SEVENTY NINE UNQUOTE   0205

TOR 0544 NRUI   RE (INTERCEPTED) 12600

UNITED STATES DEPARTMENT OF JUSTICE
FEDERAL BUREAU OF INVESTIGATION

WASHINGTON, D.C. 20535

In Reply, Please Refer to
File No.

January 27, 1969

Mr. Joseph Gervais
1905 Theresa Avenue
Las Vegas, Nevada 89101

Dear Mr. Gervais:

Your letter of January 20th has been received.

In reply to your request, information in our files must be maintained as confidential pursuant to regulations of the Department of Justice. I hope you will not infer either that we do or do not have material in our files relating to the individual you mentioned.

Sincerely yours,

John Edgar Hoover
Director

(Top) U.S. Coast Guard dispatch describing last contact between cutter *Itasca* and Earhart. *(Bottom)* FBI refusal to grant Gervais confidential data on Amelia Earhart.

THE EARLY BIRDS OF AVIATION, INC.

Secretary's Office
4 Weybridge Road
Mineola, Long Island, N. Y. 11501
516 742-3949

August 9, 1967

Mr. J. Gervais
1905 Theresa Avenue
Las Vegas, Nev 89101

Dear Mr. Gervais:

Replying to yours of August 1st, inquiring about Irene Craigmile.

I have known this lady for the past thirty years. In fact she lived just two doors away from me at one time here on Weybridge Road in Mineola.

Shortly after she was married to Mr. Craigmile, he suddenly died and shortly thereafter she married an aviator flying out of Roosevelt Field here in Mineola, named Al Heller. A son was born to them, who is now about 30 years old. She learned to fly under instructions from her husband Al Heller at Floyd Bennet Field. After a few years they were divorced and a few years later she married a man named Guy Bolam here in New York, who was engaged in the export business. She has two homes, her summer home is P.O. Box 195, Jamesburg, N.J.. She also has a beautiful summer home on Littletown Lane, Bedford, N.Y. P.O. Box 31.

When she was flying at Floyd Bennet Field and Roosevelt Field, she was a pal of Amelia Earhart and Viola Gentry, all of whom were flying at Roosevelt Field at that time. This was at the time Amelia and Viola were getting the 99 Club organized and going.

I can't speak too highly of Irene as she is a very fine person to know and is well liked by everybody who knows her. I hope this answers your question. Kind regards.

Sincerely

E. N. Pickerill

AN ORGANIZATION OF PIONEERS IN AERONAUTICS WHO FLEW SOLO BEFORE DECEMBER 17, 1916

DEPARTMENT OF TRANSPORTATION
FEDERAL AVIATION ADMINISTRATION
AERONAUTICAL CENTER
P.O. BOX 25082
OKLAHOMA CITY, OKLAHOMA 73125

December 5, 1967

AIRMAIL

IN REPLY
REFER TO: AC-260

Mr. Joseph Gervais
1905 Theresa Avenue
Las Vegas, Nevada

Dear Mr. Gervais:

This is in response to your letter of December 2, 1967, concerning Irene Craigmile.

The information you requested may be released only when the airman or someone legally competent to act for her specifically consents to its release in writing.

Sincerely yours,

Eddie E. Kjelshus
Chief, Airman Certification Branch
Flight Standards Technical Division

(Top) Reply to Joe Gervais from *The Early Birds of Aviation*, concerning early flying days of Irene Craigmile (Mrs. Guy Bolam) at Roosevelt Field, Long Island. *(Bottom)* The Federal Aviation Administration turns down Joe Gervais' request for copy of Irene Craigmile's pilot's license.

(*Above, left*) During an interview on Guam, Joaquin Seman, left, of Saipan, and Ben Salas both indicated that they knew the location of the unmarked gravesite of Earhart and Noonan. (*Above, right*) Nubuo Tanaka was the English-speaking interpreter who interrogated Amelia and Noonan on Saipan in the summer of 1937. (*Below, left*) Thomas Blas, a construction worker at the main Japanese Chico Naval Base, was an eyewitness to the crash-landing of the Lockheed 10 near the base. (*Below, right*) Harry Balfour, Guinea Airways' radio operator at Lae, New Guinea, the last person to have radio contact with the ill-fated duo.

(*Above*) Saipan prison guard Ramon Cabrera, standing, shown here in an original Japanese photo, described life in prison for Earhart and Noonan when he was stationed south of Garapan in 1937. (*Below, left and right*) Carlos Palacios and Antonio M. Cepada, interviewed on Guam, remembered the "American Spy Girl" in and around the Kobayashi-Royokan Hotel on Saipan during the summer of 1937.

U.S. Navy 16mm footage taken in July 1937 off Hull Island during search for Noonan and Earhart. Note Japanese "meatball" flag (arrow) in top frame and scattered plane wreckage in bottom of each frame.

(*Top and middle*) Official F.A.A. photos taken on the California mountainside which clearly show the registration N-16020, the same as that of the Lockheed Electra of Amelia's last flight. (*Bottom*) The exhaust manifold plate found in the above wreckage. Note the delivery date, May 5, 1937.

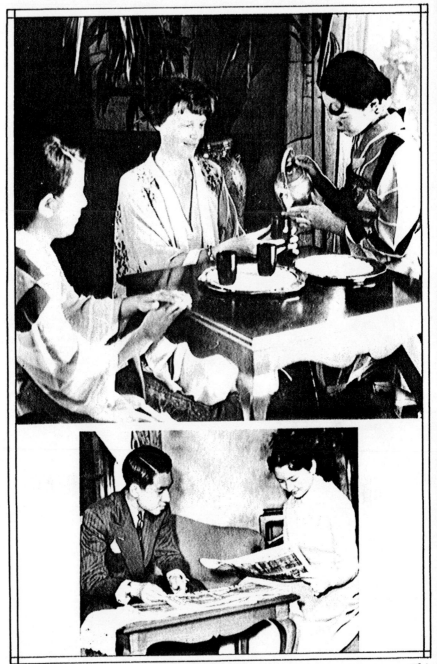

(Top) Kimono-clad Amelia Earhart being served in a Japanese tearoom. This unique photo was planted and recently found in Joe Gervais' safe. (Bottom) Honeymooning Prince Akihito and his wife with the Sunday papers. Note the similarity between this tea table and the one above.

Mystery woman Irene Bolam and her husband Guy at East Hampton Beach, Long Island, August 8, 1965. The photo was taken by Joe Gervais at the meeting of the Long Island Early Fliers' Club.

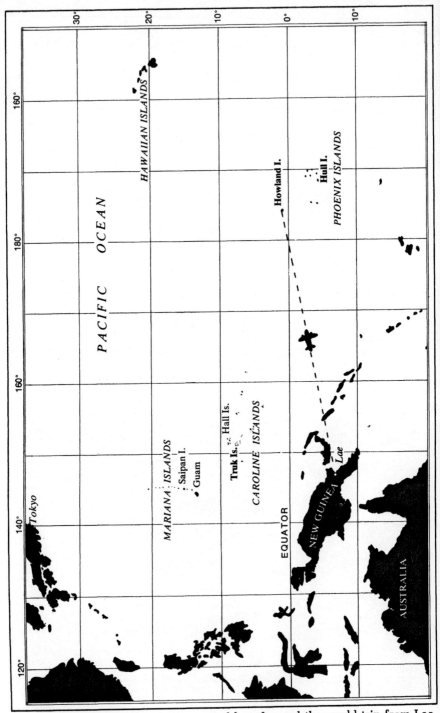

Map of Pacific Ocean showing proposed leg of round-the-world trip from Lae, New Guinea, to Howland Island.

had died on Saipan. All persons who had died were local natives, and all entries were properly recorded.

"If the flyers were not Catholic, they would have been buried in unconsecrated ground adjacent to the regular cemetery," Father Arnold explained. "There were many unidentified graves in that area when the cemetery was relocated."

"Relocated?"

"Yes, a warehouse now stands on the site of the original cemetery for non-Catholics, and there are no records today to establish who was buried there."

Gervais looked up from his futile search of the records. "If they were buried there, would there be any way in the world to locate their graves?"

The priest shook his head sadly. "I don't believe it would be possible . . . not even if you found someone who witnessed the burial. Did anyone see them buried?"

"As far as we know, no one saw them dead *or* buried," answered Gervais.

They thanked the priest and left.

Gervais then suggested that they find out who owned the hotel where Amelia Earhart was supposed to have been kept prisoner.

The land on which the Hotel Kobayashi Royokan had stood was owned by Antonio G. Cabrera, who was now a sixty-two-year-old farmer on Saipan. Cabrera had lived on the main floor of the hotel in 1937.

"An American woman and an American man lived in the hotel about that time," remembered Cabrera, "and they were under surveillance by the Japanese."

"How long did they stay there?"

"Only for about a week, and then they were taken away by the Japanese."

Gervais showed the old man a photograph of Amelia Earhart and Fred Noonan standing with a group of people.

"The girl looks just like the American girl at the hotel," said Cabrera, "but I can't be positive about her. I can only be positive about this man." He pointed at Fred Noonan in the photograph. "I am positive that this is the man who stayed at the hotel."

Gervais swallowed. "Where did they come from?"

"Jose Comacho said they crashed in the Tanapag area."

"Are you sure?"

The old man smiled. "Why don't you ask him? Jose still lives there."

Camacho still lived in the same area he had lived in back in 1937.

"The plane crashed in the Sadog-Tasi area next to the Chico Naval Base," Comacho confirmed.

"The two Americans in the crashed plane were taken away in a car toward Garapan," his wife added.

"When was this crash?" Dinger asked.

"When did it happen?" Camacho asked his wife.

She thought for a minute. "It was about seven or eight years before the invasion," she said.

At Chalan Kanoa, a village on Saipan, the investigators located Mrs. Joaquina M. Cabrera, fifty-one, who during 1937 and 1938 had been employed as a servant in the hotel.

"I used to have to take a list of the persons staying in the hotel to the island governor's office each day," Mrs. Cabrera remembered. "One day when I was doing this I saw two Americans in the back of a three-wheeled vehicle. Their hands were bound behind them, and they were blindfolded. One of them was an American woman."

Gervais showed her a photo of Amelia Earhart and Fred Noonan. "Are these the two you saw?"

She squinted at the photograph. "They look like the same people I saw, and they are dressed the same way."

"What happened to them?"

"I only saw them once in the three-wheeled truck. I don't know what happened to them."

Jose Pangelinan, a merchant at Chalan Kanoa, remembered the American flyers. "I saw a white man and woman at Japanese military police headquarters at Garapan," he offered. "Someone told me they were flyers and spies. Later I heard that the woman had died and the man had been executed shortly thereafter."

Antonio A. Diaz, a member of the Saipan legislature, remembered something about the pair. "In 1937 I was employed as a chauffeur for the commanding officer of the Japanese Chico Navy Base," he said. "I was one of the very few Chamorro natives who had access to this base. One day I overheard a conversation in the sedan between the commander and another Japanese officer concerning an airplane that crashed at Sadog-Tasi, right next to the base, and that two American pilots were apprehended. One was an American woman."

"When was this?" asked Gervais.

"In late 1937. Why don't you speak to Jose Baza, who was employed at the Chico Base at that time?"

Baza had been a stevedore at the time of the incident. "I didn't see anything," he said. "I was stacking oil drums and didn't see anything."

"You were stacking oil drums when you didn't see what?" demanded Sheriff Sablan.

"I don't know anything," answered Baza, frightened.

They returned with Diaz, who reassured Baza that it would be all right to tell what he had seen.

"I saw the airplane crash at Sadog-Tasi and the Japanese arrest the two American pilots, and one of them was a woman."

"Tell us about it," asked Gervais.

"That's all there is," said Baza.

"What happened to the Americans?"

"They were arrested and blindfolded and taken away by Japanese officials to Garapan. That's all I know." Baza would say no more.

Sheriff Sablan received word from one of his patrolmen that a Mrs. Matilda Ariola Saint Nicholas had heard that the Air Force officers were on Saipan and she wanted to talk to them. But when the investigators arrived at the Saint Nicholas home, her husband objected strongly to her divulging any information.

"It can only lead to trouble," he said. "You men will be leaving soon, whereas we will have to stay and live with this thing forever."

The investigators asked Father Arnold to go see Mr. and Mrs. Saint Nicholas and reassure them that it would be safe to talk. He did so, and the next morning "Operation Earhart" returned to the Saint Nicholas home. Mr. Saint Nicholas had stayed home from work to be present while his wife was interviewed.

"In 1937 an American girl stayed at the military-operated Hotel Kobayashi Royokan," Mrs. Saint Nicholas said. "At that time I was a young girl living with my family next door to the hotel. I saw the American girl in the hotel, and twice during the seven days she stayed there she visited me and my younger sister at our home."

"What did she look like?" asked Gervais.

"She was thin with short hair like a man's," remembered Mrs. Saint Nicholas. "She was dressed in a cloth trench coat. The first time I saw her she looked very pale as though she were sick. She wore no make-up. My sister and I offered her food. She accepted it but ate very little, only a little fruit."

"What about the second time the American woman visited you? How did she look then?"

"The next time the American girl visited from the hotel she had bandages on her left forearm," said Mrs. Saint Nicholas. "Also bruises or burns on the right side of her neck. The American girl liked my younger sister very much, and on this second visit when my sister was doing a geography lesson, the American girl helped her draw correctly the location of the Marianas Islands in relation to the other islands in the Pacific."

"Was she free to come and go as she liked?"

"I don't think so. There were two Chamorro detectives who watched the hotel daily."

"What happened to this woman after the seven days she stayed there?" asked Gervais.

"A bus boy who worked at the hotel told me the American girl died there. He said the bed she slept on was soaked with blood and that before she died, the American girl had been going very often to the outside toilet. Later the bus boy asked me to make two wreaths for a burial."

"Did you make the wreaths?"

"Yes."

"Where did the burial take place?"

Mrs. Saint Nicholas, now forty, shook her head. "I don't know. I didn't see it. I never saw the American girl again."

Gervais laid several photographs of Amelia Earhart out on the table.

"It looks like the same girl," said Mrs. Saint Nicholas.

Gervais, Dinger, Quintanilla, and Sablan then returned to the quonset hut to discuss what they had so far learned in four days of interviewing Saipan witnesses.

"Many people remember a plane crash," said Gervais. "Many people remember an American woman and an American man apparently being held prisoner. Some say they were executed. Some say the woman died, apparently of dysentery, and the man was executed. Some say they were taken away to Japan."

"But no one we have talked to actually saw an execution," said Dinger, the skeptic force of Operation Earhart. "No one saw a corpse. No one saw them leave the island bound for Japan. And no one at the time heard the name Amelia Earhart."

"And there's no record of the graves," pointed out Quintanilla.

"No one," continued Dinger, "knows for sure who the American man and woman were or what positively became of them."

"Look," said Gervais, his dark eyes flashing. "Nearly everyone who saw the American woman who was here in 1937 . . . ."

"Or 1938," interrupted Dinger.

"All right, 1937 or 1938. Nearly everyone who saw her said she looked like the photographs we showed them of Amelia Earhart. Their descriptions fit Amelia Earhart."

Dinger frowned. "I don't know . . . ."

Gervais threw up his hands. "How many American women were there flying out here in the Pacific in 1937 or 1938?"

"I'd still like to find someone who would have known for sure," Dinger mused. "Someone like that interpreter for the police here at that time . . . the Japanese officer whose wife wore a Western-style wedding ring. Or this guy Kumoi. What ever happened to this detective everyone calls Kumoi?"

"Jesus De Leon Guerrero was his name," related Sheriff Sablan.

"I replaced him in my present job. The Navy fired Kumoi as sheriff in 1952 after he had nearly beaten a man to death with a rubber hose during an interrogation. Kumoi's theory always was: if you beat a man long enough and he tells you nothing, it proves he is not lying."

"Where is Kumoi now?"

"He is a junk dealer travelling from island to island gathering bits of war scrap metal and shipping it for sale to Guam. But he's not here now."

Dinger sighed. "I wish he was here now. I'd like to talk to this Kumoi."

Dinger was to get his wish and then wish he hadn't.

CHAPTER ELEVEN

THE WALL

Operation Earhart got off to an early start on the fifth day of interrogating witnesses on Saipan. It was also a bad start. By 10 o'clock that night they had contacted seven persons who had been on Saipan in 1937, and none of them would cooperate at all.

"They all seemed afraid of something," Gervais complained to Dinger back at the quonset hut. "It's like a wall of fear had suddenly gone up."

Quintanilla and Sablan had gone to the sheriff's headquarters to see what might have happened to cause all doors to the investigation to slam shut.

Dinger and Gervais were asleep when Quintanilla returned at 2 A M and turned on the light.

"The shadow of the Rising Sun is once again cast over Saipan," Quintanilla reported seriously to the suddenly wide-awake Air Force officers.

"What do you mean?" asked Gervais.

"It's Kumoi. He's come back."

Dinger grinned. "The hell you say?"

Quintanilla shook his head. "It's not good. He's managed to put the fear of God into these people. That's why they wouldn't talk to us all day."

"You mean he didn't just come back now?" Gervais asked.

"Yesterday morning at 4 A.M"

"How did he get here?"

"On the Navy supply vessel *Hope* from Guam."

"What do you mean . . . he put the fear of God into these people?" asked Dinger, skeptically. "What power has he got over them?"

Quintanilla shrugged. "Kumoi has no official status either here or on Guam, but his prestige through fear is tremendous. Remember, for many years he was the 'jungkicho'—top investigator for the Japanese and the number-one Chamorro on the island of Saipan. The older people here still fear him."

"What's the Navy doing bringing him back here right now?" demanded Gervais.

Dinger still grinned. "Well, I'm glad they did. I wanted to talk to this Kumoi."

"And I want to talk to the Navy," added Gervais.

Just then Sheriff Sablan arrived at the door of the quonset hut. "Did you tell them?" he asked Quintanilla.

"Yes," answered the Guam detective.

Sablan frowned. "You may not get much out of Kumoi."

Dinger smiled. "Why not?"

"Kumoi worked for the Japanese a long time. There are a lot of things he won't talk about. Haven't you noticed how frightened some of the people we questioned have been?"

Dinger stopped smiling. "What were they afraid of?"

"They are afraid of Kumoi."

"But why? Kumoi is only a junk dealer."

Sablan nodded. "There have been three governments in charge here during Kumoi's lifetime. The Germans, the Japanese, and now yours. Kumoi was a cop—and a mean one at that—for many years. The older Saipanese still fear him. And he may not be willing to talk."

"How can we persuade him?" asked Gervais.

Sablan shrugged. "He might only understand his own kind of questioning." Sablan looked at Quintanilla and smacked a fist into his palm.

Quintanilla nodded.

"Well, we won't question him that way," said Dinger firmly. "Let's just hope that he tells us what he knows if we're nice to him about it."

Sablan shook his head pessimistically. For at least another hour they discussed how they would go about the questioning of Kumoi. Finally they agreed to meet Sablan in the morning by the courthouse.

The Saipan courthouse was a one-story masonry building with a long veranda and shuttered windows without glass.

"While I'm looking for Kumoi," Sablan said, "why don't you go see the mayor?" He indicated a nearby building similar to the courthouse. "Mayor Benivente is an old man who lived here in 1937, and he is now married to the widow of Cruz, who was an investigator along with Kumoi for the Japanese. Maybe the mayor will let you talk to her. I'm going to bring Kumoi back here to the courthouse."

Mayor Benivente opened four bottles of orange soda for them and once more told them he remembered nothing of any American flyers before the war.

Gervais showed the mayor a letter of introduction from the civil authorities on Guam which requested courtesy and cooperation. "We talked to your wife's sister on Guam," he told the old man. "She said that once back about that time when your wife asked Cruz about a rumor that two American spies had been apprehended, he told her to keep her mouth shut and never mention a word about it again."

"I never heard anything about that," Mayor Benivente said vaguely.

"We would like to talk to your wife," Gervais said.

The old man shook his head. "I am sorry."

Dinger's eyes widened in his tan face. "Why can't we talk to Mrs. Benivente?"

The old man gazed out of the open window. "My wife is not well. She can talk to no one."

All they got out of the mayor of Saipan was the orange

soda pop. Sablan returned to interrupt the futile questioning. "Kumoi is waiting for us in the courthouse," he said simply.

Jesus De Leon Guerrero, also known as Zuse, and even better known as Kumoi, sat at the head of a long table in the empty courthouse. The former "jungkicho" was over six feet tall and looked older than his fifty-three years. His face was wrinkled and parched and he had a bull-like neck. He wore open sandals, faded G.I. pants, and a limp white shirt open half way. Dinger and Gervais sat on one side of the table, Quintanilla and Sablan on the other.

"I remember nothing," he said, glaring nervously down the table.

They questioned Kumoi for four hours.

"I remember nothing," he repeated for the hundredth time at the close of the session. More at ease than when the fruitless questioning had begun, Kumoi agreed to meet them at the courthouse again next morning.

In the afternoon, "Operation Earhart" found Joaquin Seman, the man Ben Salas at Guam had said was with him when they witnessed the burial of two Americans in 1937 at Liang on Saipan. Salas had "guaranteed" that Seman could and would lead them to the graves.

This time Seman actually shook when asked about it. "I will say nothing," he said, hanging his head.

"But did you or did you not see such a burial?" asked Gervais.

"Please go away." Seman breathed hard.

Gervais pleaded with the man. "Your friend, Ben Salas, said you would show us where you saw the two Americans buried."

Seman turned away. "Leave me alone." His voice trembled.

"Look," said Dinger reassuringly, "no harm can come to you now. Just tell us if you saw such a burial or not."

The Chamorro was near to tears and apparently slightly nauseated. "Go away. Go away."

The detectives and Air Force officers looked at each other helplessly and left.

"That is the most scared man I have ever seen," Sablan said. Quintanilla agreed.

The next morning Kumoi again sat at the head of the courthouse table. Now he wore a slightly leering expression of confidence that from here on out things would be under his, not his questioners', control.

"Let's try it from the beginning," suggested Sablan. "Do you remember, in 1937, when the Japanese Navy was building the Chico Naval Base?"

"No," he contradicted. "In 1937 there were only the Japanese naval administrators of the island here. There were no military personnel on Saipan, and the island had not yet been fortified."

Sablan looked at the former policeman in amazement. "You don't remember the Chico Base in 1937?"

Kumoi's head shook on its thick neck. "It wasn't started yet. The only work being done here in 1937 which was anything like military was the construction of three huge oil tanks by a battalion of about thirty Japanese civilians."

"Why, man," argued Sablan, "the Japanese Army and Navy were both pouring in here in 1937 and you know it."

"No," denied Kumoi. "The military did not start pouring into Saipan until 1938."

Sablan spoke to Dinger and Gervais in English.

"How do you like that?" he said in awe. "He's still protecting the Japanese secret construction in 1937 as if we didn't all know about it."

Kumoi grinned at them. They questioned him for awhile longer, getting the same kind of obviously untrue answers. Finally Sablan lost his temper in English.

"This fool is driving me crazy," he shouted. "What he needs is his own kind of medicine . . . a good roughing up before he'll start to make sense."

Gervais and Dinger rose in alarm. "We are Air Force officers, not the Gestapo," Gervais said.

"There'll be no roughing up," asserted Dinger.

Sablan calmed down. "No. Of course not," he sighed.

Kumoi laughed aloud. Sablan shooed away two Chamorro boys who were leaning in at the open window behind Kumoi to see what all the shouting was about.

After four more hours of questioning, Kumoi's answers were basically the same. "I don't know anything." He agreed to meet them again the next morning.

While lunching at the U.S. Navy mess, they received word by one of the sheriff's patrolmen that Elias Sablan, a Caroline who once was mayor of Saipan, wanted to see them at his home.

When they arrived at the home of Elias Sablan in the pickup truck, they found four men who were employed with Sablan by the Japanese administration in 1937.

One of the men had been a guard at the Garapan prison. The other three had been construction laborers at the Chico Naval Base.

"There were two American spies apprehended in 1937 by the Japanese, but neither of them was Amelia Earhart. They were both men," Sablan said in English.

"What about the American lady Antonio Cabrera said he saw under guard at the hotel?" interrupted Gervais.

The former prison guard spoke up quickly. "There never was any such woman."

"Then who were the two American spies?"

"We don't know," answered Elias Sablan.

"What became of them?"

"We don't know," Sablan said again.

"But you say there were two American spies?"

"Yes."

Further questioning netted them nothing more.

They next called upon Judge Ada of the Saipan District Court, who during the Japanese administration had been the High Commissioner of the local Chamorros.

"What are you doing in my office without an appointment?" Judge Ada demanded irritably.

"We've come to ask you about two American flyers who crashed here on the beach in 1937," Gervais replied.

"No such incident happened," answered Judge Ada flatly.
"You never heard of it?"

"I heard the rumor, but it simply didn't happen," insisted
the judge.

"Let's talk about the rumor," began Gervais.

"I see no point in talking about something that never happened. I have work to do now."

They next drove down to the naval supply ship U.S.S *Hope*
to find out how Kumoi happened to be aboard as a passenger
from Guam. The manifest showed Jesus De Leon Guerrero
traveled as a cook on the crew. Captain Bridwell said he
would look into the matter, since he had had Kumoi under
observation for some time regarding past dealings with the
Navy.

That night in the quonset hut, Dinger, Gervais, Sablan,
and Quintanilla decided on new tactics for the third and
final questioning of Kumoi.

"We are not going to start out asking you any questions
today," Sablan explained to Kumoi at the courthouse next
morning. "Tell us anything you want to . . . anything at all
that's on your mind."

Kumoi was silent for awhile, smiling at his obvious complete control of the situation. He talked about the weather,
airplanes—and then began to tell his version of the "spy
lady" incident.

"There was no American spy lady in 1937," he said. "I
would have known about the alleged Earhart incident. I was
one of the top officers in the police force, and I would have
been one of the persons to know if an American had been
captured."

Kumoi glanced at the attentive faces appreciatively.
"An American-born Japanese woman was hanged as a spy
in 1938. She was the one everybody thinks was Amelia
Earhart."

What did she look like?" asked Gervais.

"Ah," Kumoi sighed dramatically, "the American-born
Japanese woman was beautiful and about twenty-five years

of age. She looked like she was part American and could have been mistaken for an American woman."

"What was her name?"

"I don't remember her name, but I learned that she was born in Los Angeles, California."

"What was she doing in Saipan?"

Kumoi grew thoughtful. "The woman came to Saipan from Japan. She said she was looking for work. She didn't look like a working girl, however, because she was very well dressed and spoke perfect English. Later she was arrested and was imprisoned for two months before she was executed," Kumoi said. "While she was in jail, I was the one who kept watch on her and fed her. Oftentimes she nearly lost her mind and would shout obscene words . . . she spoke only English."

"She was alone?" Gervais pressed. "No one was arrested with her?"

"There was no one with her," replied Kumoi.

"Then why do so many people here say there were two American flyers in July, 1937, and that they were imprisoned in the hotel, and maybe later executed?" asked Gervais.

"Oh, that," shrugged Kumoi. "It was in July, all right, but not 1937. In July of 1942 an American fighter plane was shot down off the eastern coast of Saipan. The two men aboard the plane apparently bailed out of the aircraft because they landed in Saipan on a rubber raft, and both were seized and taken to jail. The two Americans were imprisoned for about eighteen months and later were beheaded when the American forces began bombarding the island. The two were buried in Garapan."

"Where were they kept before they were executed?" Gervais asked.

"They were kept in the hotel," Kumoi said.

"But you just said they were taken to the jail."

"No," answered Kumoi. "I said the hotel. I was in charge of the two American prisoners myself."

"They were both men?"

Kumoi grinned. "But of course."

"What happened to them?"

"The Japanese cut off their heads."

"Did you see the beheading?" Gervais asked.

"No," smiled Jesus Guerrero, the former insular police-man for the Japanese. "But I was in a position to hear about such things."

Kumoi was dismissed. Dinger shook his head, perplexed. "During the past three days," he said, "I have never had the slightest doubt that that man could tell us the truth if he wanted to."

After lunch, they went to dockside to see Gregorio Mago-fua, the young man whose boat Fred Goerner had rented to find the "mistaken" generator from Amelia Earhart's air-plane.

Gervais told him that he wanted to rent his outboard motor boat and be taken where Goerner went skin-diving to find the generator.

The young Chamorro's eyes widened. "I did not take Mr. Goerner skin-diving," he said.

"Where did Goerner dive down to find the plane wreck?" Gervais asked.

"I took him across to the reef's edge where the wreck of an old Japanese Betty bomber sits in a few feet of water," the young man said. "But he didn't go swimming."

"That's the wreck Goerner thought was Amelia Earhart's airplane?" Gervais asked.

"No. I told him it was a Japanese plane. He asked me to wade into the water and see if I could pry some parts loose, so I did. That's all."

"You knew it was Japanese?"

The young man shrugged. "Everyone knew it was a Jap-anese wreck. It's been sitting there for years."

Dinger laughed, gazing in the direction of the reef. "You know how we could get a scoop on that network guy? We oughta dig up some old bones—any old bones—take 'em back to the States, and announce that we have found the bones of Amelia Earhart and Fred Noonan."

"Leave that sort of stuff to those show biz guys," Gervais growled. "All I want is the truth."

Ten months later in September, 1961, Fred Goerner of KCBS, San Francisco, paid another visit to Saipan and dug up some bones. In November he had them shipped to San Francisco, where another press conference was arranged. Before the TV cameras and radio microphones and the assembled press, the bones were presented as "possibly the remains of Amelia Earhart and her navigator, Fred Noonan." From coast to coast and around the world the story was sensational. A few days later, Dr. Theodore D. McCown, an anthropologist at the University of California, identified Goerner's second sensational find as the bones of three or four Chamorro natives.

As yet, no one had positively identified "Tokyo Rosa," the mysterious "Spy Lady" of Saipan, as Amelia Earhart.

No one had uncovered the graves of Amelia Earhart and Fred Noonan.

No witness had been located who had actually seen them die either by natural or accidental causes, or by execution.

No wreckage of Amelia Earhart's plane had been found.

And then—on December 16, 1961—an ancient Lockheed Electra bearing Amelia Earhart's number, N-16020, fell out of an early morning, black sky and crashed in flames against the side of a desert mountain in California.

Twenty-four years, five months, and fourteen days had elapsed between the disappearance of the Electra in the Pacific and the crash of the Electra in the Mojave.

When Joe Gervais found the crash remains on the mountain, he did not call a press conference.

CHAPTER TWELVE

THE SWITCH

I sat in the den of the Gervais home in Las Vegas not long ago fondling an ancient faded flying helmet he had recovered from the crash debris. Its yellowing leather ear pouches held snap-in bakelite radio earphones such as were used by aviators during the thirties. The frayed fabric-wrapped cord that had once plugged into the radio receiver dangled between my knees near an aluminum rudder pedal resting on the rug by my feet. Beside me on the couch was a door from N-16020 with its small plexiglass window still intact and quite transparent.

"We decided to hold no more press conferences no matter what we discovered," Gervais said, leaning back in a chair against his desk. "When you announce to the world that you've found evidence that indicates Amelia Earhart and Fred Noonan died and were buried in Saipan, you are apt to spend the rest of your life sticking to that story just to prove you were right in the first place."

"You don't believe they crashed at Saipan?" I asked.

Gervais nudged the rudder pedal with his foot. "They didn't crash there in this bird."

"Maybe . . . if they were on a photographic mission . . . maybe they crashed there in the XC-35?"

Gervais shook his head. "The XC-35 was test flown by Lockheed on May 7, 1937, *before* Amelia Earhart's round-the-world adventure; it was 'officially' delivered to the Army in August of that year, *after* she vanished." On one flight from Chicago to Washington, D.C., it averaged more than 350 miles per hour, and it won for the Air Corps the 1937 Collier Trophy for the most valuable contribution to aircraft during the year.

"But that was it," Gervais continued. "The XC-35 disappeared forever. I have asked the Air Force, the Army, and Lockheed what ever became of the XC-35. The answer is always the same. No record exists today as to what final disposition was made of the XC-35."

Photographs were published in the newspapers in 1937, showing Amelia Earhart sitting in the cockpit of the airplane in which she was supposed to fly around the world. In all the photos, Gervais explained to me, the smiling, freckled face of Amelia is the same. But the cockpits are different. The photos show her sitting at the controls in two similar, but definitely different cockpits. The instrument panels are different. Furthermore, in some of the pictures her plane is equipped with fixed-pitch propellers without ·spinners. In others the propellers are hubbed with spinners such as are used to streamline the feathering gear of variable-pitch props. Apparently not one, but two Lockheed airplanes were involved in the disappearance of Amelia Earhart. And neither of them disappeared with her.

There is no record of what happened to that XC-35.

Gervais studied my silent confusion anticipating that soon I would have to speak.

"One thing is obvious," I said at last. "We are talking about more than one airplane. We are talking about at least two airplanes . . . maybe three. There's the airplane in which she tried to radio her position. That one was somewhere in the neighborhood of Howland Island at 8 o'clock in the morning of July 2, 1937. Then there's an airplane in which an

American man and woman were reported to have crashed on the beach at Saipan, and that was at noontime, four hours later."

"A long time for a bird to travel that's out of gas, and nearly two thousand miles from Howland."

I patted the door with its plexiglass window on the sofa beside me. "And there's this one with the Earhart registration number N-16020 which crashed in California twenty-four years later. That makes three airplanes. My God! And there's the XC-35. That makes four."

Gervais grinned. "Don't forget the one that Ajima, the Japanese trader, said came down with an American woman aboard. That was between Jaluit and Ailinglapalap Atolls in the southeastern Marshall Islands, where she was supposed to have been picked up by Japanese fishermen."

I snorted. "That makes five."

Gervais nodded. "To pursue this investigation with an open mind, you've got to resist the temptation to accept only the reports that fit your favorite theory."

"She could have crashed twice," I mused. "She could have crashed somewhere in the plane she was piloting, been picked up by the Japanese, flown to Saipan, and crashed again as a passenger on landing."

Gervais grinned. "Now you're getting somewhere."

I continued to theorize aloud. "If she was on a photographic mission, she would have had to be flying a plane faster and with more range than her own Electra in order to take pictures of Truk and Saipan and arrive anywhere near Howland Island on schedule. Maybe Lockheed built two XC-35's—the one Amelia Earhart and Fred Noonan flew and another that later won the Collier Trophy back in the States. Maybe she switched from her own Electra to an XC-35, flew the photographic mission, and maintained radio silence until she could get back on her publicized course near Howland Island, where for the first time she started talking on her radio. That way, the *Itasca* direction-finders, if they had been working, would have indicated her to be coming in toward Howland on a direct course from Lae, New Guinea. Could be that's why she didn't use her radio all night. It would have given her position away when she was hundreds of miles north of where she was supposed to be."

"Then what?" Gervais prodded.

"Then she missed Howland and the Japs got her and took her back to Saipan, where the Japanese plane made a bad landing on the beach."

"And then?"

I shrugged and then said, "She died in captivity, either from dysentery or by execution, or she was taken to Japan. The Japs kept quiet about it because she was the most popular woman in the world and her imprisonment would have made them look bad. If she were a prisoner of the Japanese and our government knew about it, our government probably would have kept quiet about it, too."

Gervais nodded. "Unless the President was ready to go to war to save Amelia Earhart. We had practically no army, a small obsolete army air force, and a smaller navy than Japan. It would have been not only embarrassing to admit we had been using a famous and beloved woman for espionage, but it would have been impossible to force the Japanese to give her back without an all-out war we were in no position to fight.

"And Japan was in no position to reveal to the world that the world's most popular woman had been captured after photographing fortifications that were so illegal and so secret they were not even supposed to exist."

State Department files reveal that in 1937 request after request for Japanese permission to allow American ships to pay "goodwill visits" to the Japanese mandated islands were turned down. The same files reveal that at no time during the naval search for Amelia Earhart did the Japanese admit that one of their aircraft carriers was in a position to find her days before the *Lexington* arrived.

"Can you believe that the United States Navy operated for two days on Jacqueline Cochran's extrasensory perception?" Gervais asked me.

I answered with conviction. "No."

"Well, then," Gervais said, "since the Japanese government was asked to send its available ships to a point west of Howland Island where Jackie Cochran's extrasensory perception 'revealed' Amelia and Fred to be drifting in the ocean in the general direction of the Gilbert Islands, while the U.S.S. *Colorado* was steaming hell-bent for the Phoenix Group of islands southeast of Howland hundreds of miles away, what does that suggest to you?"

I thought it over. It seemed to suggest that our State Department was using the information from Jackie Cochran's extrasensory perception as a diversion to keep the Japanese Navy away from where the United States expected to find Amelia Earhart . . . somewhere near the Phoenix Islands.

"Right. And while the U.S.S. *Colorado* and its seaplanes are trying to pick her up in the Phoenix Islands, the U.S.S. *Lexington* is coming all the way from San Diego directly for the extrasensory position toward the Gilbert Islands to make it look good." Gervais laughed. "Can you imagine our biggest carrier, the *Lexington,* meeting up with that Japanese carrier, the *Akagi,* out there near the Gilbert Islands?"

"Did they meet up?" I asked.

Gervais shook his head, chuckling. "No. If they had, World War II might have started right then and there. It could have been combat time."

"Where was the *Akagi?*"

"Good question. Amelia disappeared on July 2. A seaplane from the U.S.S. *Colorado* landed in a lagoon at Hull Island in the Phoenix Group on July 9. The *Akagi* had seven days to get there first."

"Hull Island," I said, amazed. "You think she crashed at Hull Island?"

Gervais reminded me that while the U.S.S. *Swan* on July 9

was looking over Canton Island with its 6000-foot runway at one end of the Phoenix Group, a flight of three catapult planes was launched from the U.S.S. *Colorado* at the other end of the Phoenix Group.

"The purpose of the flight in the afternoon," according to the captain's report, "was to search the water ahead of the ship to locate Hull Island and to search the island and the water in the vicinity for any signs of the Earhart plane."

Gervais searched through the files in a metal cabinet jutting from a closet beside his desk. "Did you ever see the movie *Flight to Freedom?*"

"The one about Amelia Earhart with Rosalind Russell and Fred MacMurray? I saw it recently on television."

Gervais grunted. "Everyone *assumed* it was about Amelia Earhart, but in the movie she was called Tonie Carter." He handed me a thick sheaf of photostated pages from the January, 1943, issue of *Woman's Home Companion*. "Here. Read the story."

I began to read, a slight chill running through me at the first sentence in the story, by-lined with the name Horace McCoy, the late author of *They Shoot Horses, Don't They?*

It was a standing joke among Tonie Carter's friends that all she had to do to disguise herself was to put on a dress. Whenever she became fed up with the extravagant curiosity of the world and the intrusions of the autograph hunters, she simply slipped into a dress, arranged her bobbed hair so that it didn't look bobbed any more and there she was—just another nice-looking girl that you glanced at once and then forgot.

My imagination was so instantly stimulated that it was a moment or two before I could read on. All Amelia Earhart would have had to do to disappear would be to fix her hair, put on some make-up, and wear a dress. Could Amelia Earhart have become so fed up with "the extravagant curiosity of the world and the intrusions of the autograph hunters" and with a publicity-minded husband that she agreed to perform espionage for her country in exchange for the permanent peace and privacy of assumed death?

"Courage is the price that life exacts for granting peace," she had written long ago. "I may have to keep some place where I can go to be myself now and then," she had proscribed in her marriage terms, "for I cannot guarantee to endure at all times the confinements of even an attractive cage." Had the eyes of an adoring but devouring world become the bars of her cage from which she had the courage to escape?

I then read how an Army officer handed "Tonie Carter" a slip of paper just before her takeoff from Hawaii on the second leg of an around-the-world flight in 1937 with instructions to destroy the note as soon as she had read it. On the takeoff, the fictional woman flyer then deliberately jammed the controls, forcing the plane to crash. While was being rebuilt "Tonie Carter" was flown from March Field to Washington, where she was asked to volunteer for a mission.

"We want you to undertake a mission—one of the most vital in the history of our country," she was told by an Admiral Graves, Chief of Naval Operations. "You are the only person in the world who can do it.

"This mission," Graves went on, "will require a year, perhaps two, perhaps three. And it will be highly dangerous.

"It will be necessary," Graves said, "for you to give up, temporarily, we hope, everything you love, because the world has got to think you are dead. Upon the success of this—and believe me, I am not exaggerating—may depend the fate of the United States of America.'"

The fictional admiral warned her, "If there is any slip-up at all, you yourself will have to suffer the consequences. This country cannot intervene. The possibility of death is very great."

"Tonie Carter" immediately volunteered to do the job.

"You will fly around the world again," she was briefed, "but this time you will reverse your direction. You will start from Florida and go to Africa, India, Australia, and hop for the Hawaiian Islands from down below instead of up above. This will give the world time to get really interested in your flight. But here, somewhere in this area you will get into trouble. You will radio an S O S—you will make it sound as hopeless as possible. But you will be sure the world hears it. That will give us the chance to do our job."

"Do I actually come down?" Tonie asked.

The admiral pointed to a spot on the map. "This is Gull Island. This island is less than two miles square and only twenty feet above sea level. But it will be provisioned and stocked for you, and there you will stay until the Navy comes and takes you off. That may be a week, a year . . . . But at any rate, it will enable us to serve our purpose. That is, a great and widespread search for you somewhere in the ocean. Only we shall look for you with photographic planes." The admiral told her that only she could cause such a search to be made by air over the fortified Japanese islands because "There is an emotional difference between a man falling in the ocean and a woman. Especially Tonie Carter."

Especially Amelia Earhart!

The fictional famous woman flyer pointed out that locating "Gull Island" would be difficult.

"We'll furnish a navigator for you," Graves said. "The finest navigating mind in the entire Navy."

The fictional finest navigating mind in the entire Navy belonged to a former boy friend of the fictional flyer.

The finest navigating mind in the real-life Navy of 1937 belonged to Lieutenant Commander Fred Noonan.

The *Flight to Freedom* story then toyed with a typical slick magazine romance between the lady pilot and her navigator all the way around the world to Lae, New Guinea, "the last stop before they set out for Gull Island, their objective—2550 miles away on the most difficult and perilous hop of the journey."

Then came the climax, in the form of Mr. Yokohata, the hotelkeeper at Lae.

"Imperial Japanese Navy reports that many provisions have been left at Gull Island for you. It may interest you to know that the Japanese government is fully aware of what you are doing and that you will pretend to disappear in the sea," boasted the smiling Japanese. "Within ten minutes after your disaster is announced, a Japanese plane will discover you on Gull Island. Within one minute the world will be notified and it will be quite unnecessary for the United States Navy to send planes to look for you over Japanese mandated islands. Thank you, please."

In the magazine story, and in the film from which it came, the famous American woman flyer deliberately crashed into the sea so that she would truly be lost, thus enabling planes from the *Colorado* and the *Lexington* to search for her over the fortified Japanese mandated islands with cameras.

George Putnam sued RKO Radio because the movie version implied a romance between Amelia Earhart and her navigator. However, the suit was later revealed to have been part of the plans for publicizing the movie.

"I wonder where the writer, Horace McCoy, got the idea for this story," I mused. "From Putnam maybe."

"I dunno," shrugged Gervais. "I looked in a writers' bibliography for Horace McCoy. Then I phoned him and he said he didn't write the story."

I studied the disclaimer at the end of the magazine piece.

Editor's Note: No reference is intended in this story to any real person, living or dead; characters and motives are presented purely as fiction. The story was written by the author specially for the *Companion* from his ninety-page original first submitted to Producer David Hempstead at RKO Radio. Rosalind Russell and Fred MacMurray are costarring with Herbert Marshall in the film, *Flight to Freedom,* currently over the country.

An idea hit me. "You know . . . a man like Howard Hughes might have stumbled onto something when he was preparing for his own round-the-world flight in 1938 just one year after Amelia Earhart disappeared. He wouldn't have flown around the world without trying to find out what happened to Earhart and Noonan. And Hughes owned RKO."

Gervais grinned. "Funny you should mention Howard Hughes," he said. "In 1935 Howard Hughes set all kinds of records with the Hughes Racer. Know who the timekeepers were for those record flights?"

"Amelia Earhart?"

"And Paul Mantz."

"It's probably coincidence," I sighed.

"What about the movie name 'Gull Island'?" suggested Gervais.

"Gull Island? I don't get you."

Gervais' voice boomed out. "Hull Island! Hull Island in the Phoenix Group! On an exact line of position of 157-337 degrees from Howland Island on any compass. Hull Island where the seaplanes from the *Colorado* headed as fast as they could get there. Hull Island. Gull Island. Do you know what was supposed to be going on when the seaplane landed at Hull Island?"

I tried to remember. "There was a resident manager and some natives . . . gathering something."

"Guano, my friend. Gull guano for fertilizer. I've looked it up. Hull Island was swarming with seagulls. There's your Gull Island."

I stared at Gervais. "How far is Hull Island from Howland Island?"

"Four hundred twenty miles on a compass heading of 157 degrees."

"Four hundred twenty miles," I gasped. "Could she have been that far off course with a navigator aboard like Fred Noonan?"

Gervais shook his head. "They wouldn't have been off course at all . . . I mean, they couldn't have been lost if they knew Howland Island lay on a straight line 337 compass degrees to the north by northwest. To send a message like that, they would have had to know exactly where they were in relation to Howland Island."

My head was spinning. "You think they were heading for Hull Island all along?"

Gervais grunted. "Not likely. There was no place for a plane equipped with wheels to land at Hull Island." He pointed to a spot north of Hull Island on the map. "But they might have been heading here—for Canton Island—with its 6000-foot runway."

I had wondered from the first time I had been told about that runway . . . two things. Why had Pan American built it in the first place, since Pan Am operated nothing but seaplanes in the Pacific? And why had Amelia Earhart and Fred Noonan chosen to try and hit the half-mile by two-and-a-half-mile Howland Island when but a slight change of course would have taken them to the much larger and easier-to-find Canton Island with its huge landing strip?

"Then why send out a message giving a line of position at all?" I asked. "Especially a line from Howland to Hull."

"Because they suddenly knew they weren't going to make it to Canton Island where they were expected to get lost," Gervais said with conviction. "Because they were going down unexpectedly over Hull Island." He handed me a sheet from the copy of the *Itasca* log. "Look at her last radio message," he directed, "and put back the period mark that was left out after the word 'wait.'"

I read aloud Amelia Earhart's last message as recorded by

the *Itasca* radio operator, trying to put "a definite rising note of anxiety" into my voice as had been described in hers.

"We are in line of position 157-337. Will repeat this message. We will repeat this message on 6210 KC. Wait. Listening on 6210. We are running north and south."

"Wait," she had said, as if she had spotted something, or as if something unexpected had happened. "We are running north and south," had been the last part of the message, as if in a cryptic attempt to clarify what she had meant by, "We are in line of position 157-337."

North, from Howland Island at 337 degrees, to the only charted land lying 157 degrees southward . . . . Hull Island. But what could have suddenly happened to cause her to anxiously try to reveal her position so that only those who knew her secret destination could possibly interpret what she meant?

"Another airplane?" Gervais suggested softly. "From that Japanese carrier that had been waiting for her for nearly four months?"

I gasped. "They shot her down?"

"Could be."

We were silent for a bit, each lost in his own thoughts. Finally Gervais spoke. "You remember that Navy seaplane that headed from Hawaii for Howland Island the night following Amelia Earhart's disappearance?"

I nodded.

"Remember where it was when it ran into snow and sleet squalls in the vicinity of the equator?" I remained silent waiting for Gervais to spring another of his surprises. Gervais answered his own question. "Within 420 miles of Howland Island," he quoted from memory. "Almost the exact distance from Howland to Hull."

Another coincidence?

"Someone was in a hell of a hurry to check on something to make a night flight like that in those days," Gervais said. "Maybe it was to see if she was all right; but there's one thing for sure."

"What's that?"

"When the battleship *Colorado* got there seven days later, she was gone!"

"I'm not as sure of that as I am of something else," I added.

"What are you sure of?" asked Gervais.

"She couldn't have flown from Lae, New Guinea, to Truk and down to the Phoenix Islands in the plane she took off in from Miami. It wouldn't fly that fast nor that far. Somewhere around the world between Florida and New Guinea she would have had to switch planes."

Gervais grinned. "There was a switch all right. And I can prove it."

"How can you prove it?"

Gervais reached into the file cabinet for one of its many folders. "I can prove she switched planes. With photographs. Come look at these pictures," he ordered with an enthusiasm that belied the clock. "I'll show you proof positive that Amelia Earhart flew more than one airplane on her flight around the world."

It wasn't going to be easy for me to concentrate. The thought had suddenly struck me that maybe Gervais had become too involved in his search for a "dead woman" and that possibly he had flipped his lid. Through the window behind the sofa I could see the lights of the Desert Inn Hotel sparkle in the Las Vegas night. It occurred to me that Howard Hughes was up there with his entourage occupying the entire top floor of the Desert Inn, which he had just purchased.

"I have lots of photographs of Amelia Earhart's airplane," Gervais said. "But look at these four here."

I pulled a chair up close to where Gervais had laid the glossies on the sofa. At first glance, they all looked the same, pictures taken from different angles, at different locations, of Lockheed Electra 10, CAA registration number NR-16020.

"What am I supposed to be looking for?" I asked.

"Notice the CAA numbers on the wings and tails."

The number painted on the wing in two of the photos

was NR-16020. In the other two pictures the painted number was R-16020.

"They could have changed the registration number," I suggested.

"Would they also have changed the positioning of the port and starboard wingtip navigation lights?" asked Gervais.

In two of the photographs the wingtip navigational lights were located halfway between the leading and trailing edge and well in from the curved wingtip. In the other two photographs the navigation lights were mounted jutting out from the forward part of the wingtip.

"Now look at this," Gervais said, laying down a photo cut from a magazine. "In all the other pictures of the Earhart plane there is no paint job on the engine cowlings."

The magazine photo showed a Lockheed Electra with the number R-16020 painted on the tail, and an artistic paint job decorating the engine cowling. Its port navigation light was recessed in from the wingtip, halfway between the leading and trailing edge of the wing. I compared the photo with an NR-16020 version photographed at San Juan, Puerto Rico, after the first lap of the round-the-world flight. The Puerto Rican photo had the wing light jutting forward from the edge of the wingtip.

"Could this photo be one taken in the middle of some kind of paint job?" Gervais suggested. "There's no painted decoration on any other photo of the Earhart plane."

I nodded. "And somebody goofed and left the N out of the registration number?"

Gervais laid down a medium-close-up photograph of Amelia Earhart and Fred Noonan sitting on a loading platform of some kind. Behind them, leaning horizontally against a wall, was the wing of an airplane.

"During the search by the Navy this AP photo was sent back by cable from Batavia. It was reported as the last picture taken of Amelia Earhart and Fred Noonan sitting beside their airplane."

I studied the photo carefully, particularly the wing and the letters which were painted there partially visible in the photograph. "That isn't part of the NR-16020 wing number."

Gervais grunted. "It sure isn't. What does it look like to you?"

"It looks like AFD or AFL." There were three letters showing on the wing. The A and F were plain enough. The long, straight, uninterrupted line at the edge of the picture would have to be the first part of a D or an L.

"I checked the registration of aircraft flying in the Pacific in 1937," Gervais said. "The wing in that photograph is of New Zealand registry, and it's a Lockheed 10 Electra just like the one Amelia was supposed to be flying. Here's a letter I got from L. F. P. Taylor, director of operation and technical services of the Department of Civil Aviation in New Zealand."

Dear Mr. Gervais,

I acknowledge receipt of your letter of 15 April 1965 and I have acquired some of the information that you requested.

The first Lockheed Electra Model 10(a) imported into New Zealand was registered ZK-AFC, followed by -AFD, -AFE, -ALH, and -ALI.

The letter included particulars of each of the mentioned aircraft. I skimmed down to ZK-AFD.

ZK-AFD

1. Lockheed 10(a), 12-passenger aircraft.
2. Constructors' Serial No. 1095.
3. Engines 2 P & W Wasp Junior S.B.
4. Registered 14 June 1937.
5. Owner—Union Airways of N.Z., Ltd.

Gervais took back that letter and handed me another dated 12 May 1967, also from Taylor.

Dear Mr. Gervais,

It is difficult to trace records after all this time, particularly with World War II intervening which caused considerable disruption to our records system. However, I am able to give some information in reply to your further questions.

(1) The Aircraft were shipped as deck cargo from the U.S.A. to Auckland, New Zealand. They were off loaded on to barges and taken to the R.N.Z.A.F. base Hobsonville, where they were assembled and flown from there by Union Airways pilots.

(2) Registration letters were in red and placed on both top and bottom sides of wings, as well as on rear sides of fuselage. I am enclosing photographs which indicate the positioning of registration letters.

The photograph was a glossy of ZK-AFD in flight. There on the starboard wing were the three letters positioned exactly as on the wing before which Amelia Earhart and Fred Noonan sat in the AP picture. AFD.

Alongside the photo of the Union Airways Lockheed 10, Gervais placed the magazine photo of the Amelia Earhart Electra with the paint job on its engine cowl.

The painted decoration on the engine cowlings of ZK-AFD and R-16020 were identical . . . the official decor of Union Airways.

"Here's a photo Lockheed released of the instrument panel of Amelia Earhart's Electra," Gervais said, "and here's another photo of Amelia sitting in the cockpit of her Electra."

The two photos revealed in detail two completely different sets of instruments arranged in two totally different ways.

"Then she must have switched planes," I concluded. "But where?"

"There was a seven-day layover for 'repairs' at Batavia, followed by an overnight stop at the Royal Australian Air Force Base at Darwin, Australia," Gervais speculated. "It was the only military base she landed at on the entire round-the-world flight. Her next stop was Lae, New Guinea. And from there she disappeared.

"Here's one more photograph to consider," Gervais said.

It was a twin-engined airplane bearing the number R-16020 that looked something like an Electra 10. But this one looked larger, standing on a concrete apron before a brick and stucco military hangar. Its fuselage seemed heavier and swollen and not quite as graceful as that in most pictures of Amelia Earhart's airplane.

"Where was this picture taken?" I asked.

"I got it from Air Force files that had been classified for twenty-eight years," Gervais said. "That hangar looks to me like March Air Force Base. And that bird looks to me like the XC-35 with its reinforced, pressurized cabin."

Gervais carefully began to pick up all the photographs and replace them in a manila envelope. I noticed one picture of a Lockheed Electra that we hadn't discussed. "What's this one?" I asked.

"That's the bird that was provided for Lyndon Johnson to fly around Australia in 1942 on his famous mission," Gervais answered casually. "Note the registration number?"

"NC-16022," I read. "Why, that's only two digits away from the Earhart plane."

"Yeah. And look at the paint job."

The decor painted onto the plane provided for Johnson when he was a temporary Navy commander, paving the way for Negro troops to be cordially received by Australia during World War II, was identical to that of Union Airways.

"What's an American registration number doing on a New Zealand airliner in Australia?" I exclaimed.

Gervais grinned. "Looks like the United States has some kind of an arrangement with Union Airways, doesn't it?"

Beyond the open window, the ball of a rising sun was just beginning to bulge over the Desert Inn. Another desert day was beginning to broil the new domain of Howard Hughes.

CHAPTER THIRTEEN

THE INTERESTED

Facts and people relating to Amelia Earhart had a way of seeking out Joe Gervais. Such was the case with William Van Dusen, senior vice-president of Eastern Airlines, the huge company headed by America's World War I ace of aces, Eddie Rickenbacker. A surviving Amelia Earhart would have been a large stockholder in Eastern Airlines, for she had been an owner of two smaller airlines which had been absorbed by Eastern. ·

One day an unexpected and remarkably thick envelope from Eastern Airlines was dropped into the Gervais mailbox in Las Vegas. Upon opening the package, Gervais found a file of duplicated correspondence stapled together and a cover letter labeled "Office of the Vice President" on Eastern Airlines letterhead.

May 18, 1964

Dear Major Gervais:
On March 12, I wrote to Colonel Robert G. Wilson at the Office of Information in Washington regarding the search for information about Amelia Earhart and was informed by him that you would be the one to help us.

I am attaching copies of all correspondence so that you will be able to follow exactly what has transpired.

Your co-operation and early reply would be greatly appreciated.

> Sincerely,
> Shirley J. Hancock (Miss)
> Secretary to
> William Van Dusen

The first letter in the enclosed duplicate file was dated November 29, 1963, from Van Dusen to the U. S. Air Force Public Information Officer at the Pentagon.

Dear Sir:

It is my understanding that some previously classified information having to do with the search for Amelia Earhart in the Pacific has recently been declassified by the Air Force.

Would you be good enough to tell me if this is the case and, if so, where the material may be reviewed or how a copy may be secured.

Lieut. Col. Robert G. Wilson, USAF Community Relations Division, Office of Information, replied to Van Dusen on December 9, 1963.

We have taken the liberty of forwarding your letter to Captain Warner K. Thompson, U.S. Coast Guard Headquarters.... His office assures me that they will be pleased to forward to you all the available information surrounding the search.

Van Dusen wrote again on January 6, 1964.

May I please refer to your letter of December 9, in which you inform me that you have forwarded my letter of November 29 to Captain Warner K. Thompson in Washington.

As of this date, we have received no information from him, and we are wondering if you would be good enough to let him know that we are awaiting word from him at his earliest convenience.

Gervais gasped. Warner K. Thompson was the name of the commander whose ship, the *Itasca,* had been sent in 1937 with a radio direction-finder to help Amelia Earhart navigate into Howland Island. But that was twenty-seven years before the date of this correspondence.

The next letter in the file was on Treasury Department letterhead from the Office of the Commandant, U.S. Coast Guard Headquarters in Washington.

Dear Mr. Van Dusen:

Your letter to the Air Force has been referred to the Coast Guard, since the Coast Guard was in charge of the search for Amelia Earhart.

The only item I have is a report from Commander W. K. Thompson, Commanding Officer of the cutter *Itasca,* who commanded the search. The report runs 106 pages, but unfortunately my copy is not suitable for copying.

I have been in contact with the section handling Coast Guard affairs at the National Archives and they have informed me that they have an extensive file on the Amelia Earhart incident. The Archives can reproduce this document by photostat or microfilm. With this in mind I have referred your letter to the Diplomatic, Legal and Fiscal Branch of the Archives. You should be hearing from them shortly.

The letter was signed by Captain W. K. Thompson, Jr., apparently the son of the *Itasca* commander, and now chief of the public information division of the Coast Guard. The letter, dated January 8, 1964, was followed by another on

January 17, 1964, from W. Neil Franklin, chief of the diplomatic, legal, and fiscal branch of the National Archives in Washington:

Your letter of November 29, 1963 to the . . . United States Air Force, asking for information about the search for Amelia Earhart, has been forwarded by the United States Coast Guard to this agency for reply.

A search of records of the United States Coast Guard (Record Group 26) disclosed the following records pertaining to the search for Miss Earhart:

Logbook of the Coast Guard Cutter *Itasca,* of which some 40 pages cover the period July 2–July 15, 1937;

Incoming dispatches to the United States Coast Guard, July 2–July 17, 1937, consisting of 102 pages;

Correspondence relating to the search, May 8, 1938–June 2, 1941, 23 pages;

Twenty-three photographs with explanatory notes relating to Miss Earhart and her crew.

These documents can be made available to you or your authorized representative in the Research Room of the National Archives upon request.

The next letter from the vice-president of Eastern Airlines was dated four weeks later on February 11, 1964:

Dear Mr. Franklin:

It was most kind of you to send along the detailed memorandum with regard to your search of the records on Amelia Earhart.

Sorry to put you through some more digging — but we believe a Major Joseph Gervais submitted a report on AE. If this is available, we would love to have a copy of it. If not, any information as to where it can be obtained will help.

Thank you again.

> Sincerely,
> Lorraine Galli
> Secretary to Mr. Van Dusen

Two curious things about the letter at once struck Gervais. Amelia Earhart was referred to as "AE." Only the intimate associates of the famous flyer habitually identified her by her initials. And Van Dusen showed no interest whatsoever in the *Itasca* log, correspondence, or the twenty-three photographs relating to the lost flyers. The sole purpose of all the correspondence was obviously to find out what Gervais alone had uncovered.

The next letter to Van Dusen was dated March 9, 1964, from Wilbur J. Nigh, chief of the reference branch, World War II records division of the National Archives:

> I have been unable to locate any information from Department of the Army records in the National Archives regarding a report on Amelia Earhart submitted by Major Joseph Gervais. If additional information as to the date of the report or the office to which Major Gervais was assigned can be furnished, further search will be made.

Amelia Earhart vanished in the summer of 1937, yet the chief of the diplomatic, legal and fiscal branch of the National Archives had referred Van Dusen's query about Operation Earhart to the World War II records division. Gervais liked that. World War II for the United States officially started on December 7, 1941, four and a half years after Amelia Earhart's last flight. Would the diplomatic branch of the National Archives forward an Amelia Earhart question to the World War II records division if she had not in some direct way been involved with the war?

On March 12, 1964, in another letter to Lieut. Col. Wilson of the Air Force community relations division, Van Dusen finally tried the direct approach:

Dear Colonel Wilson:
    The information we are trying to locate was submitted to the Air Force by Major Joseph Gervais.
                    Sincerely,
                    Lorraine Galli
                    Secretary to
                    William Van Dusen

And the final letter in the packet was the May 18, 1964, letter to Gervais.

The man wanted to know what Gervais knew. It was as simple as that. But why? None of the letters in the file which Van Dusen enclosed "so that you will be able to follow exactly what has transpired" gave a reason why the information was sought in the first place.

Gervais was excited that such a man was taking Operation Earhart very seriously and with inordinate interest. At the same time, Gervais was wary. Amelia Earhart's attorney had also been most interested, as had the security chief of Lockheed Aircraft Corporation. What an Air Force information officer had once described to the press as "rubbish" was making garbage collectors out of some interesting people. Gervais was not of a mind to casually reveal what he had thus far learned about the disappearance of Amelia Earhart and Fred Noonan. Step number one was to find out more about this Van Dusen who wanted so persistently to learn the progress of Operation Earhart.

Who's Who in America portrayed Van Dusen as an airline executive, born in Toledo, Ohio, on September 19, 1901. He earned an A.B. from the University of Denver in 1924, having already assisted in the establishment of transcontinental airmail service during his senior year in college. Van

Dusen was employed by the New York and Buenos Aires Line, which was absorbed by Pan American Airways South American division in 1929. He served as director of public relations for Pan American World Airways from 1930 until 1946.

Gervais placed his finger on the page while he remembered that Fred Noonan also joined Pan Am in 1930.

Van Dusen explored Mayan ruins by air with Charles Lindbergh in 1931 and 1932 in Central America, the report continued. He made survey and trans-Pacific flights during 1935 and 1936.

Gervais paused in his reading again. Fred Noonan was the navigator for Pan American's trans-Pacific survey and passenger flights in 1935 and 1936. Could William Van Dusen *be* Fred Noonan?

Not according to *Who's Who*. Because William Van Dusen pioneered trans-Atlantic flights in 1939, and South Pacific Flights and the first round-the-world air service in 1940, while Fred Noonan in 1938 was declared legally to have died on July 2, 1937.

Who's Who listed no occupation for Van Dusen from 1946 until 1949, when he became a private business consultant; and in 1951 he was made Eastern Airlines vice-president in charge of public relations, advertising, news bureau, and public affairs.

Van Dusen served in two wars—as a lieutenant commander, U.S.N., on a special mission on the staff of General Eisenhower for the Normandy Invasion, and in the 32nd Division, United States Army, during World War I.

Gervais stopped reading again to do a little figuring. Born September 19, 1901. Served in the 32nd Division in World War I, which ended November 11, 1918, less than two months after Van Dusen's seventeenth birthday. Graduated from an academy in 1921 and from university with an A.B. degree after three years of college, having helped establish transcontinental airmail service during his senior year. Gervais realized he was dealing not only with a distinguished gentleman, but an honest-to-God genius who had taken at least one or two interesting vacations with none other than Charles Lindbergh for a pilot and had held top executive positions under Juan Trippe, Eisenhower, and Rickenbacker. Obviously Van Dusen also must have known Fred Noonan and "AE." But still the thought persisted—Van Dusen could *be* Fred Noonan . . . .

But then, could he also, in pseudonym, be a member of the Institute of Aeronautical Science, the National Aeronautics Association, Sigma Delta Chi professional journalists' fraternity, the Explorers, Wings, and New York Athletic Clubs, the Coffee House in New York City, and the National Press Club in Washington, D.C.? Not if he attended their meetings, Gervais reasoned, but the whispering persisted in his mind. Van Dusen was also credited with authoring *Exploring the Maya with Lindbergh* in 1932, contributing an article to the *Saturday Evening Post* in 1930, and the Maya Series published in *Scientific American* in 1931.

Gervais got a quick letter off to the city hall at Toledo, Ohio, requesting a search for a birth certificate for William Van Dusen. Then he reviewed the few known facts about Fred Noonan.

Gervais had been unable to learn the exact age of Fred Noonan. A search of the records in Chicago, Noonan's reported birthplace, revealed no birth certificate on file. Noonan, according to all information available, attended public schools in Chicago, and a private military academy, name unknown, and the London Nautical College. He took up a flying career after twenty-two years ocean travel as a maritime navigator. During World War I Noonan served as American volunteer officer aboard munitions ships of the Royal Navy between New York and London. He survived three separate torpedo sinkings in the Atlantic and assisted in the rescue of distressed seamen on two other occasions. During the 1920s he learned to fly when ashore from sea duty.

Noonan also joined Pan American Airways in 1930, as a transport pilot and instructor in aerial navigation. A few years later he became Pan Am manager of the Port au Prince Airport in Haiti, and then became inspector of all Pan Am airports.

In 1934, Noonan was transferred to the newly established Pan Am Pacific Division with headquarters in San Francisco. He was navigator on many survey flights across the Pacific, and on the first trans-Pacific airmail flight from San Francisco to Manila on November 22–29, 1935, and on the first trans-Pacific passenger flight on October 14–23, 1936, from San Francisco to Hong Kong. After twenty-nine years of an incredibly distinguished career navigating the oceans and skyways of the world, he left Pan American Airways because of a reported drinking problem and joined Amelia Earhart as navigator on her round-the-world flight attempt in order to "make a comeback." Noonan also held a reserve commission in the United States Navy. He was a lieutenant commander, just like Van Dusen. If in the unraveling of this mystery, Van Dusen and Fred Noonan turned out to be one and the same swashbuckling individual, it would have been a "comeback" all right.

A letter came back from Toledo. There was no birth certificate on file for William Van Dusen in the city that *Who's Who* listed as his birthplace.

Gervais wrote to Pan American World Airways in Los Angeles asking for the birth date and birthplace of Fred Noonan. He received a letter in reply from Pan Am headquarters in New York.

Dear Mr. Gervais:

Your letter of January 15th (1965), sent to our Los Angeles office, has been forwarded to the writer for reply.

Unfortunately we do not have any records on the birth date or place of Fred J. Noonan, who was navigator on the final Amelia Earhart flight, as he left Pan American in early 1937, to the best of my recollection. Since that was about twenty-eight years ago, personnel records have long been disposed of.

The letter reviewed what little, and no more than, Gervais already knew of Noonan's career with Pan American. And then the letter closed with another of the unexpected turns which again and again seemed to draw a cast of distinguished characters into a tight little knot around the mystery of Amelia Earhart.

> We are sending a copy of your letter, and also a copy of this one, to Mr. William Van Dusen who is vice-president in charge of Public Relations for Eastern Airlines, so that he may answer your questions directly. It may be, too, that he has some information on Fred Noonan!
>
> Sincerely,
Althea Lister
Curator - Clipper Hall

No personnel records at Pan American for Fred Noonan, the company's most distinguished trail-blazing navigator who vanished in one of the ten greatest news stories of the century? No fingerprints at the FBI for Fred Noonan, a lieutenant commander in the U.S. Naval Reserve, or for Amelia Earhart? No birth certificate for Fred Noonan? No trace of Wilbur Rothar, discharged from the records of New York State's mental hospitals after twenty-six years of incredible confinement for having claimed to have "found Amelia Earhart"? No trial for Rothar, and no dismissal of the extortion charges against him? No record anywhere of the Lockheed XC-35's final disposition? No trace of what had become of the main body of wreckage of N-16020, the Electra 10 bearing Amelia Earhart's registration number, which carried two U-2 pilots to flaming death against a California mountain twenty-four years after it was supposed to have borne Amelia Earhart and Fred Noonan to a watery tomb? No birth certificate for William Van Dusen, who had contacted the Air Force, the Coast Guard, and the National Archives trying to find out how much Gervais had learned, and then had finally contacted the only one who knew that . . . Gervais himself?

And when Gervais asked Pan Am in Los Angeles about Fred Noonan, the historian for Pan Am in New York referred the matter to Van Dusen.

Gervais wrote to the Navy in Washington for information about Van Dusen. He received a reply dated April 22, 1965, from the Office of the Chief of Naval Operations.

Dear Mr. Gervais:

In reply to your letter of recent date concerning William Van Dusen, who was a Lieutenant Commander, USNR on General Eisenhower's staff during the Normandy Invasion, the following information is provided.

William I. Van Dusen was in the U.S. Naval Reserve for a very short time — just long enough for his special mission — and is now a vice-president of Eastern Airlines.

This data was provided by his son, William B. Van Dusen, who was also a naval officer during World War II and at the present time is employed by the Bureau of Naval Weapons, Navy Department, Washington, D.C.

Sincerely,
F. Kent Loomis
Captain, USN (Ret.)
Asst. Director of Naval History

Gervais recalled that Amelia Earhart's husband, George Putnam, had also served briefly in the war, having been commissioned a major in Army Intelligence to perform the special mission in China of monitoring Japanese broadcasts by such exotic propaganda voices as Little Orphan Annie and Tokyo Rose.

Could a person with no fingerprints on file be identified by voice? Gervais wondered how he would go about identifying Amelia Earhart if she turned up alive but chose to deny her own identity. Not by fingerprints. Not by voice, for although her voice had doubtless been recorded for radio and sound film, recording techniques were imperfect during the thirties, and a voice could change after two or three decades. By dental work? Not if she should be wearing dentures or should choose not to submit to an oral examination. Probably the only physical means left in such a hypothetical case would be to compare the facial bone structure revealed in photographs of a younger Amelia Earhart with photographs of any suspect who might turn up thirty years later.

To George Putman, who knew her as a wife, the voice would have been as sure a means of identification as fingerprints. And to William Van Dusen, whoever he was in Amelia Earhart's life, could not the same have been true?

CHAPTER FOURTEEN

THE MEDALS

Gervais made a trip to Truk in the spring of 1965 for two reasons. One, because it would have been the photographic target of the espionage mission flown by Amelia Earhart; and two, to check out a report he had received during three separate interviews with Toyo Takahashi, a middle-aged woman at Sukiran, Okinawa, who believed she had seen Amelia Earhart crash at Truk in May or June of 1937.

"I was then a young schoolgirl of fourteen," she related in her home on Okinawa. "I was living in 1937 on the island of Truk for the summer. One day I saw an American plane which had two pilots aboard crash-land in the southern seaside swamp of Truk Island. The plane was trailing smoke. It went down in the shallow swamp grown thick with mangrove about ten o'clock one summer morning. Forty or fifty of us, mostly women, saw it. We were excited and horrified and ran toward the mangrove swamp. But we were stopped outside the mangrove area by men as we approached the downed plane, which had then caught fire. A short time later I saw one of the pilots who was taken prisoner by the local men. He was brought to a house garden not very far from where the plane crash-landed."

Toyo recalled that the captors, who were Japanese civilians, told the crowd that a female co-pilot met her death inside the burning plane.

"Then one of them displayed a woman's shoe which he said was salvaged from the aircraft," she said. "It was high-heeled and yellow colored with a pink pompon clipped at the tip of the shoe.

"The arrested aviator was rather tall and rather handsome. He was bruised on the cheeks but was looking fine otherwise. He was the first American I had ever seen in my life. His hair was yellowish, and he wore a long khaki coverall with a zipper at the front. For some reason, he was blindfolded with a towel, and when Japanese police officials arrived at the garden twenty minutes later, he was led afoot to the police station two miles away, still blindfolded."

"Were there any Japanese troops present?" Gervais asked her.

"No," she replied. "There were not Japanese troops on Truk Island then. They did not come in real large numbers until 1941 for the buildup for war."

Toyo could not tell what happened to the pilot after he was whisked away by the police.

"He could have been executed there," she suggested, "or moved to some other islands, or possibly Saipan, which was then the seat of administration for the Japanese South Sea Development Company."

Toyo said she did not go into the mangrove swamp to look at the wreckage or at the occupant who died in the crash.

"It was very hard to get into that swamp . . . a very bad place," she said. "The mangroves were so thick hardly anyone ever went in there. Most people used the path which went around this swamp when they traveled north and south on the island. I am sure the wreckage is still in there. Some men were carrying pieces of metal of the downed plane, and they were still hot when I saw them at the time. The isle where the plane went down was called Natsushima, or summer island, by the Japanese."

Gervais and the woman, in two subsequent meetings,

mapped the area in detail. The isle was now called Dublon in the Truk Island group of the Caroline Islands.

If Toyo Takahashi had indeed seen the Earhart crash, then only Fred Noonan had survived. Gervais felt it was worth a trip from his home at Las Vegas to Truk to check it out.

Gervais spent three days at Truk, wading and cutting his way through the mangrove swamp described by Toyo Takahashi, to finally peer, through eyes swollen nearly shut by insect bites, at the aircraft which had indeed crashed there. It had remained there, a battered twin-engine wreck hidden from human view by jungle growth for twenty-eight years until Gervais found it . . . but it was still easily identified as another Japanese Betty bomber, similar to the one in Saipan from which Fred Goerner had removed a generator.

Upon his return to the States, Gervais received a letter from Viola Gentry.

> Will you be our guest August 7–8, then speak to the Early Fliers' Club?? We meet at West Hampton Air Force Base at the officers' club on Sunday, August 8, 1965. You will make me the proudest Friskey in the world. Can do?
>
> Arrive at the Sea Spray Inn on Saturday, Aug 7 — and I can fill you in on A.E. questions. . . .
>
> I think she went down near or on one of the Ellice Group south of her course — namely Nui in the Ellice Group. . . .
>
> At the club, most everybody knew A.E. — and we will invite all of the 99's on that day — Aug 8 — so let me hear as soon as possible if you can be our guest and speaker.
>
> > lovingly,
> > Your friskey granny Grunt
> > Viola

The letter was written on The Long Island Early Fliers' Club stationery. Fine print at the bottom of the page stated that the club was "An organization of those who participated in aviation sometime during its first thirty years. December 17, 1903—December 17, 1933."

On August 7, 1965, Gervais and his wife, Thelma, left Las Vegas to fly to New York the day before he was to speak at West Hampton. This gave him time to first visit William Van Dusen at his Ridgefield, Connecticut, estate.

Gervais found Van Dusen, dressed in a suit of flying coveralls, working in the garden.

"I was instantly startled at a remarkable resemblance between Van Dusen and Fred Noonan, whom I had come to talk about," Gervais told me later. "There was a deep crease on Van Dusen's left cheek, the same as in old photographs of Noonan. Of course, Van Dusen was a lot older and grayer— but then, more than a quarter-century had elapsed."

Van Dusen displayed great interest in what Gervais' investigation was turning up, and offered to help in any way he could. He told Gervais that he had been a friend of Amelia Earhart.

"What makes you think Amelia Earhart didn't just miss Howland Island and crash in the ocean?" Van Dusen asked.

"With an experienced navigator like Noonan aboard?" Gervais countered. "You knew him, didn't you?"

"I knew him," Van Dusen said scoffingly. "Noonan was a bum."

"But a good navigator, nevertheless."

Van Dusen laughed. "Noonan couldn't navigate his way across my duck pond. What other reasons do you have for thinking they didn't go down in the drink?"

Gervais was astounded. Van Dusen spoke with authority, as if he might be a master navigator condemning a lesser navigator. Gervais told of finding the wreckage remnants of N-16020 on a California desert mountain, and submitted to Van Dusen's interested cross-examination about that discovery. Van Dusen also evinced great interest in the strange case of Wilbur Rothar, his long confinement, and subsequent disappearance without a trace. He made the offer to plant the story of Rothar with a New York newspaper columnist to see if its publication might turn up any leads.

"Perhaps the man will see it—or someone else will—and come forth with some information as to his whereabouts."

Van Dusen kept this promise. The story of Gervais' hunt for Wilbur Rothar appeared in two parts in Allan Keller's column in the *New York World-Telegram and Sun* of August 31 and September 2, 1965.

Any information turned up by readers of the two columns was to have been given over to Van Dusen at Eastern Airlines, who promised to forward it to Gervais. According to Van Dusen, there was no response from readers.

There was also very little response from Van Dusen. Whenever Gervais asked a pertinent question about *his* part in the Earhart affair, he had a way of smoothly changing the subject without giving any answers.

"Why don't you tell Major Gervais what he wants to know?" his attractive young wife impatiently asked at one point.

Van Dusen's eyes flashed. "All right," he thundered at his wife, "let's see you work your way out of this one." There was a tense moment of silence. Then the gray-haired Van Dusen became the charming host again. "How much are you going to tell when you talk to the Early Fliers tomorrow?"

"Mostly about my latest expedition to Truk," answered Gervais. "Why don't you come and hear my talk?"

"Drop by before you go back to Las Vegas. Let us know how the talk goes."

Over dinner, the subject of Fred Goerner's CBS investigation came up. Van Dusen laughed. "Goerner isn't even looking for her in the right ocean."

Gervais frowned. Once again, Van Dusen had made a belittling remark, and the remark had been made as if from a position of some absolute knowledge. "Where do you think she landed?" Gervais asked.

Van Dusen ignored the question. "You know, Amelia used

to fool around with code a little . . . if you knew Amelia's code you might be closer to the truth than you think. But keep up the good work, and you'll find what you're looking for," he smiled benignly. "You're doing a great job."

At the doorway while saying goodnight, Gervais asked suddenly, "Bill, do you ever have any trouble proving who you are?"

Van Dusen didn't blink. "What do you mean?"

Gervais smiled a little too casually. "You ran a search on me all over Washington, so I ran my own on you," he answered. "But I can't find a birth certificate on you in Toledo, Ohio. That where you were born?"

Van Dusen grinned. "Yes, as a matter of fact . . . sometimes I do have a little trouble proving who I am. Be sure and check back with us after your talk tomorrow."

Gervais looked back at the lighted driveway after he was seated in his rented car. Flanked by his pretty young wife, Van Dusen stood there, cheek creased deeply like Fred Noonan's, hands on hips as Noonan stood in so many photographs. Driving away from the country estate, Gervais began to realize just how many questions he had answered, and how few Van Dusen had answered, and how many, many questions there were still to be asked.

There was a festive reception and buffet honoring Joe and Thelma Gervais the next noon, August 8, 1965, at the Sea Spray on the Dunes, East Hampton, Long Island, New York. Nearly three hundred well-dressed, prosperous-looking Early Fliers, Ninety-nines, and their escorts bubbled with enthusiasm for aviation even though thirty to forty years had passed since most of them had won their wings barnstorming about in open cockpits of wood-and-fabric biplanes. All the talk was of the wonder of flying. Glass doors were open onto a sandy beach and sun deck, and the senior citizens of the sky moved lightly in and out, gray and white hair gleaming in the sun. Gervais, only in his early forties and with more than

8000 hours as a pilot, felt like a fledgeling for the first time in years.

These pioneers of man's quest outward had obviously done well for themselves. They bore themselves gracefully and smiled with the confidence of wealth, the inward knowledge that they had possessed the courage to conquer the elements, and the luck to survive day by day the first half-century of leaving the earth at will and soaring like the birds.

Gervais stood in the sun-filled doorway with Carl A. "Slim" Hennicke, program chairman for the Long Island Early Fliers' Club; Elmo N. Pickerill, who had been the first man to take a two-way radio aloft in 1910; and a slim, gray, lively Viola Gentry, who still raced airplanes more than thirty years after her famous flights beneath Brooklyn Bridge.

Gervais shook hands with each of the early flyers as they were introduced.

"I was thrilled and extremely happy," Gervais remembers. "These were the real McCoy . . . the fliers who made aviation what it is today. They were a proud and exclusive group, and you could feel it. They understood one another and had a deep love for flying. Aviation was not just a business to them."

And many of them had known, and some had flown with, Amelia Earhart.

Gervais, a camera loaded with color film hanging from his neck, snapped pictures of veteran flyers as a kid would take snapshots of movie stars. Viola Gentry turned smiling away from the noonday sun and glanced into the reception room. Suddenly the elderly aviatrix's eyes widened and she gasped.

"Why, there's Irene Bolam," she said in a voice filled with surprise and awe. "It really is Mrs. Bolam," she repeated, almost with reverence.

Gervais turned to look at the distinguished-appearing, silver-haired man and woman who had just entered the room. A chill ran through Gervais and he trembled slightly.

"I don't know if I can describe what happened to me," he recounts. "For five years I had been living with this Earhart thing. I had been reading about Earhart, asking about Earhart, speculating about Earhart, studying photographs of Earhart . . . and then, all of a sudden, right there across a room in the Sea Spray Inn, I thought I recognized her."

A feeling came instantly at first sight to Joe Gervais. Was he looking at Amelia Earhart? Had his search ended? Was Amelia Earhart . . . alive?

"Was this the same face that I had studied in so many photographs? The same face twenty-eight years older than in her last pictures? The hair was silver now . . . but shaped the same way, short around her head. It was even parted the same way. But this was ridiculous. It was too much to believe."

Gervais tried to cast the feeling from him and compose himself. He found it difficult to speak.

"Viola," he stammered almost in a whisper, "could I please meet that woman?"

"Oh yes," Viola answered thoughtfully, "you must meet Mrs. Bolam."

They crossed to the smiling couple, and Viola introduced them as Mr. and Mrs. Guy Bolam. Gervais became very wary in his amenities, unable to shake the subconscious impression that he was talking to someone he knew or had known.

"I'm most delighted to meet you, Mrs. Bolam," he said, glancing down at her bosom, which was much fuller than the younger Amelia Earhart's. "Were you a friend of Amelia Earhart?"

The incredibly familiar face smiled to a far-off memory.

"Yes," Mrs. Bolam replied. "I knew her."

Gervais, feeling as if the whole situation were progressing in strange slow motion, tried not to be too obvious in his questioning.

"I'll bet you knew Amelia rather well," he smiled.

"Yes." Her eyes twinkled mischievously. "I knew her rather well."

Suspended on a chain around her neck was a silver medallion and pinned to her dress front near where the silver medal hung were a miniature major's oak-leaf insignia and an enameled miniature metal replica of the red-white-and-blue ribbon which can only be officially worn by those who have been awarded the American Distinguished Flying Cross.

There were still nearly three hundred people about the room, but not to Joe Gervais. To him there were only the two of them.

"Were you a pilot, Mrs. Bolam?"

"Oh yes." Her voice was soft and friendly.

"Did you ever fly with Amelia Earhart?"

"Yes, Major. I flew with Amelia."

Gervais could feel the adrenalin rising in his body. He had to interrupt what he felt must be obviously suspicious questioning. He turned a forced smile toward Mr. Guy Bolam.

"What business are you in, Mr. Bolam?" he asked in a polite tone.

Guy Bolam had a jaunty face and spoke with a British accent.

"Oh, well, you chaps have A.T. and T. over here."

"American Telephone and Telegraph?"

"Yes." Bolam smiled beneath a trim gray mustache. "I'm in communications. Something like your A.T. and T."

Gervais turned back to Irene Bolam.

"I'll bet you made a lot of flights with Amelia Earhart."

A puzzled quiver touched her smile. "Yes. We flew together quite a bit," she admitted.

"I'm so pleased to meet someone as charming as you are who knew Amelia Earhart," Gervais maneuvered. "I wonder if you would be willing to give me your address so that I might write to you sometime."

She glanced at Mr. Bolam as if for advice. His eyebrows lifted just a touch. Then he gave the hint of a shrug. She reached into her purse, brought forth a pen and calling card, and scribbled something quickly across it.

"I should be happy to hear from you, Major," she said, handing him the card.

Gervais stepped back and raised his camera.

"May I take your picture?"

"Oh no, please," she smiled.

"Oh, come on," Gervais persisted, "just one."

She glanced again at her husband. "What do you think?" she asked him.

"I don't know . . . ," he began.

Gervais snapped the shutter.

"Just one," he said. "I'll send you a copy."

Irene Bolam was looking with slight confusion toward her husband. Viola Gentry gasped. Guy Bolam shrugged.

"Oh, well. I suppose just one picture is all right," he relented, not that there was much choice. Gervais had already snapped the picture and was smiling as ingratiatingly as he knew how to.

"Are you a Ninety-nine?" he asked Mrs. Bolam.

"Yes," she replied.

He also asked her if she belonged to Zonta, a feminists' sorority of which Amelia Earhart was a member.

"Yes," she replied again.

Guy Bolam made an excuse to break up the conversation and then led her away.

"Have you known her long?" Gervais asked Viola Gentry.

"Irene Bolam is a wonderful woman," came the reply.

"She's a Ninety-nine and a Zonta?"

"Oh yes."

Viola quickly intercepted someone else to introduce him to. Gervais shook hands automatically, and closed up the leather case of his camera. He would take no more pictures with that roll. He would not risk spoiling the shot he had just snapped. He resolved to try and get Irene Bolam apart from her husband sometime during the afternoon.

At lunch, Mrs. Bolam was seated next to Thelma Gervais, who amiably chatted with her, totally unaware of her husband's incredible hunch.

That afternoon at the West Hampton Air Force Base officer's club, Gervais delivered a color-slide presentation of his expedition to Truk. One by one he studied each of the nearly three hundred attentive faces in the audience. Neither Irene Bolam nor Guy Bolam was among them. They simply were not there.

At the conclusion of the talk, there was a pleasant surprise ceremony in which Thelma Gervais was presented the Amelia Earhart Award for Outstanding Contribution to Research in the History of Aviation for her invaluable assistance to her husband in his strange quest. The award was symbolized by a bronze replica of a silver medallion which had been awarded to Amelia Earhart by the City of New York after her first successful solo flight across the Atlantic.

It was the first constructive recognition that there might be any value in what had become the obsession of Joe Gervais. The Air Force had already shown its appreciation of the wave-making young major by prematurely retiring the thirty-eight-year-old Gervais, a combat-ready squadron commander with more than 8000 hours of military flying experience, against his will.

To her proud husband, the medal hanging by a bronze chain around the neck of Thelma Gervais looked exactly the same size and shape as the silver medal which he had seen Irene Bolam wearing earlier.

After the meeting Gervais returned to the Sea Spray Hotel. There was a phone call that evening for Gervais. It was Mrs. Bolam.

"We would be pleased to have you and Mrs. Gervais come to dinner tomorrow night."

Caught completely by surprise, and having let common sense persuade him that his original hunch about Irene

Bolam was simply too fantastic to be true, Gervais reacted in a way which seemed only logical at the time.

"Mrs. Bolam," he replied, "I would love to come visit you. But our plans are already made. We have to pick up my children, who are staying at my sister's house on Long Island, and catch a plane which leaves tomorrow at three in the afternoon."

"Oh, that's too bad." The disappointment in the voice of Mrs. Bolam was unmistakable. "I would very much like to talk to you."

"About anything in particular?" Gervais asked.

"About your investigation into Amelia Earhart's disappearance."

"Perhaps we could do it another time," Gervais suggested. "Can you give me a raincheck on your kind invitation?"

"Of course," she replied. "Please come and see us the next time you are in New York. Consider it an open invitation."

"Thank you. It's a date then. Tell me, Mrs. Bolam—you knew Amelia Earhart. Do you think she is dead?"

There was a brief silence at the other end of the line. "I believe Amelia Earhart will live as long as people remember her," said Mrs. Bolam. "I wish you good luck and hope you find what you are looking for."

Gervais learned nothing new when he stopped in to see William Van Dusen at Eastern Airlines before departure the next day. Van Dusen offered to use his influence to help Gervais get a look at any classified Amelia Earhart information in Washington and said he would let him know if the story he was planting in a New York newspaper column turned up any trace of Wilbur Rothar.

"Do you know this lady?" Gervais asked, handing Van Dusen Irene Bolam's card.

Across the top of the card she had written the name "Irene Craigmile" and across the bottom of the card was her phone number.

"No."

"You ought to meet her. She's a very nice lady and was a good friend of Amelia Earhart's," Gervais suggested.

"I'll look her up," said Van Dusen and changed the subject.

Later as Gervais was leaving, he asked, "Are you going to look up Mrs. Guy Bolam?"

"Yes," answered Van Dusen.

"Well, don't you want her address and phone number, then? They might not be listed in the phone directory."

"Oh. Yeah. Let me copy that."

Gervais got the distinct impression that Van Dusen might have already known Mrs. Guy Bolam and her address and phone number. Gervais was filled with this suspicion all the way to Kennedy Airport.

High above the earth in the jetliner, Gervais began to chastise himself, as he reviewed the new and exciting data he had just acquired. Mrs. Guy Bolam wore a silver medal that looked like Amelia Earhart's trans-Atlantic solo medal. Mrs. Bolam wore a major's oak-leaf insignia. Amelia Earhart had been made an honorary major in the Army Air Corps by a reserve squadron in San Francisco. Mrs. Bolam wore a miniature Distinguished Flying Cross ribbon, and Amelia Earhart had been awarded the DFC... for the solo flight across the Atlantic. Amelia Earhart was a member of Zonta Sorority and the Ninety-nines, and so was Mrs. Guy Bolam. Mrs. Bolam must know a great deal about her friend Amelia Earhart.

If Gervais had not had his wife and children along and a planned departure at 3 P.M., would he have changed his plans and gone to dinner at the Bolam house? How could a man dedicated to what was becoming a fanatical hunt for a dead woman have failed to make a simple change in plans to check out such an intriguing source of information available twenty-eight years after the purported death of Amelia Earhart? Gervais had the depressing feeling that he would regret for a long time not having accepted Mrs. Guy Bolam's invitation.

And he was right.

Some of the passengers on the jetliner were watching the movie. Some read. Some snoozed. Not Gervais. If he had been up front in the pilot's seat, he would have turned the plane around and headed it back to New York.

There is no passenger in any airliner more uncomfortable than a master pilot who is along for the ride. And there was no one aboard that jet craft more frustrated than Major Joseph Gervais, USAF (Retired).

CHAPTER FIFTEEN

THE UNINTERESTED

Mr. and Mrs. Guy Bolam, interested enough in the prime mover of Operation Earhart to seek out a meeting with Joe Gervais, appeared to be uninterested in what he had found on Truk. They had not stayed for the slide presentation.

No one with or without knowledge of the matter, according to William Van Dusen, had responded to the two New York newspaper columns which had sought more. information about the mysterious Wilbur Rothar.

Repeated requests by Gervais for an interview with Amelia Earhart's best friend, Jacqueline Cochran, were rejected. The nearest thing to an interview was when Gervais succeeded in contacting her husband, Floyd Odlum, by telephone at their Indio estate one afternoon.

"I am sorry," said Odlum, who had ostensibly put up the money for the Lockheed airplane in which Amelia Earhart was supposed to have disappeared. "My wife is simply too busy to see you."

The Air Force clearly wanted nothing more to do with the investigation. And an article by Paul Briand, Jr., based upon the interviews Dinger and Gervais had obtained from natives of Saipan and Okinawa, had been forwarded by the Secretary of the Air Force to the Navy Department, which had bottled up the manuscript in an Amelia Earhart file which was restricted for thirty years.

In 1966 Gervais and his wife had flown a rented private plane to West Medford, Massachusetts, to show Amelia Earhart's sister all the information so far gathered: the statements of those who had seen Amelia Earhart at Saipan . . . the crash of N-16020 in California years after it had "disappeared" in the Pacific . . . the evidence that her sister had been undertaking a photographic espionage mission against the Japanese when she vanished . . . the fruitless hunt for Wilbur Rothar.

"Please do not open your briefcase, Major Gervais," Mrs. Morrissey pleaded nervously. "I have no wish to see, nor can I agree to the publication of any material which might in any way conflict with the rights of my late brother-in-law's widow, Mrs. Margaret Putnam."

Mrs. Morrissey, a high school English teacher and wife of many years to a Cambridge manufacturer, bore a marked resemblance to her famous sister.

"Mr. Fred Goerner of KCBS in San Francisco has prepared an excellent history of the last tragic flight of my sister," she said, "and although I do not agree with his conclusion — the Japanese capture and death on Saipan theory — both my husband and I have confidence in his accuracy and integrity. We really fail to see what is to be gained by further pestering the aged natives of Saipan and by bulldozing a few more acres of their sad little graveyards."

"Do you agree that there is a mystery about your sister's disappearance?" Gervais asked.

Mrs. Morrissey sighed. "Yes," she admitted, "but the only intelligent approach to a possible solving of the mystery of Amelia's disappearance is to explore all possibilities — but to withhold judgment until tangible, irrefutable evidence is produced. Personally, I incline toward Admiral Black's theory of the plane's ditching beyond Howland Island and its immediate submersion in the twenty-foot waves he reported. However, we have no *proof* either."

"Are you sure you wouldn't like to see some of the evidence I've gathered?" Gervais asked, patting his briefcase.

She smiled in a troubled fashion. "No. Thank you very much. I'd rather not."

Mrs. Margaret Putnam Lewis, remarried since the death of George Putnam, maintained the lack of interest in assisting the investigation that she had expressed originally in a letter to Paul Briand, Jr., dated May 1, 1960.

She wrote now from the Stove Pipe Wells Hotel she owned and operated at Death Valley:

> In my silence regarding the Earhart material you were hoping for, I did not purposely wish to deal you such a blow, nor do I want the years to go by any further without some comment from me on my long silence, and lack of cooperation, but even now though I wish to say something, it is difficult to put into writing the various emotions I have had, and continue to have, over the Earhart material, a part of my inheritance to which I have theoretically the "rights."
>
> It would surprise you to know what out-and-out STRUGGLES there have been here on the West Coast to get that material away from me, and you would also be surprised, I think, to know that I have had three different high-priced attorneys helping me protect and defend the material until such time as it can be used as it should be used.

Putnam's widow concluded her apology by stating that "the ramifications of this whole Earhart chapter of history have been more than I could successfully contend with and even now I am in an uneasy calm awaiting another gale from an unscrupulous source."

Gervais had color prints made of the photo he had snapped of Mr. and Mrs. Guy Bolam. Her hair was gray and parted in the same manner as her friend's . . . and the cheekbones . . . and there was the medal suspended from her throat . . . and the major's miniature oak leaf . . . and the tiny, blurred detail of decoration which he remembered as the red-white-and-blue of the Distinguished Flying Cross.

Gervais began his search. He looked in every book on early aviation he could lay his hands on for a photograph of Mrs. Guy Bolam, Irene Bolam, or Irene Craigmile.

He addressed an envelope, wrote a short friendly note, and sent a copy of the color photograph to Mrs. Bolam at her address in Bedford Village, N.Y. At the same time, he wrote to Zonta International and to the Ninety-nines, inquiring about her claimed membership in those organizations in which Amelia Earhart had been so active. Both groups sent back past and present membership lists with messages that no Irene Bolam, Mrs. Guy Bolam, or Irene Craigmile had ever been recorded as a member of either organization.

CHAPTER SIXTEEN

WINSLOW REEF

Late one night the telephone woke Dinger from a sound sleep at Hamilton Air Force Base, California.

"How would you like to sail the South Seas with me in an open boat?" the voice of Gervais teased through the phone. "I've discovered something that may crack this case wide open!"

"Wh-what?" stammered Dinger, half awake.

"Remember Amelia Earhart's last message?" Gervais asked excitedly. "'We are on the line 157-337. We are running north and south.'?"

"What time is it?" asked Dinger, rubbing his eyes in the dark.

"Who cares what time it is? Listen, Bob. I have found land that no one has ever looked at. And if she were flying from north to south on a line 157 degrees by compass from Howland Island, then she could have spotted this land that no one has ever checked out. Remember she said 'Wait . . .' like maybe she had spotted someplace to land just as she ran out of gas?"

"What land are you talking about?" demanded Dinger, waking up at last.

"It's 157 degrees southeast of Howland Island," exclaimed

Gervais. "Howland Island is 337 degrees northwest. A line 157-337 from Howland runs right alongside it, and no one has ever been there to look for the wreckage."

"Joe, I don't understand," Dinger said into the phone. "We've always known there was land 157 degrees southeast of Howland. You mean Hull Island 420 miles from Howland."

"No . . . no . . . ."

"But a seaplane from the U.S.S. *Colorado* landed there during the search . . . landed in the lagoon and found a European overseer and some natives gathering gull guano."

"No . . . no," Gervais interrupted. "I'm not talking about Hull Island."

"What *are* you talking about, Joe?"

"Winslow Reef," Gervais replied. "Winslow Reef. It's a pattern of sand bars at zero degrees 59 minutes south latitude, 174 degrees and 43 minutes west longitude. That's 170 miles southeast of Howland Island. The reef sticks six feet out of the water at low tide, and the sand bars are only visible at low tide. I've checked the tide tables. And the tide was out at 8 A.M. She would have seen the sand bars if she were flying there . . . and she would have been able to make a landing. Want to have a look at them with me next summer? No one else has ever checked them out."

"Why not?" Dinger demanded. "The Navy checked out everything on the map."

"That's just it. These particular sand bars weren't on any map at the time. They weren't even charted until passing ships reported them in 1945 and 1954."

"And nobody went ashore to have a look?"

"What for?" Gervais countered. "Nobody was looking for Amelia Earhart in 1945 or 1954. Sailors avoid shallow water and sand bars. They were reported so other ships could avoid them, too. I'm going to hire a shallow-draft boat and have a look. Want to come along?"

Dinger sighed. "Let me sleep on it."

But there was no more sleep for Dinger that night. He had flown too many missions over the endless Pacific not to put himself in Amelia Earhart's place again on that morning of July 2, 1937.

The Earhart plane had been equipped with a fixed-loop antenna ... an early-model radio compass which required her to turn the entire airplane in order to get a fix on any radio transmission. Just suppose, Dinger reasoned, that Amelia Earhart had just passed to the south of Howland Island and then established a fix on the Coast Guard cutter's transmitter there. It could have indicated that the signal was emanating either from 337 degrees, which would have been correct, or from 157 degrees, which would have been in the wrong direction ... away from Howland Island to the southeast. She wasn't familiar with the direction-finding loop antenna, because it was new, and she had been a "seat-of-the-pants" flyer right up until her preparation for the round-the-world flight. One fix obtained from a loop antenna will indicate the angle at which a radio signal is traveling, but not the direction from which it is being sent. The signal could be coming from either end of the line of angle indicated.

The procedure for determining from which direction the transmitter is sending the signals is to continue on course, take another fix to obtain a new line of angle for the signal, and then determine upon which side of the aircraft the two lines of angle would join at the transmitter.

If she had been south of Howland Island when she overshot it, Dinger reasoned, a second fix of, say, 334-154 would have told her on which side lay Howland Island. To a plane flying east, two fixes of 337 and 334 would have indicated that she had overshot Howland Island on her left and to the rear in a northwesterly direction.

In other words, a single fix indicates two opposite directions and is therefore ambiguous information. A second fix indicates which of the two directions, 180 degrees apart, is the right direction. Pilots call this technique "solving the 180-degree ambiguity."

Could Amelia Earhart and Fred Noonan have failed to solve their 180-degree ambiguity, flown 180 degrees in the opposite direction from their planned destination for more than an hour past their estimated time of arrival and then run out of gas?

If so, they would have still been looking for Howland Island, and when the gas ran out, a sand bar suddenly appearing ahead on the limitless surface of the Pacific would have been better than nothing. And a crash landing was nothing new to Amelia Earhart.

Winslow Reef and its pattern of four uncharted neighboring sand bars gleaming white and smooth out of a low blue tide 170 miles along the line she frantically called out . . . "157-337" . . . actually 157 degrees southeast of Howland Island . . . would have been a welcome sight to the pilot of a powerless plane. Any old land in the sea.

Gervais plunged full-throttle into preparations for journeying to the unexplored sand bars 170 miles southeast of Howland Island in the uninhabited equatorial center of the South Pacific Ocean. He booked a seat on a Pan Am flight to Pago Pago and paid a $250 deposit to owner-skipper Charles Carr for passage in his 28-foot open yawl from Pago Pago at Samoa to Winslow Reef via Tokelau in the Union Islands, and Canton and Hull Islands in the Phoenix Group—a planned voyage of close to 2000 miles, starting from Pago Pago on July 2, 1966, the twenty-ninth anniversary of Amelia Earhart's disappearance.

It would be winter south of the equator. The Environmental Science Services Administration of the U.S. Department of Commerce advised Gervais that:

Although there is no danger from hurricanes or tropical storms during these winter months, there is danger of rough weather associated with a phenomenon known as the Intertropical Convergence Zone. This zone meanders back and forth across the equator and pro-

duces areas of severe thunderstorms. This is the major
weather feature which would affect your planning. Since
it is a synoptic feature and subject to frequent changes,
we are enclosing a schedule of weather broadcasts for
the area. With the information obtained from these
broadcasts you should have very little trouble planning
your trip. Actually, you have selected the best possible
season as far as weather is concerned. We hope this information is of value to you. Have a good trip.

Dinger, chief of information and a pilot still on active duty
with the 6th Air Force Reserve Region headquarters at Hamilton Air Force Base, was suddenly stricken with arterial
sclerosis in both legs. He entered surgery at the Presidio in
San Francisco to have plastic arteries installed and was
scratched from the expedition.

Gervais proceeded solo with his plans and wrote to tell
Viola Gentry what he was doing.

"I am real proud of you and Thelma for carrying on *re*
A.E.," she replied.

I am glad that you are going into uncharted waters.
As I told you, I am sure you will find something in the
Ellice Group, like at Nui, nearest to Howland about
250 miles south of her course. I have forgotten how
many miles to Howland and the Phoenix Group. I asked
AE to take CW (code wireless) instead of voice, knowing
she could not talk if in the water. Nui, if I remember, is
about 15 miles long, about one mile wide . . . .

In my sleep a few years ago, I was given longitude and
latitude. When I woke in the morning I looked up both
and found Nui of the Ellice Group . . . .

Extrasensory perception! Nui was nearly a thousand miles
west of where he planned to go. Gervais marveled again at
the faith these early women pilots demonstrated in ESP.

Amelia Earhart had been interested in ESP even before she

learned that her best friend, Jacqueline Cochran, claimed to possess remarkable powers of supernatural vision, according to the Cochran autobiography, *The Stars at Noon.* "I found that Amelia was following interestedly the work in the extra-sensory field being done at Duke University and I told her a little bit about some of my own experiences."

The Cochran book told of a series of experiments in which Jacqueline's ESP led Amelia Earhart to the location of a crashed and missing airliner, followed by the successful location "by vision" of another crashed airliner, and how she subsequently "accompanied" Amelia Earhart and George Putnam on a coast-to-coast flight by ESP.

With all this ability and preliminary work with Amelia, why didn't I locate her when she went down? The answer is that I did, or at least I think I did, but can never prove it one way or the other, and besides it was all to no purpose. George Putnam was in my apartment in Los Angeles almost as soon as he could get there after the news of her nonarrival at Howland Island. He was extremely excited and called on me for the kind of help Amelia thought I might be able to give. I told him where Amelia had gone down; that with the ditching of the plane, Mr. Noonan, the navigator, had fractured his skull against the bulkhead in the navigator's compart-ment and was unconscious; but that Amelia was alive and the plane was floating in a certain area. I named a boat called the *Itasca* which I had never heard of at the time, as a boat that was nearby, and I also named an-other Japanese fishing vessel in that area, the name of which I now forget. I begged Putnam to keep my name out of it all but to get planes and ships out to the des-ignated area. Navy planes and ships in abundance combed that area but found no trace. I followed the course of her drifting for two days. It was always in the area being well combed. On the third day, I went to the Cathedral and lit candles for Amelia's soul, which I then knew had taken off on its own long flight. I was frustrated and emotionally overcome. If my strange ability was worth anything it should have saved Amelia. Only the urging of Floyd ever prompted me to try my hand at this sort of thing again and he hasn't urged me for several years for he knows it upsets me.

The area indicated in these visions had been near the Gilbert Islands, hundreds of miles west of where Gervais planned to look. If the information from Jacqueline Cochran's ESP had been used by the State Department in 1937 in an attempt to divert the Japanese Navy's offer of assistance to a point hundreds of miles west of where Amelia Earhart actually went down, could Viola Gentry in 1956 be using ESP as a dodge to persuade Gervais to explore nearly a thousand miles in the same general wrong direction?

"I will say this," the lady who once flew under Brooklyn Bridge wrote. "To the best of my knowledge you are on the right track. I am also sure you will find something that will reward you for all of your years and efforts."

On June 6, 1966, Gervais sent a progress report to Dinger in the hospital.

Have been swimming one mile every day for a week now, trimming off a little flab. Three more weeks of this and some daily hot sun and I will look like an Admiral ready to take on the Pacific. I expect to be in 7-level [Royal Canadian Air Force 5BX physical fitness tables] condition because there's nothing easy about any of it.

Rest easy, Ace, the best is yet to come—think positively. Did you know that there is in every man an islandic core of inner self which no other man can fully explore or know?

Then a cablegram was delivered collect, a few minutes past midnight of July 2, 1966, a few hours before Gervais' scheduled takeoff from Las Vegas.

MAJ J GERVAIS
PLEASE WAIT BOAT BROKEN I WRITE YOU LETTER NEVER MIND
RESERVATION MAYBE NEXT TIME YOU HEAR FROM ME HONO-
LULU
CHARLEY CARR

It was from Pago Pago, and there was no additional address. The letter arrived a few days later by airmail special
delivery.

Dear Mr. Gervais,
I am sorry that I got you all shook up with my tele-
grams, but we arrived in Pago Pago in a sinking boat.
First, before I can sail anymore, the boat must be repaired; second, before I can leave Pago Pago these repairs must be paid for; third, as yet, I do not know
what the total cost will be. For sure this will mean a
3-week delay. All drydock work in Samoa is done strictly
by the native workers. Next week I should know what
the cost will be. Meantime, I will be contacting Honolulu
for the funds I will need. However, if the cost should be
too great I will have to go to work here—or perhaps sell
the boat and fly back to Honolulu. Either way I'll send
your $250 to you and by all means will stay in close con-
tact with you.
I appreciate the confidence and trust you have shown
in me. Please do not get on the airplane until everything
is ready; there are no accommodations here except at
the hotel for $15 a day. My sailing spirits are very low at
this time and these too will have to be repaired.
Charley

The last word Gervais ever heard about the unfortunate
yawl appeared in the November, 1966 issue of *Pacific Islands
Monthly*, a news magazine published from Australia.

NO BUTS, 28-ft yawl, arrived unexpectedly in Fiji
waters in late September after a series of mishaps which

started when she broke her anchor chain off Late Island, Tonga.

Owner-skipper, Charles Carr, of Honolulu, had taken a three-man seismological survey party to Late from Vavau; and while the yawl was anchored off the island, the anchor chain broke in heavy seas and high winds. Carr then found the clutch would not engage.

When he managed to get the engine going, he found the yawl was taking water.

Bailing was of no avail, but just when he was about to abandon ship, he found the leak.

Having made temporary repairs, he tried to sail back to Late. But the current was too strong.

Vavau also seemed out of the question, even though it was only 35 miles away. So Carr made for Fiji, 450 miles away.

He called at Lakeba to radio to Suva about the three men marooned on Late, and then sailed to Suva, via Lautoka.

After *No Buts* was overhauled at Suva, Carr planned to sail for Auckland.

Needing something to do in his frustration, Gervais sent a print of the color photo of Mr. and Mrs. Guy Bolam to Viola Gentry, just to see what her reaction would be.

She wrote on September 22, 1966, from Mackinac Island, Michigan.

Thank you for the picture of Guy and Irene. Met Irene at a banquet the Zontas gave for Amelia. Think it was 1928. However it was when she got back from her ride [first woman to fly the Atlantic] with Bill Stultz and Glen Gordon in the "Friendship." How do you know them?

Could she have forgotten so soon that she had introduced them to Gervais only the year before at the Sea Spray Inn?

Read Goerner's story *(The Search for Amelia Earhart)* in *True* Magazine. I do not believe much of it. I know he must have had all the trips and went places and such— but where are the bodies? Admiral Nimitz told him she landed in the Marshalls. That would keep her almost on her course—which I was proud to see in print.

What about the plane in California that has her serial numbers on it? That interests me....

Sorry you had no luck this summer, but surely next year.

One more thing. The island Nui of the Ellice Group is about 150 to 200 miles from the place in Marshall Islands—Yes?

Then one day several months later Bill Van Dusen, the unusually interested vice-president of Eastern Airlines, flew into Las Vegas from Indio, California, especially to see Joe Gervais.

"About this expedition to have a look at Winslow Reef for the Earhart wreckage," he began, "is it still on for next summer?"

"If the boat doesn't sink again," Gervais confirmed.

"You intend to travel 1600 miles in an open boat?"

"I have to. That's all I can afford."

"That's what I came to talk to you about," said Van Dusen. "I spent last night with the Odlums at their ranch in Indio. At dinner, I was telling Floyd and Jackie about your theory. Jimmy Doolittle was there, too. You know, they all knew Amelia Earhart very well. They're quite interested in what you are doing."

"I'll bet they are," grinned Gervais.

"Don't you think it's kind of risky going all that way in open sea by sailboat?" asked Van Dusen.

"There's no other way," explained Gervais. "The water is too shallow there to get in close to the sand bars, even in a sailboat. We have to get as close as we can, and then launch an outboard motorboat to get right up to the sand bars."

"How about a helicopter?" asked Van Dusen. "Would that work?"

"Sure," exclaimed Gervais. "If I had one. But I haven't."

"Forgetting about what you have and what you can afford, what would be ideal in the way of equipment to explore your sand bars?"

Gervais thought for a minute. "Why, a larger, diesel-driven ship with a helicopter on the fantail. Then we could stay in deep water and look over the sand bars and even land on them in the chopper."

"Right," said Van Dusen. "You know, Floyd Odlum might be willing to finance an outfit like that for you. Would you be willing to explain your whole theory . . . the 180-degree ambiguity . . . the line of position, and all that on a tape recorder so that I can play it tomorrow for Floyd Odlum and Jackie Cochran? If you make a tape, I might be able to persuade Floyd to finance your expedition complete with helicopter on the fantail and anything else you need."

"You think he would?" gasped Gervais.

"If you can convince him on tape the expedition stands a good chance of settling this Earhart thing once and for all," Van Dusen nodded. "Will you make the tape?"

Gervais made the tape, and Van Dusen departed, ostensibly back to Indio, California.

"Did you say anything about your contact with Mrs. Guy Bolam on that tape?" Dinger asked in the long-distance telephone conversation that followed Van Dusen's departure.

"Negative. All we talked about was getting to Winslow Reef."

"They could be merely trying to find out everything you know," mused Dinger.

"I thought of that," Gervais agreed. "I let 'em think the only thing we've got on our minds is getting out to Winslow Reef."

"Why the tape?" asked Dinger skeptically. "What's the matter with your going down to tell the story in person?"

"I suggested that, but Van Dusen said the Odlums are too busy for that. It's the tape or nothing."

Dinger grunted. "I don't get it"

"I don't get it either. You know what I think?" Gervais asked. "I think it was an exercise to find out if we're on the right track, too. But I'm not going to sit back and do nothing but wait for a helicopter on the fantail. I'm still working on that woman back in Bedford, New York."

CHAPTER SEVENTEEN

THE BONES

Joe Gervais and I were having a cup of coffee one evening in February, 1967, while awaiting Gervais' jet departure for Las Vegas.

"I can't seem to find out anything at all about Mrs. Guy Bolam," Gervais said. "No reference to her in any books or articles about the early days of aviation. No early photographs of her. No answer to my letters or Christmas cards. No acknowledgment of the photograph I sent her. No record of her ever having belonged to the Ninety-niners or to Zonta. I simply can't get a line on her. It's beginning to bug me."

"What about her husband?" I asked.

"Guy Bolam? He told me he was with Amalgamated Telephone and Telegraph. They never heard of him. There's a Guy Bolam Associates, Incorporated in New York. I've had my brother-in-law and others in his office in New York City call the number to try and find out what kind of business Guy Bolam Associates is. The woman who answers the phone won't say. Most of the time there is simply no answer."

"How about the property?" I asked.

"What property?"

"That house you were invited to."

"In Bedford Village? What about it?"

"There must be a deed recorded someplace," I suggested.
"Why not have your brother-in-law check the county records
to see who owns the house they are living in?"

It was just a suggestion. Investigators in the movies always
seem to have limitless funds to hop on a plane and head anywhere in the world at any time. In real life, a brother-in-law
seemed more practical. Before Gervais took off, we agreed
to meet again in April at Los Angeles.

It was a trying time for Gervais. Fred Goerner, whose
Search for Amelia Earhart was enjoying bestsellerdom, had
been less than kind in the book to Gervais and Dinger. Goerner was on a lecture tour of the United States demanding a
Congressional investigation, gruesomely maintaining that the
bones of Amelia Earhart and Fred Noonan had been smug-
gled back from Saipan by the U.S. Marine Corps and were
being kept under a conspiracy of silence in some dark recess
of the National Archives in Washington.

William Van Dusen forwarded to Gervais a copy of a letter
from Linton Wells, director of Storer Broadcasting Company's Washington news bureau, which cast some light on
Goerner's confrontation with the Marine Corps regarding
the alleged bones:

> Talked for almost half an hour with General Greene's
> aide who was with the General when he talked to
> Goerner. The General categorically denied any knowl-
> edge about AE's plane, or the supposed digging up of
> her bones. Goerner wasn't convinced, and when the Gen-
> eral offered to swear on the Bible, Goerner said he
> wouldn't believe him. The General gave Goerner the
> names of Marine officers to contact but Goerner said
> he would not call them because he knew the General
> would order them not to say anything. The General
> offered the use of his telephone right then. Goerner
> declined the offer. I feel sure you can discount the

Goerner Marine stories. The General won't say anything more for publication because he feels that Goerner would just exploit it for his own use.

Another Marine general who requested that his name not be disclosed wrote to Gervais:

> I met with Mr. Goerner on two or three occasions when he visited Headquarters in an attempt to run down additional information in connection with his project of reporting Amelia Earhart's disappearance. The Navy and Marine Corps both went to considerable lengths to investigate claims which Mr. Goerner had made that the Marine Corps had been involved in the recovery of Miss Earhart's body and the wreckage of her aircraft. The Commandant of the Marine Corps himself held a lengthy conference with Mr. Goerner and directed that appropriate members of the staff at Headquarters assist in determining whether there was any information which might be useful to Mr. Goerner. As I remember it, extensive research and several letters to retired personnel all produced negative results, and I honestly believe there is nothing known to any Marines that would contribute anything to Mr. Goerner's questions.

But if the "American Spy Lady" known by so many natives at Saipan in 1937 as "Tokyo Rosa" had, as nearly half the Saipanese remembered, died there and been buried, then why had no one reported ever having seen her corpse? And why could no one of Goerner's team or the team of Operation Earhart locate her grave or remains?

In reviewing the interviews Gervais and Dinger recorded on Saipan regarding the mysterious "Tokyo Rosa" it is easy to overlook the fact that about as many people believed she had "been sent to Japan" as thought she had died. The assumption that Amelia Earhart is dead causes the mind to tend to skip over any evidence that she might have survived. Besides, if Amelia Earhart had lived, why would it have remained a secret for thirty years?

That was the sort of assumption which caused Gervais to methodically search in other directions for the answers to Amelia Earhart's disappearance. It also caused the more flamboyant and emotional Goerner to ask Senator Thomas Kuchel of California to launch a Congressional investigation into what he believed to be a government conspiracy to conceal both the secret files and the actual bones of Amelia Earhart and Fred Noonan.

The now-famous, bones-in-the-archives "solution" in Fred Goerner's book was actually proposed a few months earlier in a Dallas, Texas, dispatch by United Press International staff writer John Drollinger on July 29, 1966.

It was enough to make any man curious . . . .

So Billy Burks, who was digging up a grave 22 years ago in Saipan, asked the officer supervising the work who was buried there.

"Have you ever heard of Amelia Earhart?" was the reply.

It was a question, not an answer.

After the answer, the intelligence officer took charge of the remains and ordered the two men not to say anything about the incident. Burks said he heard that the remains were taken to Washington secretly.

According to Army graves registration figures, there were an awesome lot of American graves on Saipan in 1944. Killed and buried there were 2189 Marines, 67 soldiers, 46 sailors, and 2 Coast Guardsmen. They had paid the price for the real estate where in 1937 the "American Spy Lady" known by the natives as "Tokyo Rosa" had spent her first days of Japanese captivity. Between 1947 and 1949, the remains of the 2304 good men who died to capture Saipan in 1944 were exhumed and returned to American ground via Hawaii and the Oakland Army Terminal.

The movement of our military corpses is the Army's exclusive job. No record exists—none of the careful paperwork involved in handling human remains—that indicates the U.S. Marine Corps either shipped or transported any dead man or dead woman from Saipan to Washington, D.C.

Gervais thought the theory rather naïve. "Where would they keep them?" asked Gervais. "In a filing cabinet or a safe? The Archives are a warehouse of documents and information—not a mausoleum.

"Then again, he could be right," Gervais said. "We have to keep an open mind."

CHAPTER EIGHTEEN

THE CODE

My sixteen-year-old son, Tony, accompanied me to Hollywood in March, 1967, for a meeting, not previously planned, with Gervais at Gene Autry's Continental Hotel on the Sunset Strip.

"I'll show you a picture of the Earhart wreck and where it went down," Gervais had called excitedly the night before from Las Vegas. "I've broken the Earhart Code!"

It sounded exciting enough to keep my number-two son interested, so I brought him along to tape the session on the recorder he usually used for rock music. Six floors down, out on the Strip, love-generation hippies milled about, but inside the room tension mounted as Gervais reviewed "the facts."

"You remember how in the movie *Flight to Freedom* the heroine was supposed to land and hide out on 'Gull Island'? Then you remember that on July 9, 1937, during the search by the Navy for Earhart and Noonan, a Lieutenant Lambrecht landed a seaplane from the battleship *Colorado* at Hull Island, which was in the direct line of position from Howland Island last called out by Amelia Earhart on her radio? And you remember that the Japanese carrier *Akagi* with three destroyers had been lying in wait four months at Jaluit, easy steaming distance to Hull Island? You recall that the *Akagi* and its planes could have gotten to Hull days ahead of any plane from the *Colorado,* which had to steam all the way from Pearl Harbor?"

We knew all that, and we waited impatiently for Gervais to get to something new.

"Remember, she called out 'wait'?" Gervais continued, "Like maybe something unexpected and frightening was happening?"

Gervais switched on a slide projector and began to pull some 16-millimeter film through it awkwardly by hand. It was Navy film shot during the search for Amelia Earhart.

"I'm going to show you a picture of what Lambrecht found on Gull Island."

"You mean Hull Island, Joe," I interrupted. "Gull is a fictional name in a fictional screenplay."

"Is it?" grinned Gervais. Old shots of Amelia Earhart, Fred Noonan, and George Putnam were projecting jerkily on the wall as he slid the film through. "Remember the one distinctive thing we know about Hull Island? Seagulls! The place was infested with gulls. There was supposed to be a European manager there and a crew of natives harvesting gull guano. That's where the name Gull Island came from. Hull Island and Gull Island! They're one and the same."

"Come on now, Joe," I complained. "Gull Island was just a movie name as far as we know."

"Or could it have come from real life?" I suddenly wondered. "Howard Hughes could have known the true story. He owned RKO, which made the movie."

"Wrong. Ah . . . here it is." He held the film and tried to focus the projector. My son helped him. On the wall appeared a photograph of a tropical island and lagoon almost obliterated by thousands of flying gulls. The water of the lagoon and the sky above blowing palm trees were thick with flying gulls.

"There, my friends," Gervais boomed. "There's a photograph of Gull Island . . . Hull Island . . . whatever you want to call it."

We stared at the projection in total bewilderment. "So what, Joe?" I finally asked. "I've seen that before. Those are the films released by the Navy to the newsreels after their search was called off in 1937."

"Sure," said Gervais. "I've run this film a hundred times without seeing anything special. But last week I projected it one frame at a time. You remember what the Japanese military flag looked like in those days?"

"The red meatball?"

"The red meatball. Just a red ball—supposed to be the sun—on a field of white. Now watch."

He drew the film upward in the slide projector. Its lens was large enough to project three frames of the film at a time, one above the other. The gulls were so thick against the island landscape, they formed patches which nearly obscured the island itself. The clouds of birds swirled this way and that. Suddenly we all saw it.

"Well, I'll be damned," I breathed.

In one frame of the movie film, and one frame alone, a patch of birds had swept aside to reveal a Japanese flag planted right in the middle of the beach . . . stretched out by the wind to reveal its ball insignia against a field of white.

"That's what the planes from the U.S.S. *Colorado* found at Hull Island," declared Gervais. "They went there to pick up Amelia Earhart and Fred Noonan. But the Japs had got there first and left their flag to taunt us."

"Wait a minute," said my son Tony, moving over to the wall for a closer look at the projection. "I see something else."

"Good boy," grinned Gervais. "What do you see, Tony?"

Tony ran his fingers along the beach in the projection. "There . . . there . . . and there. Could be the wreckage of the plane."

We all crowded around the remarkable projection, passing a magnifying glass from hand to hand, trying to make the details in the blow-up even larger.

"I see what could be a wing section."

"This could be a tire."

"How about this? Left engine and broken wing?"

"What are these things?"

"I don't know what to make of this right here. Might even be a salvage hook?"

But unmistakable in the center of the beach, jauntily flew the Japanese flag.

"I don't get it," I sighed. "Why would the Navy release a picture like that to the newsreels?"

"Because it only shows up in one frame," Gervais explained. "Running through a projector at regular speed, you can't even see it. The birds are in the way. To a film editor, it would seem to be perfectly harmless footage of a tropical island infested by seagulls."

My head was throbbing. "What did you mean I was wrong when I said Howard Hughes might have written *Flight to Freedom* because he owned RKO, which made the movie?"

"Because the movie was made in 1942. Howard Hughes didn't buy RKO until 1947 after the war."

"Who did he buy RKO from? Who owned it in 1942?"

Gervais shrugged with exaggerated calmness.

"Jacqueline Cochran and Floyd Odlum."

"What?"

"Howard Hughes in 1947 purchased controlling interest in RKO Studios from Floyd Odlum and Jacqueline Cochran!"

It was past midnight. There was no conversation for awhile. Each of us was lost in exercises of deduction while we waited for room service to send up some coffee. Gervais put away the projector and film and began spreading a chart of the South Seas and a stack of clear plastic transparencies on the table.

"Now," he proceeded as we sipped our coffee, "you recall that Bill Van Dusen once suggested I should look for Amelia Earhart's code? That she liked to fool around with code, and if I learned hers I might be nearer to the truth than I think?"

We remembered.

"Well, for about three years now I have been spending

my spare time trying to discover a code. I have printed the names of everyone we have ever run across on these transparencies. I have put down all the numbers, miles, fuel consumption, headings, addresses, telephone numbers, plane registrations . . . all are on transparencies. I have made transparencies of the names of all locations involved, and the names of all the islands she would have reached in the Pacific.

"Recently I made transparencies of the names Irene Bolam, Irene Craigmile, and Guy Bolam. One by one I began applying these names to groups of islands in the Pacific . . . trying to see if I could spell out the names using letters from the names of the islands, and if I could, whether it would mean anything. I don't know why, but I left the Phoenix Group until last. Then here is what I found."

Gervais spread out a piece of paper so that the name Guy Bolam was spelled vertically:

G
U
Y
B
O
L
A
M

Alongside he lined up transparencies inscribed with the names of the eight islands of the Phoenix Group.

"There are an awful lot of ways you can stack them up," he explained, "but this is the way that paid off."

GARDNER
ENDERBURY
SYDNEY
BIRNIE
PHOENIX
HULL
CANTON
MCKEAN

"What we do now is slide the names of the islands of the Phoenix Group over each of the vertical letters spelling out the name of our mystery woman's husband."

<u>G</u>ARDNER
ENDERB<u>U</u>RY
S<u>Y</u>DNEY
<u>B</u>IRNIE
PH<u>O</u>ENIX
HUL<u>L</u>
C<u>A</u>NTON
<u>M</u>CKEAN

We stared at it.
"Hey, that's fine," said my son
"I don't get it, Joe," I said.
Gervais underlined it for us.

<u>G</u>ARDNER
ENDERB<u>U</u>RY
S<u>Y</u>DNEY
<u>B</u>IRNIE
PH<u>O</u>ENIX
HUL<u>L</u>
C<u>A</u>NTON
<u>M</u>CKEAN

I felt annoyed. "So it spells out Guy Bolam. So what? You could do that with the names of almost any eight places on earth."

Gervais grinned. "Count how many letters in we go in each island name. The first is G and one letter in. The second is U, the seventh letter of Enderbury. Go ahead. You do it, and mark the numbers alongside."

I did as he asked, counting carefully.

<u>G</u>ARDNER   1
ENDERB<u>U</u>RY   7
S<u>Y</u>DNEY   2

BIRNIE	1
PHOENIX	3
HULL	4
CANTON	2
MCKEAN	1

Gervais let us stare at it some more. He wrote the numbers out horizontally.

17213421

"It doesn't mean anything to me," I sighed finally.

"It means something on the chart." He punched a finger against the map. 172 degrees and 13 minutes west longitude . . . 4 degrees and 21 minutes south latitude!"

We all gasped. "Hull Island?"

"Not just Hull Island," exclaimed Gervais. "172 degrees and 13 minutes west, and 4 degrees 21 minutes south on Hull Island." He laid a detailed map of the island over the Pacific chart. "That's right there on the northwest shore of Hull Island. The lagoon—exactly the lagoon where the U.S.S. *Colorado's* seaplane landed to look for Amelia Earhart!"

"That is the goddamnedest thing I have ever seen in my life." I said it several times. I couldn't seem to find any other words.

We made Gervais go over the whole thing again. It came out the same. There was no changing it.

Gervais pulled a letter from his pocket. "I received this only this morning. It's from my brother-in-law. I didn't know whether to come here for this meeting or hop the first jet east."

"What is it?" I asked.

"You remember you said I should have someone check to see whose name is on the deed of the property Mrs. Guy Bolam lives on in Bedford Village, New York. To see who the legal owner is?"

"Yeah?"

"My brother-in-law went down to the courthouse and took a look at the name on the deed."

"Who owns the property?"

"Floyd Odlum. Jacqueline Cochran's husband. Floyd Odlum."

He handed us photographs in color of the house, taken by his brother-in-law. It was a beautiful house with what looked to be about a four-car garage. It wasn't just a house. It was an estate.

And the name painted clearly on the mailbox of the house next to the estate owned by Floyd Odlum and lived in by Mrs. Guy Bolam was: Rakow.

"Have you heard any more about Floyd Odlum fixing you up with a boat and helicopter to search Winslow Reef?" I asked.

"Negative."

"Are you still going out there?"

"Negative. I've got a raincheck to visit Mrs. Guy Bolam. The Pacific expedition is off. I'm going to New York."

CHAPTER NINETEEN

THE ROSE

"Let me say this about all my research for *Daughter of the Sky* and my conversations since," Paul Briand, Jr., wrote Gervais in early 1967 from the Air Force Academy:

The closer you get to friends and family of Amelia Earhart, the more you feel a conspiracy of silence. Do they all have something to hide, something so big or embarrassing to the Earhart name and fame that they are reluctant to tell the truth? They are and were: Muriel Morrissey and her mother, Paul Mantz, Clyde Holly the attorney, and Jacqueline Cochran. Is the truth so fantastic that the courts readily declared Amelia Earhart and Fred Noonan legally dead long before the mandatory seven years?

In writing *Daughter of the Sky,* I proceeded from the understanding that Amelia Earhart was one of America's greatest heroines; indeed, my heroine had no feet of clay. Could I be wrong? What did Amelia Earhart know of Tokyo Rose? There is evidence to indicate that she was in Tokyo during the war, hearsay to be sure, but evidence nevertheless. Why did Jackie Cochran rush into Tokyo right after the war and before the occupation forces? Was it to find her old friend and bring her back to the States as quickly and quietly as possible? What did Major George Putnam of Intelligence overhear in monitoring Tokyo Rose programs in the CBI theater? His own wife's voice? What is Holly afraid of if you think AE is still alive? And Fred Noonan? Here, my friend, is where I would like to dig.

> Cheers and luck for 67,
> P. Briand

My own comment on this was: "I don't buy that. Why, it's ridiculous. If the Japanese had used her to make broadcasts, the whole idea would have been for her to start right out saying, 'Hello. This is Amelia Earhart.' "

"Yes," Gervais agreed. "The whole propaganda value would have been in who she was. There would have been no point at all in Amelia Earhart broadcasting Japanese propaganda under the name of Tokyo Rose."

But what *was* her husband, George Putnam, doing in China listening to Japanese radio?

Amelia Earhart's sister, Muriel Morrissey, in her book *Courage is the Price*, published in 1963, wrote:

> George Putnam, who served as a major in the Air Force in the Burma-Chinese sector, flying B-29's, spent most of his off-duty time following clues and listening to often-harrowing tales.

One could form an incorrect impression from Mrs. Morrissey's statement that Putnam had been a B-29 pilot, or at least a crew member. Actually, Putnam was granted a direct commission as a major in Army Intelligence, and sent to China without any prior military training.

> After the European D-Day when the collapse of Japanese resistance was imminent, a woman's voice was sometimes heard, broadcasting from Tokyo false information to the American forces. Could this "Tokyo Rose"

possibly be Amelia, brainwashed to the point of leading her countrymen into enemy traps? Every fiber of GP's being denied the possibility, but he alone in all that vast area could without question identify Amelia's voice, even though weakened and tense from psychological mistreatment. He made a dangerous three-day trek through Japanese-held territory to reach a Marine Corps radio station near the coast where the broadcast reception was loud and clear. After listening to the voice for less than a minute, GP said decisively, "I'll stake my life that that is not Amelia's voice. It sounds to me as if the woman might have lived in New York, and of course she had been fiendishly well coached, but Amelia—never!"

It's a remarkable narrative. Only Putnam could identify Amelia Earhart's voice, "even though weakened and tense from psychological mistreatment." A strangely precise statement: "even *though* weakened . . . ." Not "even *if* weakened and tense from psychological mistreatment." And there was no hypothetical suggestion that if the voice had been Amelia Earhart's, she might have been broadcasting because she had been mistreated physically. The mistreatment was mental.

Putnam's statement, after listening for "less than a minute" to the suspect voice, was also strange.

"I'll stake my life that that is not Amelia's voice," he was quoted by the sister of Amelia Earhart as saying. "It sounds to me as if the woman might have lived in New York, and of course she has been fiendishly well coached, but Amelia—never!"

Fiendishly well coached to do what? To sound like Amelia Earhart? Why would the Japanese coach Tokyo Rose to sound like Amelia Earhart? Would the United States give Putnam a major's rank and send him to China for "a dangerous three-day trek through Japanese-held territory" to listen to a voice that did not sound like Amelia Earhart?

Could Mrs. Morrissey's Freudian slip be showing? Possessing knowledge that the reader would never dream of, was Mrs. Morrissey subconsciously claiming that Japan was trying through a "fiendishly well coached" voice to trick the United States into believing Amelia Earhart was alive in Tokyo?

Mrs. Morrissey's text continued:

> The theory that Amelia and Fred had been captured and were held by the Japanese authorities during the hostilities was not abandoned until after their capitulation and the occupation by General Douglas MacArthur in 1945. At that time Jacqueline Cochran, who had done heroic service in organizing American women fliers to ferry new planes from the United States to the European air bases, was given a final mission by General "Hap" Arnold: to make an official investigation of the activities of Japanese women in the Imperial Air Force. In doing this research Miss Cochran, the first American woman to land in Japan after the surrender, had access to many government files which were later taken to Washington for microfilming. Jacqueline's friendship for Amelia led her to delve into a folder when she saw pictures of Amelia and newspaper clippings presumably about her. There were data about other American fliers including Colonel James Doolittle and Jacqueline herself also. Nothing indicated that Amelia had been a prisoner. As the file was still "open" in 1945, it seems unlikely that the Japanese government had any knowledge of her being "liquidated" by their orders . . . .

That Jacqueline Cochran had been the first woman to land in Japan, ahead of the occupation forces, was duly reported in the press at the close of World War II—as was her mission for General "Hap" Arnold "to study the role Japanese women played in aviation during the war." No one questioned it. The war was over! No one gave a damn. A good excuse was not even needed for a famous woman flyer to be aboard the first B-29 to land in a country that had been waging a fanatic, religious war against us. No one even thought to question why, in that passionate spasm of victory, the chief of the Army Air Force would dispatch a woman to do research on the activities of Japanese women in aviation.

In her own book, *The Stars at Noon,* published in 1954, Jacqueline Cochran tells how, having completed her task as a member of the General Staff in the Pentagon as head of the WASPs (Women's Airforce Service Pilots), she became a correspondent for *Liberty* magazine in order "to get to the Orient and see what was going on there" as the war was about to end.

"At the last minute I was given a Priority No. 1, an unusual rating for a correspondent," she wrote, "but General Arnold had signed orders making me a Special Consultant for the duration of my trip and had given me some specific assignments to perform while in the Pacific."

En route, in Guam she socialized with such notables as General Jimmy Doolittle, General Carl "Tooey" Spaatz, General Curtis LeMay, General Kenneth McNaughton, General Nathan F. Twining, and General Thomas Power, all of whom have since become Chiefs of Staff of the Air Force. She was also on hand to welcome on arrival at Guam the Archbishop Francis Spellman, Vicar General of the Armed Forces, who later became America's most famous cardinal and at the time of his death in 1967, the world's greatest collector of philatelic Amelia Earhart memorabilia.

She was kissed by General Jonathan M. Wainwright, the hero of Bataan, and again welcomed the arriving Archbishop Spellman to Manila.

"All available planes at Guam were ordered to proceed to Japan immediately to evacuate the released American prisoners in bad health," she wrote. "In one of these planes, I became the first American woman to land in Japan after the war."

Coincidentally, if it was a coincidence, Jacqueline Cochran's arrival in the Philippines and in Japan was timed perfectly with the first liberation and screening of American prisoners of war and interned American civilians. Not only was she the first and only American woman to arrive and witness these repatriations, she also became the first, and possibly the only, American pilot to have a close look inside the Imperial Palace grounds at Tokyo.

"General Arnold had directed me to make an official investigation of what the Japanese women had done in the Imperial Air Force," she wrote. "This took me to the Dai-Ichi building which served as the General Headquarters."

As to what Muriel Morrissey referred to as Jacqueline Cochran's "access to many government files which were later taken to Washington for microfilming," her own version is: "My search of the records found no evidence that the Japanese women had participated in any active war effort beyond factory or home production. It did, however, find numerous clippings and photographs about Amelia Earhart and Jimmy Doolittle and other American pilots, including myself. There were several files on Amelia Earhart."

The files she reported finding on Amelia Earhart, whether microfilmed or not, have never since been located by Joe Gervais, Paul Briand, Jr., nor Fred Goerner, even though all of these investigators have sought information about these mysterious files from both the Japanese and United States governments. Where are the Amelia Earhart files found by Jacqueline Cochran at the Dai-Ichi General Headquarters and why does it appear that they have ceased to exist from the date she reported finding them?

For the first time it seemed important that chronologically the earliest appearance in history of the name "Tokyo Rose" was not in propaganda broadcasts by Japan to our troops in the Pacific. The first time Tokyo Rose appears in history is in Saipan in the summer of 1937 when the "American Spy Lady" became known to all the natives of Saipan as Tokyo Rosa.

But Tokyo Rose was tried for treason in San Francisco

during the summer of 1949 and convicted and sent to the Federal penitentiary for women at Alderson, West Virginia for ten years. Or was she? I took it on myself to locate and read the more than seven thousand pages of official transcript of what the press called "The Trial of Tokyo Rose."

After the laborious business of selecting a jury was completed, "The Trial of Tokyo Rose" began with actual testimony on July 12, 1949, in the Federal Northern District Court in San Francisco. The U.S. government had brought nineteen witnesses from Japan to appear at the trial at a cost of more than $23,000.

From the outset and throughout more than two months of testimony and the presentation of evidence which followed until the jury adjourned to deliberate on September 29, it appeared that there may have been as many as fifteen different women who could have been "Tokyo Rose" or that there was no "Tokyo Rose" at all.

The woman on trial was Mrs. Iva Ikuko Toguri D'Aquina, an American citizen born July 4, 1916, of low-income Japanese immigrant parents in Watts, California. While attending the University of California at Los Angeles she became interested in radio script writing, although after obtaining a B.A. degree from UCLA in 1940 she went to Japan in July, 1941, to live with a sick aunt and attend a Japanese medical school. She traveled with a visitor permit issued by the Japanese consul in Los Angeles, but without an American passport. She was in Tokyo when the Japanese attacked Pearl Harbor on December 7, 1941, failed to obtain passage on the few ships available to stranded American and British citizens, and took a job with the Japanese government-operated Domei news agency as a monitor of Allied radio broadcasts. Iva Toguri, unmarried at that time, spoke no Japanese.

In August, 1942, the Broadcasting Corporation of Japan, a privately owned company operated by the Japanese government under direct control of Emperor Hirohito's wartime cabinet, summoned Iva Toguri to audition for a job as

212 / AMELIA EARHART LIVES

English-speaking female disk jockey for short-wave propaganda broadcasts directed at British and American troops. She was employed as an announcer for *The Zero Hour,* a program actually named after the famed Japanese Zero fighter plane. But she was not the only woman broadcasting in English from Japanese radio stations during World War II.

The defense attorney, Wayne M. Collins of San Francisco, lost no time in establishing that there were a number of sultry voices pitching propaganda at women-starved Allied troops throughout the Pacific.

Names of other Japanese programs which broadcast in English using female voices to entice Allied troops were *Humanity Calls, The Postman Calls, Light from Asia, The German Hour, Prisoners Hour, Hinomura Hour,* and *The Women's Hour.* Also engaged in preparing and broadcasting the programs were no less than forty Allied prisoners of war quartered in such Tokyo housing as the Dai-Ichi Hotel, the Sanno Hotel, and Bunka Prison Camp.

Iva Toguri, who might have avoided trial by claiming Portuguese citizenship through her marriage to Portuguese national Felipe D'Aquina of the Domei news agency in April, 1945, before the war ended, did not do so. Having chosen not to renounce her American citizenship, she was indicted on eight counts of overt actions against the United States, constituting treason during wartime, by a Federal Grand Jury in San Francisco. The charges carried the possibility of a death penalty.

Six large disk transcriptions made from monitoring Japanese short-wave broadcasts by the Office of War Information in Portland, Oregon, were used by the prosecution to prove that Iva Toguri, who used the theme song "Strike Up the Band," made such statements as this, after the United States Navy had virtually wiped out all that was left of the Imperial Japanese Fleet in the Battle of Leyte Gulf in the fall of 1944:

"Now you boys have really lost all your ships," Iva Toguri's voice chided. "You really are orphans now. How do you think you will ever get home now?"

She was charged with having "told troops that their sweethearts at home in the U. S. were unfaithful to them, that they lacked fidelity, that their wives and sweethearts were running around with 4-F's and with shipyard workers, all of whom had plenty of money in their pockets to give the wives of the soldiers a good time; and she told the boys over the air to lay down their arms, stop fighting, that it was futile to go on, that the Japanese would never give up, that the Japanese had a will to win, and that there was no reason in the world why the American soldiers should stay out there and wage a futile battle, risk their lives, and probably get killed."

She was accused of calling American troops she was talking to "boneheads of the Pacific" or "suckers."

Nine out of ten Pacific veterans asked if they ever heard the broadcasts of Tokyo Rose will answer yes. Asked specifically if they heard her identify herself as Tokyo Rose, they will still answer yes. Such is the tricky way of mass memory.

The fact is that no female voice on Japanese radio at any time before, during, or after the war ever identified itself as "Tokyo Rose." No radio voice ever said anything like: "This is Tokyo Rose."

Iva Toguri always identified herself as "your Orphan Anne" or "Orphan Annie"—never as Tokyo Rose during any of her broadcasts. Nor did the United States government ever actually accuse the hapless UCLA coed from Watts of being Tokyo Rose, although the press labeled her so; and her defense endlessly and correctly maintained that she was not Tokyo Rose.

A copy of *Time* magazine arrived at Radio Tokyo in the summer of 1944 by way of Sweden. It described how American G.I.'s in the Pacific were listening to a female voice known as "Tokyo Rose" over Japanese radio. This article caused considerable discussion among the English-speaking staff of female announcers at Radio Tokyo, and between them they decided that the article might be referring to Iva Toguri on *The Zero Hour.*

There was one period of at least six weeks in 1945 when Iva Toguri's voice was not heard at all. In the latter part of April, 1945, in a Roman Catholic ceremony at the Sofia University Chapel in Tokyo, Iva Toguri became the wife of Felipe D'Aquina, a Eurasian citizen of Portugal who was employed by the Domei news agency as a linotype operator. During a leave of absence from *The Zero Hour* for a month and a half prior to the marriage rites, she had studied Catholicism to be admitted to the Catholic Church.

At the same time Jacqueline Cochran rushed ahead of the U.S. occupation forces into Tokyo to "study the role Japanese women played in aviation during the war," a Hearst team of writers, Clark Lee of International News Service and Harry Brundidge of *Cosmopolitan* magazine, hurried ahead of our troops to the Domei news agency to hire Leslie Nakajima, whom Lee had known there before the war, to locate "Tokyo Rose" for an exclusive *Cosmopolitan* interview. Nakajima received $200 and Iva Ikuko Toguri D'Aquina identified herself as the mythical Tokyo Rose in exchange for an offer of $2000 for an exclusive interview.

The U.S. Army occupation forces arrested Iva Toguri in October, 1945, and held her for questioning in Sugamo Prison. She was eventually released, but while there she consented to grant J. Richard Eisenhart, a guard, the "autograph of Tokyo Rose." She signed the slip of paper:

Iva I. Toguri
"Tokyo Rose"

The Tokyo Rose interview by Harry Brundidge never appeared in *Cosmopolitan,* but in August, 1948, the Hearst writer, accompanied by FBI agents, flew to Japan and put the finger on Iva Toguri.

After four days of deliberation the jury in San Francisco found her not guilty on seven of the eight counts of treason. The verdict of guilty on one charge of having committed an overt act detrimental to the United States during wartime resulted on October 6, 1949, in a sentence of ten years' imprisonment. She was released from the women's Federal penitentiary at Alderson, West Virginia, in 1955 with four years off for good behavior.

Lack of funds prevented an appeal to the higher courts, but today Iva Toguri lives in an expensive Chicago apartment house with her father and brother, who operate a grocery store, a book store, and an import mercantile business.

But the United States was not the only country against which an overt act had been committed by one of the fifteen-or-more Tokyo Roses on *The Zero Hour*. Treason was committed against Japan itself over Radio Tokyo on June 15, 1944 —enough treason to cause the dreaded Kampeitei secret thought police to launch a full-scale investigation of the Emperor's own English-speaking voices of Japan.

"Colonel, do you recall that Saipan fell to the American troops on June 15, 1944?" Defense Attorney Collins asked the former commander of Radio Tokyo during the trial of Iva Toguri.

"It was probably about that time," replied Colonel Shigetsugu Tsuneishi.

"Now," continued Collins, "it was not the practice of the Japanese government to make prompt announcements of losses of territory that had been under Japanese control during the war, isn't that true?"

"*That* was generally reported fairly promptly," said Tsuneishi.

"It was? But when you say that the broadcasts would be made rather promptly, you mean they would be made after the Japanese Army high command permitted such news to be broadcast, isn't that true?"

"That is true," admitted Tsuneishi.

"And yet, when the news of the fall of Saipan came through *that* was announced by a flash break-in on Radio Tokyo, wasn't it?"

"I don't remember." Tsuneishi squirmed.

"You don't recall," persisted Collins, "that not only was the news broadcast by flash report that Saipan had fallen, but that there immediately followed over *The Zero Hour* the martial music entitled 'The Stars and Stripes Forever'?"

The idea that "The Stars and Stripes Forever" had been played over Radio Tokyo more than a year before the war ended was so incredible that the court interpreter couldn't believe his ears. "Will you read that, please?" the interpreter asked the court reporter. Eventually the question was put in Japanese to the former director of Radio Tokyo.

"I don't remember that incident clearly," he claimed, "but I have a sort of vague idea that there was something of that nature."

"Yes, you do have a recollection, Colonel, haven't you, that a full-fledged investigation was immediately conducted of the persons on *The Zero Hour* as a result of playing 'The Stars and Stripes Forever' on that occasion?"

"I believe there was something of that type, but investigation was not a result of my direct order or anything like that," Tsuneishi answered. "It was just a general warning that was given."

"It was a fact, wasn't it," asked Collins, "that a Lieutenant Reyes was taken immediately thereafter from Radio Station Tokyo to the headquarters of the Kampeitei, together with George Ozasa?"

"I don't remember that," repeated Tsuneishi.

After further questioning, Colonel Tsuneishi admitted that the Radio Tokyo news flash of the Americans capturing

Saipan, followed by the playing of "The Stars and Stripes Forever," had been investigated by the Japanese secret police.

"I remember vaguely that there was such an incident or trouble," he concurred, passing off the remarkable occurrence, "but I do not recall who was investigated."

No such exultation burst through the airways from Radio Tokyo when Iwo Jima fell to the Americans, or Tarawa, or Okinawa, or any of the other bloody island victories by American troops which led to the downfall of Japan. "The Stars and Stripes Forever," at first mistaken by the Kampeitei for "The Star-Spangled Banner," was only played one time over *The Zero Hour,* to celebrate the American capture of Saipan.

Was the female voice that caused the Japanese secret police to raid Radio Tokyo on June 15, 1944, the same voice George Putnam trekked through enemy territory to the coast of China to listen to in the first part of 1945?

The name Tokyo Rose first appeared in the United States press in the April 10, 1944, edition of *Time* magazine, which found its way that year via Sweden to those unfortunate American-born women who, either willfully or under duress, broadcast Japanese propaganda beamed at our troops in the Pacific. The article appeared under the classification:

RADIO

By Any Other Name

Tokyo Rose is the darling of U.S. sailors, G.I.'s and Marines all over the Pacific. She is a Jap propagandist, but her broadcasts are popular among American listeners: she gives them humor, nostalgia, news, entertainment and good U.S. dance music. In a very feminine and friendly voice she murmurs:

"Good evening again to the all-forgetting and forgotten men, the American fighting men of the South Pacific. *The Zero Hour* to the rescue once again, taking up a few vacant moments you may have to kill. And since this is Monday and therefore Old Timers' night,

these few moments will be filled with music for you Old
Timers who perhaps like another kind of music. So
here's our beginning number tonight. It is the Waltz
King, Wayne King . . . ."

No one knows for sure who Tokyo Rose really is.
OWIsters incline to think she is a Japanese, born on the
island of Maui, Hawaii, and educated there. Her voice
is cultured, with a touch of Boston. She would be a very
good propagandist if G.I. Joe had more tendency to
believe her.

Uncomfortably Close. Tokyo Rose's voice is wafted
over the Aleutians and the South Pacific on a stronger,
clearer signal than any provided by U.S. Radio. She can
usually be heard around 8 P M daily, Australian time,
short or medium wave, on a 65-minute show designed
for U.S. armed forces in the South Pacific. Her special-
ties, assisted by a male announcer who sounds not unlike Elmer Davis, are *News from the American Home
Front* and the jazzical *Zero Hour. News* purports to be
a rehash of U.S. domestic broadcasts. It is angled, but
has some basis in fact.

Tokyo Rose is sometimes uncomforably close to the
truth. Last Aug. 5 she announced that U.S. forces would
land on Kiska on Aug. 17. The landing was Aug. 15.
Her broadcasts almost never exaggerated U.S. losses.
She has built a reputation on accurate broadcasts like
the following: "Well, you boys in Moresby, how did you
like that ack-ack last night over Rabaul? Your commu-
niqué didn't say anything about losing those two For-
tresses, did it? But you fellows know, don't you? You
know what did not come back . . . ."

Rose's U.S. idiom is consistently accurate: "Back in
your old home town, remember the old juke box and
what you got out of it? Remember the cheese sandwiches
and the cokes with the gang? It's pretty hard to remember, but your juke box once had this piece: *Crosstown*
(music). . . . And whenever that came out of the juke box,

somebody started an impromptu rumba and boy, did the manager kick. But that was only when your mood was good, whether it was the moon, the coke, or the girl. . . ."

There are other roses in Tojo's garden, but none so fair as Tokyo. Like her, they remain unidentified. Sometimes they are mistaken for her . . . .

The *Time* article specifically spelled out the exact time of broadcast and precise words that either had been used or were to be used by a voice "cultured, with a touch of Boston." The story could be straight reporting, or it could be a plant giving cryptic instructions as to when and how to present a particular voice on Radio Tokyo for positive identification.

To suggest that Amelia Earhart's voice was used for regular propaganda broadcasts is as absurd as to suggest that a voice "had been fiendishly well coached" to sound like Amelia Earhart's voice, as reported by her husband, George Putnam.

But to suggest that Amelia Earhart was placed on the air by the Japanese for positive identification of her voice by the only person who could with certainty recognize it is pure logic. And to recount that George Putnam was commissioned a major in Army Intelligence by the United States and sent to a remote and dangerous part of the China coast to listen to *The Zero Hour* and make that identification is pure history.

It is our opinion that in 1937 an American spy was intercepted and captured in the Pacific by the Japanese, who tried to use her to blackmail the United States into signing a consular treaty favorable to Japan. Her name was Amelia Earhart. The Japanese gave her the code name of Tokyo Rose. President Franklin Delano Roosevelt refused to be blackmailed, refused to admit to American espionage by demanding her return, and left her to the fate traditionally reserved for spies who are caught—total abandonment by her country. The Japanese, who could not admit they had caught Amelia Earhart spying without owning up to flagrant violation of international law in secretly building the huge naval base she was spying on at Truk, allowed her to survive in anonymity for one reason, and one reason alone. She in turn possessed a secret that was vital to Japan.

And allowing that history-changing secret to fall into the hands of a belligerent nation even then planning the attack on Pearl Harbor was so embarrassing to an American President and his political party that it enabled the Japanese to use Amelia Earhart in obtaining one of the greatest concessions for silence in history.

In the years that passed did it become necessary for the powerful forces who knew the secret to find a way to persuade any candidate of an opposing political party to willingly join in the conspiracy of silence? When he became President did he, too, keep the faith?

The language and legend of flowers describes the rose as the emblem of "silence and secrecy."

Would it be against the national interest to break the silence . . . to reveal the secret? We of Operation Earhart searched our souls for the answer and decided that our nation would not be harmed by the truth. We believe that history has a right to be recorded . . . mankind a right to know.

CHAPTER TWENTY

THE MOTIVE

If Amelia Earhart was alive, there had to be a powerful motive for those who knew it to keep it secret for these more than thirty years.

The immediate motives were obvious. The Emperor of Japan could not reveal it in 1937 without disclosing what she had photographed—illegally constructed naval facilities on Truk intended for use in war against the United States. Nor was the President of the United States in a position to admit he had used the world's most beloved woman for an aggressive act of espionage and to risk war for her release.

On July 7, 1937, five days after Amelia Earhart's last flight, all the aircraft carriers in the Imperial Navy of Japan, with the single exception of the *Akagi,* participated in the invasion of China. The Japanese task force immediately became pinned down along the coast because fighter planes sold to the Chinese by France and England proved to be superior to those which had been made in Japan. Without a reasonably rapid procurement of a fighter plane which could outclass those of China, Nipon's ambitious adventure against mainland China would almost certainly fail.

Emperor Hirohito, who slightly more than one year earlier on June 1, 1936, had been the first Japanese ruler to have himself proclaimed a living god, now had two problems on his hands: how to get himself a fighter plane which would give the Japanese invaders air superiority over China . . . and what to do with a famous lady prisoner who was an embarrassment to both her captors and the nation responsible for her illicit acts.

Ministers of the Emperor exerted diplomatic pressure on the U.S. State Department for a consular treaty which would enable Japan to purchase what war materials it needed. This treaty was rejected by the American government in the fall of 1937.

However, there was a superior fighter plane, the prototype of which had already been built and was sitting protected by civilian security guards in a California hangar. The multimillionaire who had designed and built the "racer" was a personal friend of Amelia Earhart. In fact, she and Paul Mantz had actually been aloft in her airplane as observers of the wealthy American three years earlier when he had piloted the plane he built to a new world speed record over a measured course.

General Hap Arnold, chief of the U.S. Army Air Corps, personally flew to California to inspect the record-breaking plane but was unable to do so when civilian security guards hired by its designer mistakenly refused to admit the general into the hangar. Subsequently, the plane was offered to the Air Corps as a fighter and was rejected.

Mitsubishi Engineer Jiro Horikoshi, who was in the United States at that time working in American aircraft engine factories on an industrial exchange program, subsequently returned to Japan where he became famous as the designer of World War II's Zero fighter—the Zero which later proved superior to anything being flown by the United States at the time Japan attacked Pearl Harbor. Books published as recently as 1967 by Lyle Stuart and 1966 by Random House say respectively that the Japanese managed to "copy the plans" of Amelia Earhart's millionaire friend "faithfully, ending up with the Zero, that scourge of American aviation in the early days of the war," and that "the men who built the Zero had borrowed heavily from" the plane which even today, more than thirty-five years after it was built, still sits under security guard in California. A 1968 *Newsweek* article describes Amelia Earhart's friend as "a designer and pilot of record-breaking airplanes, one of which was copied by the Japanese in building their formidable fighter, the Zero."

Since the President of the United States had publicly "accepted" the death of Amelia Earhart and also had denied Japan a consular treaty to trade for what it needed, there remain two speculations: Did Emperor Hirohito try to induce Amelia Earhart's friend, whose plane had been irrevocably turned down as inadequate for the defense of his own country, to make such plans available to Japan—and failing in such endeavor then arrange for the theft of such plans for a plane desperately needed in his China war?

In the foreword to *Zero!* by Masatake Okumiya and Jiro Horikoshi, America's leading aviation writer, Martin Caidin, assesses the importance of the Zero to the Japanese in making war against the United States.

The Japanese lacked the scientific "know how" necessary to meet us on qualitative terms. . . . This was by no means the case early in the war when the Zero fighter airplane effectively swept aside all opposition. In the Zero the Japanese enjoyed the ideal advantage of both qualitative and quantitative superiority. The Japanese fighter was faster than any opposing plane. It outmaneuvered anything in the air. It outclimbed and could fight at greater heights than any plane in all Asia and the Pacific. It had twice the combat range of our standard fighter, the P-40, and it featured the heavy punch of cannon. Zero pilots had cut their combat teeth in China and so enjoyed a great advantage over our own men.

In the text itself, Okumiya wrote:

The unforgivable error of "underestimating the enemy" made by the Americans and the British was perhaps best illustrated in the reliance placed upon the antiquated Brewster F2A Buffalo fighter plane, which American aviation experts boasted was "the most powerful fighter plane in the Orient" and a "fighter plane far superior to anything in the Japanese Air Force." . . . Against the Zero fighters, the Buffalo pilots literally flew suicide missions.

In the first twenty-four hours of war with the United States, waves of the deadly Zeros won absolute air mastery over the successful Japanese attacks on the Hawaiian Islands, Malaya, the Philippines, French Indochina, Palau, Wake Island, and Guam. The commander of the Zeros recalled:

> Without exception, every combat report recorded only smashing victories. Our successes exceeded by far even the most optimistic preattack estimates.
>
> What I would like history most to record, however, is that this abrupt reversal of the Asiatic-Pacific balance of power was accomplished with the total of only approximately one thousand planes of the Japanese Naval Air Force and that this same force suffered only the barest minimum of losses.

By March of 1942, with Zero fighters easily ridding the skies of all Allied planes, Japanese forces took control of Tainan, Bali, Jolo Island, Tarakan, Balikpapan, Bandjerdari in the Celebes, Makasar, Timor Island, and Amboina. By the close of this Java operation, naval land-based South Pacific Japanese airpower had destroyed 565 Allied planes. Eighty-three per cent of these, or 471 planes, were destroyed by Japanese pilots flying the fighter copied from the "racer." Throughout the entire Pacific theater in these first months of the Pacific war, land- and carrier-based Zeros destroyed

65 per cent of all Allied planes that were put out of action. From Pearl Harbor to Singapore, a war front 6000 miles long, the Zero patterned after the plane which had been turned down by U.S. Army brass absolutely massacred our pilots, who were sent to slaughter in the kind of fighter planes preferred by our brass to the "racer" design.

What did this mean at Pearl Harbor?

Okumiya wrote:

> The nature of the Hawaiian Operation prevented the Zero fighters from demonstrating fully their exceptional combat performance. Our planes so quickly eliminated all enemy aerial opposition that the Zeros confined their sweeps mainly to strafing attacks.

What did it mean in the Philippines and the Dutch East Indies?

> In the Philippine Islands and the Dutch East Indies campaigns, however, our success rested directly on the ability of the Zero fighters to establish control of the air. *Neither campaign could possibly have achieved its success with a fighter plane of lesser performance than the new Zero which so completely surprised the enemy.*

The scandal of World War II has long enough been considered to be that American commanders lined up our Pacific Fleet in Pearl Harbor and then took the Sunday of December 7, 1941, off for a day of rest only to be caught by a sneak attack. The mystery of World War II is what happened between July 2, 1937, and that December morning four and a half years later which made that infamous attack possible and successful... how did the Emperor of Japan manage to obtain plans for a superior fighter plane remarkable in its similarity to one which Amelia Earhart had personally watched being piloted on its maiden flight by her friend who had designed and built it?

The attack on Pearl Harbor and Japan's war on the United States would have appeared even to Emperor Hirohito and his military leaders too hopeless to have begun without the fighter plane design which became the Zero.

In 1935 the American racer, with Amelia Earhart and Paul Mantz flying observation above it, set a new world record for a measured course of 352.46 miles per hour. Top speed of the Zero, as published in *Airviews*, "The 50 Years of Japanese Aviation" by Kohri and Naito, was 351.10 miles per hour. The engines were 1100 and 1130 horsepower respectively. Kohri and Naito describe how American Intelligence first got its hands on a captured Zero:

> During the Aleutian Islands campaign a Zero fighter crash-landed on one of the Aleutian Islands. It had been launched from a two-carrier task force against the Americans. It was captured in U.S. hands rather intact. The slight damage of the downed fighter was repaired and the plane contributed greatly to the U.S. pilots and designers in finding out the weak points in the formidable Japanese fighter.

Why did they wait so long? Why wasn't a comparable plane in a hangar in California examined for its capabilities and weaknesses? Why wasn't its designer called upon for his expert opinion?

Ten thousand Zero versions of this aircraft were built before the war ended in 1945. Of more than three thousand Kamikaze planes, many of which dove into the sides of more than fifty ships, including six aircraft carriers, more than one thousand five hundred were Zeros. Throughout the entire war it was essentially the same plane which was first tested by Japan in combat against China in September, 1939, and was comparable to the Army-rejected fighter that set speed records in America in 1935 and 1936. The Japanese, unable to make improvements on a design they had not truly developed, saw the Zero surpassed at last by an American Army and Navy that had to learn how the hard way.

Had Amelia Earhart been used in any way to obtain the plans for a weapon without which Japan could never have attacked the United States? Is the thought so incredible? To prove her very existence, her voice was put on the air for positive identification by the one man who "alone in all that vast area could without question identify Amelia's voice, even though weakened and tense from psychological mistreatment," as her sister wrote in *Courage Is the Price*.

If Amelia Earhart was alive, had she been "brainwashed" to reveal the existence of an American-designed fighter plane that had been rejected by our government, which might be copied and built by the Japanese to fill their need for airpower against China and ultimately to make it possible for them to launch the attack on Pearl Harbor which got the United States into the whole bloody war?

It was a thought to pale the oncoming victory. A scandal, if true, to be avoided at all cost.

Why was the name Tokyo Rose revived years after it had first been used in 1937 by the Chamorro natives of Saipan for Amelia Earhart during her first days of captivity?

There could be no secret without a code, and an article in *Time* had suggested the code name Tokyo Rose. Once more negotiations were under way by the Emperor of Japan. Something of considerable value to the Emperor of a crushed and burning country was to be obtained in exchange for the preservation of a secret.

With priority orders from General Hap Arnold, Jacqueline Cochran headed for the Far East to be there when the fighting stopped. The late Francis Cardinal Spellman, another friend and admirer of Amelia Earhart, followed after her, catching up with her in Guam and again in the Philippines. Onward she traveled as all the Allied nations of the world, including Russia who had just belatedly invaded Manchuria, cried out for the "unconditional surrender" of Japan.

"I intend to hang the Emperor and ride his white horse through Tokyo," Admiral William "Bull" Halsey had boasted.

With his country in smoking ruins about him, his navy at the bottom of the oceans, his air forces scattered wreckage, his armies beaten to their bloodied knees, and huge mushroom clouds slowly dissipating their fearful atomic radiation over Nagasaki and Hiroshima, Emperor Hirohito waited confidently for a prearranged reply to a message which was being relayed by Sweden and Switzerland to the United States, Great Britain, China, and the Soviet Union. His reply to Allied demands for "unconditional surrender" included an exceptional condition considering the extent of his defeat:

> The Japanese Government are ready to accept the terms enumerated in the joint declaration which was issued at Potsdam on July 26, 1945, by the heads of the Governments of the United States, Great Britain and China and later subscribed to by the Soviet Government, with the understanding that the said declaration does not comprise any demand which prejudices the prerogatives of His Majesty as a sovereign ruler [referring to himself as both government and god]. The Japanese Government hope sincerely that this understanding is warranted and desire keenly that an explicit indication to that effect will be speedily forthcoming.

All he was asking in defeat was that he not only be spared from trial and probable hanging as a war criminal, but that he be allowed to remain on after surrender as the Emperor of Japan! In exchange for what? An American heroine for an Emperor?

Hirohito's surrender condition was less than popular with the Japanese Prime Minister, the Foreign Minister, the War Minister, and the Navy Minister, all of whom faced the certain choice of ceremonial self-disembowelment or being tried and probably hanged as war criminals by the Allied Powers.

And in Washington, early on the morning of August 1, 1945, Secretary of War Henry Lewis Stimson, whose Army Air Corps had turned down the plane which later evolved as the Zero, was the only one of the four top advisors summoned by President Harry Truman who urged that Japan be notified at once that the Emperor would be allowed to remain in power. Secretary of State James F. Byrnes, who had been chairman of the interim committee on the atomic bomb, on the other hand, pointed out that both the deposed Prime Minister Churchill and the late President Roosevelt had again and again publicly and privately specified that the surrender of Japan would have to be unconditional . . . that to allow the Emperor to continue as the ruler of Japan instead of facing war crimes charges would certainly not be unconditional, as had been demanded by all the Allied nations. He said the United States could not concur with the Emperor's request for his own survival without consulting the British and Chinese governments, which had joined us in the Potsdam Declaration demanding that Japan's surrender be as unconditional as had been Nazi Germany's. Secretary of the Navy James Forrestal, who later committed suicide, and Fleet Admiral William D. Leahy were also present, but neither was particularly anxious to agree to the condition that Emperor Hirohito be permitted to continue to rule Japan.

Under Secretary of State Joseph C. Grew, who had been Ambassador to Japan from 1931 to 1941 and was privy there to any secret prewar negotiations regarding Amelia Earhart, had proposed nearly four months prior to this meeting, in early May, 1945, that the Emperor of Japan be assured that he would be allowed to remain in power after surrender. As acting Secretary of State, Grew urged throughout June and July that the condition of the Emperor's pardon actually be presented in the form of an offer to Japan.

Both the Secretary of War and Assistant Secretary of War John J. McCloy urged on July 3, 1945, that President Truman persuade China and Great Britain at Potsdam to join the

United States in offering, without even being formally asked, to spare the Emperor of Japan. But the President waited until after Amelia Earhart's newly commissioned spouse, Major George Putnam, had time to get into China to listen to a radio voice, code-named Tokyo Rose, for purposes of positive identification. Coincidence?

The liberal Labor Government in London chose to follow whatever decision the United States reached about Emperor Hirohito, although the general British feeling was somewhat stronger, as reported in an August 10 dispatch to *The New York Times:*

> At the same time, there is a strong opinion among the British military leaders who have been most closely concerned with the prosecution of the Japanese war that the Emperor should be treated exactly the same as the Nazi hierarchy and condemned as a war criminal.

A London *Times* editorial on August 11, 1945, took a dim view of Japan's insistence that the Emperor be protected, concluding that "even if the war should have to be continued for a few more days, the Allies cannot afford to accept, without utmost scrutiny, a stipulation which might once again create a threat to the peace of the world."

The Soviet People's Commissar for Foreign Affairs Vyacheslav Molotov on the night of August 10, 1945, in Moscow told U.S. Ambassador W. Averill Harriman and British Ambassador Archibald Clark Kerr that the Japanese offer of surrender was "neither unconditional nor concrete" and that the Red Army would give the Soviet answer by continuing to advance into Manchuria.

New York Times news analyst Hanson W. Baldwin wrote:

> We have been told by those in this country who advocate Hirohito's retention that, first, he could command surrender everywhere and make the task of stabilizing

and governing Japan far easier; and second, that he is a figurehead anyway and did not lead Japan into this war. Both things cannot be true. . . . We should accept no conditions to unconditional surrender, and probably many Americans would like to see Admiral William F. Halsey, Jr., ride Hirohito's white horse.

On August 11, 1945, in Chungking, China, the official organ of the Kuomintang, *The Central Daily News*, said that "Japan offered the kind of conditional surrender which we cannot accept. We are confident that America, Britain and the U.S.S.R. are unable to accept it either."

The Dutch, the Australians, the British, the Chinese, the Russians, and even General Douglas MacArthur, who, as Supreme Allied Commander, was soon to take over as the new "shogun" of Japan, indicated at the time of the surrender that Emperor Hirohito should be prosecuted and punished as the number-one war criminal of Japan for the brutal atrocities committed in his name. Later MacArthur found it more provident in his own royal fashion to deal shogun-to-shogun with the Son of Heaven during the occupation.

President Truman knew the Emperor's terms, and he accepted them. In exchange for what?

During the ecstatic spasm of celebration which followed victory, nobody questioned anything. The war was over at last, and that exquisite fact was enough. No reporter even thought to question why Jacqueline Cochran was among the first to land in Japan aboard a B-29 sent for the liberation of important military prisoners of war and civilian hostages being held by the Japanese.

But her previous meetings on Guam and Manila with Cardinal Spellman suggest that the problem of how to get anyone as easily recognizable and as big news as Amelia Earhart past the curious eyes of aircraft crews and reporters might have been solved by evacuating her in the concealing garments of a Catholic nun.

If Amelia Earhart's anonymous release from protective custody in Japan was a factor which contributed to the thoroughly defeated Emperor's survival, then how has it all remained a secret for more than three decades? Surely subsequent Presidents in the White House, with less to lose politically by disclosure than the administration in power at the close of World War II, would have no personal or national stake in preserving the secret.

This sort of speculation led Operation Earhart, in seeking logical reasons for continued secrecy throughout both Republican and Democratic administrations, to wonder, for instance, why President Eisenhower would be discreet about something that could be embarrassing to the opposition party. My wife, Betty Jane, came up with an interesting coincidence one morning while reading General Eisenhower's memoirs, *Mandate for Change.*

"I ran into the name of Jacqueline Cochran in Eisenhower's book," B.J. remarked.

"What did Jackie have to do with Eisenhower?" I asked.

"She persuaded him to run for President," my wife answered calmly.

Early in 1952, she went on at my urgent request, Eisenhower, unconvinced that the American people wanted him to be President, was living in Paris. In *Mandate for Change* he wrote about many visitors there who later became publicly active in "Citizens for Eisenhower" groups:

> Many were good friends; I could question neither their dedication nor their integrity . . . . On February 10 Miss Jacqueline Cochran arrived on a special mission. Two days earlier there had been a mass meeting at midnight in New York's Madison Square Garden, arranged by supporters who were hoping by this means to add weight to their argument that I should become a candidate. The entire proceedings were put on film. As soon as the film was processed, Miss Cochran flew the Atlantic and brought it immediately to Paris. Her second task

was to get me to sit still long enough to view it. By the time she reached our house, she had gone thirty-five hours without sleep.

Indeed, Jacqueline Cochran gets around, often on "special missions" by plane. Going thirty-five hours without sleep to carry a can of film across the Atlantic in 1952 was an effective and dramatic way to get Eisenhower to "sit still long enough."

As we conferred, Miss Cochran told me about the opposition of the so-called "pros" in politics, who, although part of the Eisenhower group, believed that no meeting of this kind, held after the completion of a Garden fight the same evening, could possibly draw a crowd at midnight. They felt that a poor turnout would slow up the "Eisenhower movement" which they thought was then gaining momentum. Miss Cochran asked that my wife be with me when we viewed the film. It was shown in our living room at Villa St. Pierre in Marnes-la-Coquette.

Fifteen thousand people had assembled in Madison Square Garden. It was a moving experience to witness the obvious unanimity of such a huge crowd—to realize that everyone present was enthusiastically supporting me for the highest office of the land. As the film went on, Mamie and I were profoundly affected. The incident impressed me more than had all the arguments presented by the individuals who had been plaguing me with political questions for many months. When our guests departed, I think we both suspected, although we did not say so, that out lives were to be once more uprooted.

I immediately got a letter off to Gervais in Las Vegas.
"Find out what political party Jacqueline Cochran and Floyd Odlum belonged to before 1952," I instructed. "Were they Republicans or Democrats?"

The reply came by return mail. "Until 1952 Jacqueline Cochran and Floyd Odlum were lifelong Democrats. In 1952 they switched their voter registration to Republican and became the prime backers of Eisenhower for President."

Tex McCrary, who as an Army Air Force information officer had been in Tokyo with Jacqueline Cochran in 1945, was co-chairman of the rally at Madison Square Garden along with Miss Cochran. His wife, Jinx Falkenberg, and millionaire Jock Whitney joined them in renting the arena. Jinx and Jackie went to Texas and other states and brought three special trainloads of supporters to the rally, including brass bands and Texas Rangers on horseback. What was filmed that night and flown by Amelia Earhart's best friend to Paris was as spontaneous as several millionaires could make it.

Miss Cochran described the Paris meeting in *The Stars at Noon:*

When I was taken into General Eisenhower's office, I told him that I believed I was carrying a message of utmost importance to our country from the common people of America and that with but a half-hour at my disposal I was going to start talking and would ask for no interruption. My words seemed effective. They kept rolling off my tongue, out of my heart. At the end of the half-hour, "Ike" asked me to continue while he arranged to have the film set up for showing at least in part. "Ike" watched that film for about ten minutes and I watched him. He had it stopped and asked me if I would take it out to his home and he and Mamie and associates would look at it in full at the close of the day's work. And there at his home I watched emotions grip General Eisenhower as he realized fully for the first time as he watched the film that he was receiving a call to duty from the people, and not just an invitation from public leaders and politicians. After we stopped the film, I sat talking to "Ike." His whole outlook had changed. I saw tears. It was apparent that he had taken a decision. He talked about his childhood and about the honors and duties he had had. He asked me to get in touch with certain people immediately on my return to New York, telling them what had happened during my visit and asking them to come over to see him immediately.

What Jacqueline Cochran described as "our little group" turned to raising the funds to win the 1952 New Hampshire primary election for Eisenhower. Her efforts on "Ike's" behalf steamrollered along from then on until Sherman Adams obtained a seat for her on the podium while Eisenhower accepted the Republican nomination for President at the Chicago convention.

"Now see what you have done," remarked Mamie Eisenhower as she kissed Jacqueline Cochran on the cheek. Floyd Odlum and his flying wife attended Eisenhower's inaugural festivities. "They were colorful like the ones four years before which Floyd and I also attended as special guests of President Truman," she wrote.

President Eisenhower could understandably have found it in the national interest to preserve discreet silence about any secret involving Amelia Earhart and the Emperor of Japan, particularly because he was elected on a platform to solve problems in the Pacific, not to cause any new ones. In fact, President Eisenhower's scheduled visit to Japan in 1961 had to be cancelled anyway because of student demonstrations there against a slowly stabilizing, United States-assisted Japanese government.

But what would have been Richard Nixon's attitude if he knew or came to know the secret? Any kind of a scandal which could have been laid on the Democratic party in 1960 might have made the hair-thin difference which could have gotten Nixon elected over John F. Kennedy in the close election of that year. A book published by Lyle Stuart in 1967 discloses that Amelia Earhart's friends made donations to the 1960 Nixon campaign for President. According to this source, one friend "apparently extended help to Nixon to the tune of $200,000 to $250,000." And there is no particular requirement for a President or a candidate for President to disclose anything thought worthy of secrecy by his predecessors unless he feels motivated in the national interest to do so.

There are secrets and secrets. The fascinating and frightening thing about the secret of Amelia Earhart is not the behavior of those who for a time live in the White House, but the fantastic lengths to which individuals outside of the government will go to keep it a secret.

Gervais and I, insignificant Air Force officers who innocently yet thoroughly undertook an investigation we romantically called "Operation Earhart" simply to find out what happened to a famous and beloved woman who disappeared under curious circumstances, are now faced with a problem. We have uncovered what may be important history that we feel must be recorded. Its importance is for historians to decide.

In telling our story of the secret of Amelia Earhart, we see with crystal clarity that we are dooming ourselves for the rest of our lives to being called liars by some of the most powerful and honored people on earth.

But perhaps, we thought, we could still clinch the identity of a woman believed to have left no fingerprints and supposedly dead for three decades. Joe Gervais had a raincheck to visit a woman in Bedford Village, N.Y., whose name appeared to be a code which spelled out in degrees and minutes of latitude and longitude the precise location of a tropical beach where Amelia Earhart and Fred Noonan crashed after being shot down on July 2, 1937, by planes from the Japanese carrier *Akagi*.

CHAPTER TWENTY-ONE

THE CHASE

In early June, 1967, Gervais flew from Las Vegas to New York to use his raincheck for a visit with Mrs. Guy Bolam. From a room in the Commodore Hotel in New York City he called the telephone number of the residence of Mr. and Mrs. Guy Bolam in Bedford Village. The phone rang repeatedly, and on subsequent calls rang unanswered. A quick automobile ride to Bedford Village disclosed that the large house had been unoccupied for some time—the furniture had been removed—but the telephone was still connected and in operating order.

While he was there, Gervais naturally took the opportunity of checking out the Rakow residence next door. Upon what he would find there depended the worth of my single effort at code breaking.

Gervais had fooled around with what he called the Little Orphan Annie Code, taken from the same comic strip that had inspired the broadcast pseudonym of Iva Ikuko Toguri D'Aquina, mistakenly publicized as Tokyo Rose.

"Here's how it works," Gervais had explained to me one night back in Las Vegas. "You print one word backwards over another word and then cancel out all the matching letters in the two words."

He demonstrated with the names Earhart and Rothar. "Earhart spelled backward is TRAHRAE. Look."

Gervais spelled it out on paper.

EARHART
TRAHRAE
ROTHAR

Then he crossed out the matching letters.

T̶R̶A̶H̶R̶A̶E̶
R̶O̶T̶H̶A̶R̶

"See what that leaves?"

AE—O

"AE could stand for Amelia Earhart. But what would O stand for?"

"Ocean," Gervais said with conviction. "Amelia Earhart— Ocean. What do you think of that?"

I didn't think much of it at the time.

But after we had learned that the name Rothar had changed to Rokar in transit from one mental institution to another, I made a suggestion to Gervais. "I assume you have now carried your Little Orphan Annie Code to its conclusion."

The only new letter in Rokar was K, I pointed out. "That makes the Little Orphan Annie Code spell out AE OK. Amelia Earhart . . . OK." And when the name RAKOW turned up on the mailbox of the house next door to the house deeded to Floyd Odlum and formerly lived in by Mrs. Guy Bolam, I added the only new letter in that name, W, and made a story plot out of the Little Orphan Annie Code.

Amelia Earhart is in the Ocean.
Amelia Earhart is OK and safe back home.
Amelia Earhart is OK and the Witness lives next door.

I was kind of proud of that contribution to coded intrigue. But you don't find something under every rock you turn over. Rakow turned out to be a perfectly legitimate electrical engineer. Mrs. Rakow, unaware of the coincidence of her last name, had known Guy Bolam casually.

"We used to run into each other occasionally out by the mailboxes," she remembered.

"Did you know Mrs. Bolam?" Gervais asked.

"Oh, I didn't know that Mr. Bolam was married," came the quick reply.

Gervais described Irene Bolam.

"Oh yes," Mrs. Rakow remembered. "There was such a woman who stayed there, but I'm not aware of her relationship to Mr. Bolam."

When Gervais dialed the telephone number of Guy Bolam Associates, Inc., in New York City, there was no answer. A friend had done some checking on the firm; and as near as he could determine, Guy Bolam Associates, Inc., was engaged in some sort of financial or investment activity, but was not listed with the Securities and Exchange Commission.

Gervais paid a call on Guy Bolam Associates. He found a suite of several offices sharing a common receptionist who knew nothing of the business in the empty office with connected telephone sublet by Guy Bolam Associates, Inc.

Most of the offices on the floor belonged to various foreign legations. Gervais began to make the rounds of these offices inquiring after their neighbor, Guy Bolam Associates. He picked up the trail from a Miss Carter, who was a secretary for the Icelandic Mission.

"Perhaps I can help you," she offered after considerable conversation. "I became slightly acquainted with Mrs. Burger."

"Who is Mrs. Burger?" asked Gervais.

"Mrs. Burger was Mr. Bolam's secretary when they occupied their office here. I have a phone number."

Gervais hurried back to his hotel to dial the number in Princeton, New Jersey. Mrs. Helen Burger answered the phone at once.

"May I speak to Mr. Guy Bolam, please?" Gervais asked.

"I'm sorry," Mrs. Burger answered. "Mr. Bolam is in Europe on business and won't return for about ten days. Can I help you?"

"Perhaps you can. You see, I have an invitation to visit Mrs. Guy Bolam," Gervais explained. "But I seem to have misplaced her phone number. I've tried their home in Bedford Village, but there doesn't seem to be anyone home."

"Oh," Mrs. Burger responded trustingly, "Mrs. Bolam is staying at the residence of her nurse and companion, Peggy Salter, in Sanford, North Carolina."

"Her nurse? Is Mrs. Bolam ill?"

"She's better now. Actually, she had a bad case of shingles and has been resting in Trinidad for four months from February through May. I believe the holiday has helped."

"I hope so." Gervais held his hand over the phone's mouthpiece and cleared his throat. "Mrs. Burger. I've come a long ways—from Las Vegas to New York—to see Mrs. Bolam. I wonder if you could give me her phone number in Sanford, North Carolina."

"Certainly, but she'll be coming back here to meet Mr. Bolam in about ten days."

"Where? In Bedford Village?"

"Perhaps. Or right here in New Jersey."

"I'd like to telephone Mrs. Bolam if I may," Gervais coaxed. "Could you give me her phone number and address?"

"All right," agreed Mrs. Burger.

When Gervais nervously dialed the North Carolina number, her voice answered almost immediately. "Hello."

"Hello, Mrs. Bolam. Major Gervais here. How are you?"

Her voice remained calm. "Hello, Major Gervais. How are you?"

"Fine. I've come to New York to see you."

She did not seem surprised. They exchanged banalities. She inquired about his family.

"I must talk to you. When can we get together for a chat?" he finally asked.

"What on earth must you talk to me about?" she countered.

"About the old days and Amelia Earhart. When can I see you?"

"Oh, I can't see you in this country," she said. "If I meet with you at all it can't be in this country."

"I beg your pardon?" said Gervais.

"I mean, I couldn't meet with you in the United States," she repeated. "Look, Major Gervais. I once had a public life. I once had a career in flying. But I've retired. I've given all that up now. As a major retired from the Air Force, you should be able to understand this."

"I think I understand, Mrs. Bolam. But I've been looking for Amelia Earhart for seven years. I *must* talk to you. Can't we get together?"

"It will have to be in some other country," she repeated. "I can't meet with you here."

Gervais frowned, intrigued. "Mrs. Bolam, I don't know what you mean by some other country. I'm willing to meet with you anywhere. But to make it easy . . . how about meeting me in Canada or Mexico?"

There was a short pause before the voice came on again. "Very well, Major Gervais. I've never liked traveling in Mexico . . . I'll tell you what. Today is June 17. I'll meet you June 23 at 7 P.M. in the lobby of the St. Laurentian Hotel in Montreal."

"All right, Mrs. Bolam. I'll see you in Canada."

It was all very mysterious, but Gervais made a plane reservation and a hotel reservation. There were several days to wait, and Gervais decided to go ahead and check out other aspects of the case. Next on the agenda was Marcia Short, who lived in New York City and was the author of the poem "Missing," the tribute to Amelia Earhart composed twenty-four hours after her disappearance in July, 1937.

Because the writing style of Marcia Short was so similar to that of Amelia Earhart, Gervais wanted to have a look at her. He even toyed with the speculation that Marcia Short and Mrs. Guy Bolam might turn out to be one and the same. This theory collapsed when Mrs. Short, an elderly widow whose husband had been an Army general, dined with him that night.

"I have a surprise for you after dinner," Mrs. Short declared eagerly. "I'm going to take you to meet Margaret Shellford, the seer." Mrs. Short's eyes twinkled beneath the red hair that belied her senior citizenship. "Margaret Shellford has agreed to help you find Amelia by extrasensory perception."

When Gervais arrived at her apartment with Mrs. Short, Margaret Shellford, dressed exotically in a long robe, reclined on a low couch, stroking a cat.

"Do you believe in ESP, Major Gervais?" she asked in a calm voice.

"I don't know anything about ESP," Gervais replied. "Naturally I am a little skeptical. But Amelia Earhart believed in it, and so did her friend Jacqueline Cochran."

"Yes," smiled the occult advisor of Park Avenue neighbors, "and Marcia here has been spiritually in touch with Amelia. Did you know that?"

Gervais grinned. "I know Marcia wrote a poem right after the Amelia Earhart crash that I figure as awfully close in describing what happened out there."

"That's because Marcia didn't write the poem."

"Huh? Then who did write it?"

"Amelia wrote it herself . . . using Marcia. Amelia wrote the poem and sent it back by instant transfiguration." Miss Shellford shrugged. "Marcia simply recorded what Amelia was telling her by extrasensory transmission."

Gervais was speechless. What could he say?

"Now, Major Gervais," she asked, changing the subject,

"Marcia has asked me to help you. What would you like to know?"

Gervais was slightly embarrassed. "Miss Shellford . . . I have to be honest with you. I really don't know much about ESP, the supernatural, instant transfiguration, and that sort of thing. I really don't know how you can help me."

"Isn't there something you want to know?" she countered patiently. "Just ask a question about something you would like to know."

Gervais frowned thoughtfully. "All right," he said slowly. "Can you tell me . . . is Amelia Earhart dead or alive?"

The medium arose from her couch. "Major Gervais," she admonished as she led them toward the door, "why do you ask me that question when you already know the answer?"

Gervais had eliminated one tantalizing possibility. Marcia Short was not Amelia Earhart. And soon another confrontation in Canada might give him an answer one way or the other. A third tantalizing question was the identity of Wilbur Rothar, escaped after twenty-five years in mental hospitals. Gervais decided to check the records of Bellevue Hospital, where the sanity hearing had committed Rothar after "ten days of observation."

"We have no record of any Wilbur Rothar as a patient here in 1937," said Charles Martin, assistant hospital administrator. "Nor do we have any record of a sanity panel."

"Would there be such a record if Rothar had been sent for observation to Bellevue?" Gervais asked.

"We have a complete record system," said Martin. "We have records of all patients treated at Bellevue, but none of Rothar in 1937." Gervais was about to turn away when Martin again spoke. "The only Wilbur Rothar in our records was in 1964."

"What?"

"Here it is," read Martin. "Wilbur Rothar, admitted to the

Bellevue emergency dressing office on September 27, 1964, and released the same day. Brought in from the Municipal Lodging House in the Bowery."

Twenty-three months after the patient known as Rothar had "eloped" forever from Central Islip State Hospital, according to their records. Eleven months after he had been returned to the hospital, according to the records of the Central Islip police . . . and eleven months after the case had been marked "closed" by the hospital.

Gervais hurried to the Bowery and talked with a Mr. McCormick, who was a social worker for the Municipal Lodging House.

"Mr. Rothar was a man in his early seventies," said McCormick, consulting a file card. "He was not one of our regular indigents. He just happened to drift in here and get into some kind of trouble that required emergency treatment at the hospital. He had a daughter somewhere in New York named Doris."

McCormick said he could provide no more information than that about Rothar. The enigmatic man of several similar names, who failed to appear in the records of Bellevue Hospital for an "observation" visit in 1937 that resulted in more than a quarter-century of incarceration in maximum security wards of state mental institutions, had been dutifully recorded for a brief emergency visit there twenty-seven years later.

That night, Gervais dined with William and Cathy Van Dusen at their estate.

"I hear you are going to Montreal tomorrow," the Eastern Airlines executive mentioned casually.

"How did you know that?" gasped Gervais.

The former Pan Am historian grinned and held out a silver cigarette case over the white table cloth.

"Smoke?"

There was one cigarette in the case . . . an old-fashioned, ivory-tipped, non-filtered Marlborough, such as was popular in the thirties. Gervais felt his skin crawl as he read the inscription inside the proffered cigarette case: "A Salute, to the man who showed us the way across the Pacific, Frederick J. Noonan, Navigator." The inscription was followed by the etched signatures of the entire crew of the first China Clipper to fly the Pacific, including the signature of the smiling Van Dusen.

"Where did you get this?" Gervais asked.

"Oh, I don't know," grinned Van Dusen, obviously playing a game with the thirty-year-old cigarette case and the single old-fashioned cigarette it contained. "I guess Fred must have left it here or something."

"But wouldn't it belong to his widow? It's a personal effect, isn't it? Wouldn't that be his widow's property as his next of kin?"

Van Dusen shrugged, still grinning. "Maybe he didn't want her to have it. Did you ever think of that?" Then he changed the subject, and simply would not discuss the cigarette case any further.

"Every time I left Van Dusen," Gervais remembered, "I felt like a mouse that had been mauled but not yet eaten by a cat."

As Van Dusen had known, Gervais caught an Eastern airliner next day for Montreal. Once there he hurried to the St. Laurentian Hotel and queried a desk clerk.

"Is there a Mrs. Guy Bolam registered here?"

The desk clerk checked his file. "Not yet, sir, but we have a reservation for Mrs. Guy Bolam."

Gervais checked in and waited in the lobby, on edge for the expected meeting at last. Minutes dragged by as he watched the lobby's main doorways in anticipation of her arrival. The minutes dragged into an hour. Gervais smoked one cigarette after another. Hours passed. It became dark outside. Gervais was too frustrated to eat. Guests crossed the lobby to go out on the town. Gervais waited . . . and waited . . . and waited. . . .

Sometime after 1 A.M. he gave up, left a message at the desk for Mrs. Bolam, and retired to his room. With a desperate optimism he lay down with his clothes on. Eventually he fell into a fitful sleep. Shortly after dawn he called the desk clerk on the telephone.

"Has Mrs. Bolam arrived?"

"No sir, she hasn't registered."

That afternoon, twenty-four hours after he had arrived in Montreal, Gervais caught a plane back to New York. During the twenty-four hours, Gervais had had her paged once every hour at the hotel. He had also repeatedly placed phone calls to the Bolam numbers in Princeton, New Jersey, New York City, and North Carolina. There had been a lot of ringing, but no one answered any of those phones until he got back to New York City. Then he reached Mrs. Burger at the Princeton number. She seemed honestly surprised when he told her how Mrs. Bolam had made the Montreal appointment and then failed to show up.

"Why, that's odd," Mrs. Burger exclaimed. "I happen to know Mrs. Bolam is still in North Carolina waiting for Mr. Bolam to return from Europe."

Gervais called Sanford, North Carolina, again. Mrs. Bolam's "companion," Peggy Salter, answered.

"Mrs. Bolam cannot come to the phone," she said abruptly.

"Look, Miss Salter, I wasted a lot of time and money to meet Mrs. Bolam in Montreal and I still want to talk to her. Would you please ask her to come to the phone."

"No, I won't. Mrs. Bolam has been ill. We went to Trinidad to improve her health and now you are upsetting her and making her all nervous again."

"Can't she talk with me just for a few minutes?"

"No," snapped Peggy Salter, "and will you please quit calling us?" She then hung up.

Angry, Gervais called Mrs. Burger at Guy Bolam's Princeton number. "I am going to visit my sister in Boston. Would you please ask Mr. Bolam when he returns to call me there?"

A few days later, Guy Bolam did call. He laughed when Gervais recounted how Irene Bolam had stood him up in Montreal. "Yes," he said in his clipped British voice. "She sometimes does things like that. But, I'll tell you what. I am going down to meet Mrs. Bolam on June 29. Why don't you fly down with me and we'll see her together?"

They arranged to meet at the Newark Airport for a 4 P.M. flight to Raleigh, North Carolina, on June 29. While making his own plane reservation by phone, Gervais made a cautious inquiry. "Does a Mr. Guy Bolam have a ticket on that flight?"

In time, the answer came. "Yes, sir. We have a reservation for Mr. Guy Bolam."

Seemingly, everything was beginning to straighten itself out. Except that on June 29 when the plane took off from Newark Airport at 4 P.M., Guy Bolam was not aboard. As his alleged wife had done in Montreal, Guy Bolam had failed to show up.

Gervais flew to Raleigh, North Carolina, alone, rented a car, and drove hastily for forty miles to Sanford and the rambling country house where Bolam lived.

"They're gone," volunteered a gardener working in the yard.

"Gone where?"

"I dunno. They just drove off."

"You don't know where they went?"

The gardener leaned on his power mower. "Don't know where they went. Know which way they started."

"Which way?"

"Started driving north."

"With baggage?"

"Yup."

"Who all went?"

"Just the two of them. You a credit man?"

Gervais shook his head.

"No need to worry about them," volunteered the gardener. "Nothing wrong with their credit. Nothing at all."

In a few days, at the Smithsonian Institution in Washington, D.C., there was to be a ceremony by the Ninety-nines and other early American flyers commemorating the thirtieth anniversary of Amelia Earhart's disappearance. A Navy file on Amelia Earhart, classified for thirty years, would become available for public inspection. Was Amelia herself now driving north to Washington? With Gervais in persistent pursuit, had the logical time come for her to personally and publicly break the story in her own way?

Amelia Earhart did not show up at the ceremony in her honor at the Smithsonian. The thirtieth anniversary of her original disappearance passed hardly noticed in the fourth of July weekend. But not by us. Gervais and I both had believed for some time that Amelia Earhart would pick her own time, place, and method of disclosing that she was alive. And we had suspected with considerable foreboding that, since we were so close on her tail now, she would select that ceremony at the Smithsonian Institution to reveal the best-kept secret of the century.

Did the fact that her thirty-year silence had not been conveniently broken on the Fourth of July, 1967, mean that we were in fact not as near to the solution as we believed? Gervais in Washington and I in San Francisco heaved a perplexed coast-to-coast sigh of relief that the time had not apparently been right for us to be scooped by the principal character in our story.

Gervais hurried back to New York and began again what was beginning to be the routine telephone search for Mrs. Guy Bolam. He called Bedford Village, Guy Bolam Associates, and Bolam's office in Princeton, New Jersey. He also tried Peggy Salter's number in Sanford, North Carolina. All he got from any of the calls was persistent ringing at the other end of the line. Every hour he called all four of the numbers in order. Finally he got an answer at the Princeton, New Jersey, number. It was Bolam's secretary, Mrs. Helen Burger.

"I am terribly sorry, Major Gervais." She sounded genuinely concerned and surprised at his remarkable tale of missing both Mr. and Mrs. Bolam in so many different places. "Have you tried Mrs. Bolam's apartment in Jamesburg?"

"No, I haven't." Gervais tried to conceal his excitement at learning of yet another residence for his enigmatic prey. "What is Mrs. Bolam's Jamesburg address?"

"I don't have the street number," Mrs Burger answered guilelessly. "Just a post office box number, Jamesburg, New Jersey, and a phone number."

Gervais quickly dialed the number. Mrs. Guy Bolam answered the phone. "How did you get my phone number? It's not listed."

Gervais evaded the answer to protect Mrs. Burger from possible reproach. "I've spent twelve hundred dollars so far trying to get together with you for a chat," he said. "I've been to Canada, where we were supposed to have a date, and to North Carolina, where I was supposed to go with Mr. Bolam. But he also failed to keep a date with me."

She made no apology. "I can't understand why anyone would go to all that trouble just to see me," she said flatly.

"I want to talk to you about the early days of your flying career."

"I've told you. I've left all that."

"I've gone to all this trouble . . . won't you please let me see you, Mrs. Bolam?"

"I'm not having any house guests at the moment."

"But I don't want to be your house guest. All I want is to talk to you for half an hour."

"What about?" she countered.

"Well, about your name," he said. "About how when the names of eight islands in a group in the Pacific are placed one above the other in a certain way, letters up and down spell out the name Guy Bolam, and give the exact location in degrees and minutes of latitude and longitude of a place where a plane went down in the Pacific thirty years ago."

"Oh that." She tossed it off as if it were a boring subject too mundane to discuss. "Well, if you know me as well as you think you do, you know I don't stand on ceremony."

"I beg your pardon," Gervais gasped. "Can't we have lunch together?"

"If I have lunch with you at all, it won't be now. It will be in New York City at the Wings Club when I invite you." She changed the subject. "Did you see Mrs. Morrissey when you were in Montreal?"

Amelia Earhart's sister, Muriel Morrissey, lived in Massachusetts, not Canada. "I didn't go to see Mrs. Morrissey," he answered. "I went to Montreal for no other purpose but to see you."

She ignored the answer and changed the subject again. "I walked in my garden this morning and I am very tired."

"Have lunch with me later this week," Gervais tried again.

"Put exactly what you want from me into writing and send it to me," she instructed coldly. "If I want to discuss it with you I may invite you to lunch at the Wings Club. I am too tired now to talk about it."

That was it.

How far can you go in trying to make positive identification of a private citizen when there are no fingerprints to check . . . no birth certificate to look at, no legal documents of any kind? How do you make a private citizen talk if she doesn't wish to?

"What do you think we ought to do now?" Gervais asked me upon his return to Las Vegas.

"She told you to put exactly what you wanted from her into a letter," I answered. "Let's do that. And let us tell her that I am writing a book. Let's be honest all the way and see if she will reciprocate in kind."

I worked for an entire day on the letter. We did not wish it to be misunderstood. Then we mailed it. It read:

Las Vegas, Nevada
July 15, 1967

Mrs. Guy Bolam
Princeton, New Jersey

Dear Mrs. Bolam:

We—Joe Gervais and Joe Klaas—are writing this letter together in a sincere effort to establish an amicable communication with you so that we may clear away a great stumbling block in our research into the disappearance of Amelia Earhart.

Joe Gervais, whom you know, is the chief researcher for what has become known as "Operation Earhart" and for seven years has devoted thousands of hours as well as thousands of dollars in an intensive and dedicated search for the truth about Amelia Earhart. Working with him on this exhaustive investigation is Major Robert Dinger. Both Gervais and Dinger were command pilots in the United States Air Force, and Gervais was also an aircraft accident investigator.

For a time they were working in cooperation with Paul Briand, Jr., author of *Daughter of the Sky*, but Briand is no longer a part of "Operation Earhart."

Joe Klaas is the author of the book which will tell the considerable results of "Operation Earhart." Klaas, a former newspaper reporter with degrees in journalism and creative writing, was also a military pilot in the RAF and USAF. He is a serious professional writer, as you may judge for yourself from his previous successful book which is enclosed for your enjoyment and information.

"Operation Earhart" was not begun with the intention of writing a book, but rather as a simple effort to pursue the truth from information which Gervais discovered while stationed in the Pacific. What began as a result of simple curiosity has become a way of life for Gervais. What has so far been uncovered is important history which must be recorded. Klaas was called in to write the book, and is well along now in the manuscript. The important thing is that Klaas is an ethical journalist, trained in the law of the press. He is not a selective writer discarding facts that would disprove a preconceived theory, but is presenting all the facts uncovered in Saipan, Truk, Guam, Japan, and in the United States. Also in Australia and New Zealand and a few other places.

"Operation Earhart" was begun by amateurs who by experience alone can now qualify as professionals. And by results.

We are going into detail in this letter in order to assure you that the work we are doing is serious business to us, and will most assuredly be taken seriously by the world.

You have stated that if we know you as we think we know you, we should know that you do not stand on ceremony. Well, then we had best not do that.

As incredible as it seems to us, we keep turning up facts which indicate that Amelia Earhart is alive.

In spite of all the information we have gathered which leads us to this amazing conclusion, we would probably still not give it credence if we had not also found the Amelia Earhart Lockheed 10 N-16020, which did not crash in the Pacific, and also the other aircraft involved.

Your DFC, your oak leaves, your name, and the secret it reveals . . . and more recently your understandable reluctance to meet with us in Canada, North Carolina, New Jersey or New York . . . our own efforts to identify Irene Craigmile in Zonta International, or the Ninety-Nines . . . your real estate arrangement with Floyd Odlum and reports we have from Japan and Chicago, etc., etc., etc. . . . and the code . . . we've even had your photographs analyzed for bone structure by an eminent orthopedic surgeon to find out if it is possible that you are Amelia Earhart.

We are doing everything we can, honestly, to try and prove that you are *not* Amelia Earhart. But if you are not, it strangely is most difficult for us to prove that you are not she.

I repeat, we want only the truth. We now have an

entire filing cabinet full of documents, photographs, letters, statements, diplomatic correspondence, records. We have entire files on Fred Noonan, William Van Dusen, Guy Bolam, Hilton H. Railey, Jackie Cochran, Floyd Odlum, Paul Mantz, Lockheed, the aircraft involved, Wilbur Rothar . . . and all the parts of the puzzle seem to be falling into place.

If you are not Amelia Earhart, please let us know enough about your background so that we may be certain that you really are someone else. Then we can get off this subject and go on with our research.

If you are Amelia Earhart . . . rest assured that we hold you in great respect as an individual . . . and that although we are now dedicated to publishing the story, we shall give every consideration to any information you may be able to give us. Since the story must now be told, could you find anyone who could better tell it than three fellow flyers who have for so long been so interested in Amelia Earhart as to have been devoting all this effort to her memory and then have the amazing luck to rejoice in her survival?

At least, we certainly hope so, because we love her.

Please write to us as soon as you can, and tell us who you are and what your relationship may be to Amelia Earhart.

> Most sincerely yours,
> Joseph Gervais
> Joe Klaas

We mailed it airmail special delivery the same day I wrote it . . . July 15, 1967. Then we waited. A week later at Hamilton Air Force Base, California, I showed a copy of the letter to Bob Dinger.

"She'll never answer that," he predicted.

"Why not?" I asked.

"Why should she?" he asked again. "What you are asking is none of our business. Would you answer a letter like that?"

I thought for a minute. "She claims to be a friend of Amelia

Earhart and to have flown with her many times. She claims to have been a pioneer aviator herself in the early thirties. I don't see why she wouldn't want to tell us who she is."

"She'll never answer it," predicted Dinger again.

Dinger was wrong. After more than two weeks of anxious waiting we received an answer postmarked July 31, 1967, at Plainsboro, New Jersey. The handwritten letter said:

Gentlemen:

Your letter came as a great surprise to me! I'm sorry if you felt I was evading your efforts to contact me personally. I could simply not imagine any reason for your taking the time or expense.

Unfortunately your quest has not ended, for I am not she. I can offer in evidence two people whom you may call for verification of this fact, because they each knew us both well as Amelia Earhart and Irene Craigmile. These folks are Viola Gentry, who, the last I heard was working at a hotel on Mackinac Is., Michigan, and Elmo Neal Pickerill, of Mineola, New York.

I wish you every success in the outcome of your investigations. It has always been my feeling the [sic] Amelia Earhart has not passed away completely, so long as there is one person alive who still remembers her.

Most sincerely,
Irene Bolam

It was not our feeling that Amelia Earhart had passed away completely. Elmo Pickerill and Viola Gentry were already known by us to be close friends of Irene Bolam. They were with Gervais when he first saw her. But we wrote to them anyway.

"Irene O'Crowley married Craigmile who passed on, now Mrs. Bolam—came from a well-to-do family in Newark, New Jersey," Miss Gentry scribbled across the bottom of our letter. "Her Aunt a well known lawyer—Never did much with her flying—just flew."

Pickerill, the first man ever to take a radio aloft in an airplane, was more explicit:

Dear Mr. Gervais:

Replying to yours of August 1, inquiring about Irene Craigmile.

I have known this lady for the past thirty years. In fact she lived just two doors away from me at one time in Mineola.

Shortly after she was married to Mr. Craigmile, he suddenly died and shortly thereafter she married an aviator flying out of Roosevelt Field here in Mineola, named Al Heller. A son was born to them, who is now about 30 years old. She learned to fly under instructions from her husband Al Heller at Floyd Bennett Field. After a few years they were divorced and a few years later she married a man named Guy Bolam here in New York, who was engaged in the export business. She has two homes; her summer home is in Jamesburg, New Jersey. She also has a beautiful summer home in Bedford, New York.

When she was flying at Floyd Bennett Field and Roosevelt Field, she was a pal of Amelia Earhart and Viola Gentry, all of whom were flying at Roosevelt Field at that time. This was at the time Amelia and Viola were getting the 99 Club organized and going.

I can't speak too highly of Irene as she is a very fine person to know and is well liked by everybody who knows her. I hope this answers your question. Kind regards.

Sincerely,
E. N. Pickerill

Shortly after writing the letter, Pickerill died. But while his letter was still fresh, we made inquiry of the Department of Transportation, Federal Aviation Administration in Oklahoma City about the pilot licenses of several women. The following information came from Eddie H. Kjelshus, chief of the airman certification branch of the flight standards technical division at Oklahoma City:

Dear Mr. Gervais:

The following is the information requested in your letter of August 18, 1967:

Aviatrix	Date Issued	Type	Number
Amelia Earhart	4–16–29	Transport	5716
Viola Gentry	3–01–28	Private	1822
Jacqueline Cochran Odlum	8–17–32	Private	26464*
Irene Craigmile	9–20–32	Student	
	5–27–33	Private	28958

* Jacqueline Cochran Odlum was originally issued number 26464. That number was exchanged for number 1498 on August 29, 1932.

We are unable to locate a record of a certificate issued in the name of Irene Heller. Perhaps the name given is either their maiden name or married name, and the certificate was issued under the other name. If you could furnish a certificate number or full name (both married and maiden), we will be happy to search our records again.

Sincerely yours,
Eddie H. Kjelshus

It was the first concrete evidence we had that anyone named Irene Craigmile existed before Amelia Earhart disappeared. Yet, why were there no pilot licenses issued to her under the names of O'Crowley or Heller, particularly if, as Pickerill stated, Heller taught her to fly?

"Let's see if we can get a copy of Irene Craigmile's pilot's license," I suggested. "It may have some other information on it."

The suggestion became a challenge to Gervais.

On December 5, 1967, Kjelshus responded to Gervais' first request for a copy of the Irene Craigmile license No. 28958:

> This is in response to your letter of December 2, 1967, concerning Irene Craigmile. The information you requested may be released only when the airman or someone legally competent to act for her specifically consents to its release in writing.

Gervais may not have been legally competent, but after nearly eight years of relentless investigation he wasn't about to let that stop him. Gervais had a money order made out, designating Irene Craigmile as the payer, and sent it to the FAA aeronautical center at Oklahoma City with a request for a duplicate of the license. A letter came back addressed to:

> Dear Miss Craigmile:
> We have searched our airman files and find that your private pilot certificate number 28958, dated May 31, 1937, has expired and is no longer valid.
> Pilot certificates issued prior to July 1, 1945, unless subsequently reissued, expired July 1, 1947. Holders of the expired pilot certificates were then given ten years to reinstate themselves without the need for a further showing of competence. The reinstatement privilege ended September 1, 1957. . . .

Enclosed was a copy of the Noncommercial Pilot's License No. 28958 issued to Irene O. Craigmile, 31. It was unsigned, and dated May 31, 1937. For some reason the date, May 31, 1937, was crossed out, and penciled in above it was the corrected date of June 1, 1937.

So . . . a license was not issued to Irene Craigmile in 1932 or 1933 as indicated in the first letter at all. Instead License No. 28958 was issued to Irene Craigmile apparently on June 1, 1937.

It was the same day . . . June 1, 1937 . . . that Amelia Earhart took off from Miami, Florida, on the flight she never completed around the world.

Did Irene Craigmile, alias Irene O'Crowley, alias Irene Heller, alias Mrs. Guy Bolam, begin to exist only as Amelia Earhart soared on wings of mystery across the horizon?

The address on the private license was in Brooklyn, New York, and it was validated neither by her signature nor by any officer of the Bureau of Air Commerce.

Apparently Mrs. Guy Bolam (Irene Craigmile), when the unsigned license was placed in the files on May 31 or June 1, 1937, never got around to picking up her license.

Also, Mrs. Bolam's letter to us did not convince us as it should have if the facts were clear. Even her handwritten grammar was strangely challenging.

" . . . they each knew us both well as Amelia Earhart and Irene Craigmile," she said of Elmo Pickerill and Viola Gentry. "I wish you every success in the outcome of your investigations. It has always been my feeling the (sic) Amelia Earhart has not passed away completely, so long as there is one person alive who still remembers her."

It was a rather plaintive, yet grateful, closing to the letter— seemingly thanking us for even remembering one of the most famous and fascinating women in history. The language moved us strangely. It had a lonely sound to it when read aloud in a quiet room. Obviously we must write another letter to Mrs. Guy Bolam.

Dear Mrs. Bolam,

Thank you for your kind reply to our letter which to one who is not Amelia Earhart would certainly have come as a shock. I hope you will consider that to be suspected of being that wonderful woman is a compliment. We are sincerely objective in our investigation and are not taken to flights of fancy not backed up by impressive evidence, so we hope you will bear with us in our pursuit of the truth.

We believe the set of circumstances which led us to our incredible conjecture about your identity to be such a remarkable set of coincidences, that we ask your indulgence in helping us to prove beyond a shadow of a doubt that you are *not* indeed she.

Would you be so kind as to tell us under what name you pursued a career in aviation, briefly what your aviation career consisted of, and where and when you did your flying? We are particularly interested in where you lived and flew during the decade between 1936 and 1946.

We hope it would not be too much to ask your birthplace, the names of your parents, and where you attended school prior to 1937.

How well did you know Amelia Earhart? Can you give us a brief description of the kind of person you remember her to be?

Do you know Wilbur Rothar? Do you know where we can contact Wilbur Rothar?

Are you acquainted with C. B. Allen, and do you know where we can reach him?

Do you know the secret purpose of Amelia Earhart's "last flight"?

If you will help us with the answers to these questions, we will be most grateful. Our book is 75,000 words along now and we shall certainly see to it that you get a first edition in consideration for your kind assistance. Please let us hear from you soon.

> Sincerely yours,
> Joseph Gervais
> Joe Klaas

In the letter we wanted to make certain she understood we were writing a book, and to give her every opportunity to clear up any mistakes at all we might be making.

It should not be difficult, we reasoned, for any woman on earth to prove she is not Amelia Earhart. We were begging in as considerate and respectful a way as possible for Mrs. Guy Bolam to clear up our thinking. All she had to do was tell us where she was born, where she went to school— any simple set of facts that could be verified to prove she was not the famous flyer presumed by the world to be dead for nearly a third of a century. If she were a loyal friend of a dead woman, why would she not cooperate?

This time Bob Dinger was right. We received no answer.

But Viola Gentry made a special trip out from the East to Las Vegas to see Gervais. It was she who let us know that Mrs. Guy Bolam had taken off again.

"I am sorry, but I've helped you all I can there," she informed Gervais before two witnesses at dinner in a Las Vegas restaurant. "Irene has gone to Paris. You'll never see her again."

"You know, Viola," Gervais commented, "there are a lot of people interested in this case. It could be worth a lot of money to find out what really happened out there on July 2, 1937."

Miss Gentry nodded. "That's what Amelia says."

Conversation stopped for a moment as all three of those with her at the table stared at the pioneer aviatrix.

"Viola," Gervais said softly. "Do you know what you just said?"

Her eyes darted about. "What?"

"You said, 'That's what Amelia says.' As if she were alive."

"Oh my, did I say that? I meant Muriel. You know . . . Amelia's sister, Muriel Morrissey. I often confuse their names."

The summer of 1968 Gervais went again to New York City, and, true to Viola Gentry's prediction, was unable to locate any trace of Mr. and Mrs. Guy Bolam. He decided to have one more stab at locating Wilbur Rothar.

"I represent one Wilbur Rothar," Gervais said to an employee of the Criminal Court of New York–Manhattan District. "I wish to see the entire file concerning Wilbur Rothar indicted for extortion in 1937."

The employee returned in a few moments from checking the old General Sessions Court records.

"This is a confidential file, case number 214079," the public servant reported. "Because it concerns the individual's sanity, a petition must be filed with the court in order to have access to this file."

"Fine," answered Gervais. "What is the procedure and how long will it take?"

"You simply petition the court for a hearing. I can put you on the calendar in about three weeks."

"That won't do," Gervais said. "I have come here from Nevada and must return in twenty-four hours. You must grant me special consideration."

The petition to look into the confidential court records of Wilbur Rothar was placed on the calendar of Judge Brust, Section 30, for hearing at 2 P.M. of August 6, 1968. Permission was granted. There was an admonishment not to take notes, and that under no circumstances could any information in the file be used for publication. The same employee of the court was assigned to watch Gervais at all times during his perusal of the file.

The file of Wilbur Rothar contained an eighty-seven-page lunacy commission report signed by the lone member of the lunacy commission, a Dr. Lonnardo. Attached to this report was an eight-page deposition signed by FBI Special Agents T. J. Donegan, G. A. Callahan, P. M. Trapani, and stenographer Louise Albaugh, dated August 3, 1937, at the FBI office, Foley Square, New York City.

With the court employee watching closely, Gervais could hardly make notes on paper, so he made mental notes.

Police forced Rothar to take the reward money offered by Putnam for information about Amelia Earhart, Rothar told Dr. Lonnardo. Rothar claimed to have been severely beaten on his arrival at the police station after his arrest. This, he said, resulted in a neck injury.

Rothar described Fred Noonan's body, legs, genitals, intestines protruding from a torso half-eaten by sharks, at least a thousand of which were swimming nearby. Noonan and the plane wreckage were lodged on a reef, according to Rothar.

Dr. Lonnardo noted that Rothar kept asking over and over throughout the examination for his sister, Muriel. Rothar said Muriel wore a brace of some sort when she was younger.

From time to time, Rothar and the doctor got off the subject of Amelia Earhart and onto the subjects of the murderess Ruth Schneider, the Lindbergh case, and other crimes. The patient claimed to know that a part-time nurse who was really the kidnap-convicted Hauptman's girl friend had run out the front door with the baby, whom she knew to be mentally defective. "Don't they know this?" Rothar asked.

Then the doctor noted Rothar's description of Amelia Earhart, mad, head bandaged, tied to the bunk of his ship, sheets badly soiled with blood and excrement, out of her mind and raving wildly.

Throughout the entire examination Rothar maintained Amelia Earhart was alive, but Fred Noonan was dead. "The Boiler was blown up by ammunition," he repeated no less than eight times.

There on a sheet among the notes of Dr. Lonnardo was a map of an island—drawn by the hand of Wilbur Rothar. On the map of the island was a circled X. It marked the spot on the beach where Rothar said he first saw four colored men cooking something like a leg and eating it. He described in vivid detail how the four men in turn repeatedly raped the woman he later learned was Amelia Earhart. He described in exceptionally obscene language the intimate and perverse acts performed, not only upon her, but upon himself, switching from acts of rape to acts of sodomy so often that the doctor could not be sure which victim of sexual mayhem he was talking about—Amelia Earhart or himself.

He used vile yet vivid language, portraying acts so repulsive that Gervais developed an instant mental block in discussing what he found in the report.

Rothar also described seeing a warship, either a destroyer or a minesweeper.

Dr. Lonnardo noted that he diagnosed Rothar to be insane at the time he committed the acts for which he was charged with extortion.

On the crude but stangely accurate hand-drawn map the doctor had scribbled: "Harl Island. Lae to Harl Island, P.I., 312–315, 425 SE Howland Island."

Wilbur Rothar, who was to spend the next twenty-five years in maximum security wards for the criminally insane in New York State hospitals, had accurately drawn a map of and a fair indication of the exact location of the now familiar "Gull Island" of the movies, or Hull Island of the Phoenix Islands, about 420 miles southeast of Howland Island. 312–315, if taken to read degrees on the compass from Howland, and 425 if taken to mean miles—and what else could they mean?—was close enough to the truth to make one wonder about both the sanity and identity of "Wilbur Rothar."

While Gervais was going through this astounding report of the "sanity commission," the court employee who had been assigned to watch over him continually tried to keep a conversation going about professional football. After reading the report of Dr. Lonnardo, Gervais suggested that a review of a copy of the original indictment of Wilbur Rothar delivered to a certain hotel room might be exchanged for some pro football tickets.

Late that afternoon, there came a knocking at the Gervais door, and pro football tickets were made available in exchange for examination of the following document:

AMELIA EARHART LIVES

COURT OF GENERAL SESSIONS
COUNTY OF NEW YORK
THE PEOPLE OF THE STATE OF NEW YORK
against
WILBUR ROTHAR

a/ka William Goodenough

Indictment NO.
214079

Defendant.

Indictment: On August 5, 1937, the defendant was indicted for the crimes of an Attempt to Commit the Crime of Extortion and an Attempt to Commit the Crime of Grand Larceny in the First Degree. The charge is that on August 3, 1937, he demanded $2000 from George Putnam, the husband of missing aviatrix Amelia Earhart, on the pretense that he had the latter in his custody and would release her only upon receipt of the money.

Evidence: On August 3, 1937, the defendant contacted George Putnam and told him that he had located his wife, Amelia Earhart. The defendant stated that he had been a member of a crew that found the missing pilot on a coral reef in the South Pacific, and that he now held her in his custody. Only for $2000, he declared, would he release Amelia Earhart to her husband. Mr. Putnam immediately contacted the police, a plan was devised, and the defendant captured with $1000 in marked bills in his possession.

Previous Criminal Record: The defendant has no criminal record other than his arrest in the instant case.

Recommendation: On August 31, 1937, in the Court of General Sessions, the defendant pleaded not guilty with a specification of insanity. A commission in Lunacy was appointed to examine him and found the defendant to be insane at the time of his examination, as well as at the time of the commission of the offense. On October 13, 1937, in Part 8 of the Court of General Sessions, the Report of the Commission was confirmed by Judge

John J. Freshie, and the defendant committed to the Matteawan State Hospital.

On March 28, 1952, a motion to dismiss the indictment was brought before Judge Francis L. Valente in Part 1 of the Court of General Sessions. The theory of the motion was that the Lunacy Commission's determination that the defendant was insane at the time of the commission of the crime was conclusive upon the court. The motion was denied on June 25, 1952.

The defendant remained at Matteawan until April 19, 1960. At that time he was considered sufficiently improved to be transferred to Harlem Valley State Hospital.

On August 30, 1960, this office received a letter from Dr. Leo P. O'Donnell, Director of the Harlem Valley State Hospital. It stated that the defendant has made a "satisfactory adjustment" at the new hospital, and was considered sufficiently improved to be released to the custody of his sister, Mrs. Mary Rago. Dr. O'Donnell inquired as to whether this office would be willing to dismiss the indictment against the defendant, stating, "He is not considered dangerous but would require after-care supervision if permitted out of the hospital."

A successful prosecution of the case is impossible. The complainant, George Putnam, who is an essential witness, died several years ago. In addition, the Report of the Commission on Lunacy, holding the defendant to be insane at the time of the commission of the crime, although an advisory report only, makes it very unlikely that the prosecution could prove that the defendant was legally responsible for his actions at the time of the crime.

The defendant has been in custody much longer than the maximum prison sentence authorized by statute for a conviction. Even if convicted, upon sentence he would be entitled to credit for the time served under the commitment and would have to be discharged.

In view of the foregoing it is my opinion that the interests of justice would be better served by dismissal of

the indictment under Section 671 of the Code of Criminal
Procedure.

No previous recommendation in this case has been
made by the District Attorney to any judge of this
court.

Dated, New York, N.Y. September 19, 1960.

Respectfully submitted,
s/ Melvin Stein
Assistant District Attorney

APPROVED:
s/ Alfred J. Scott
Chief Assistant District Attorney

Our previous research, of course, indicated that this, the
first action by the district attorney's office after twenty-four
years, was not wholly successful. The patient, who may
or may not have been responsible for his actions in 1937,
still had a year or more maximum-security-ward time to
serve at Central Islip State Hospital on Long Island. After
more than twenty-five years' incarceration in such institutions under indictment on charges that were never brought to
trial, it is doubtful if anyone, including the patient himself,
knew exactly who it was who either escaped or was discharged into a world which must surely have become alien.

Mary Rago was the name given as his sister in the document filed by the assistant district attorney in 1960. But
the 1937 report filed by the Lunacy Commission consisting
of one doctor referred over and over again to a sister named
Muriel . . . and of course Amelia Earhart had a sister named
Muriel whom Viola Gentry said she called Amelia occasionally by mistake.

Could well-meaning and dedicated psychiatrists have convinced a man that it was all an hallucination? . . . that he was
not the person he believed himself to be? Is an insane man
less certain of his sanity than a sane man? Could twenty-
five years of hospitalization convince a navigator, possibly
half-crazed from a crash injury already, that he was not a

navigator at all? . . . that he had never been terrorized by sharks or abominably mistreated by men of a different color than his own . . . but that indeed he was merely a janitor, father of eight, from a fictitious home in the Bronx, who had been arrested once in his life for one dishonest act and stashed behind bars and padded walls for a quarter of a century?

Could a psychiatrist in a hospital for the criminally insane believe a patient who, for instance, kept repeating, "I'm Fred Noonan, chief navigator for Pan American Airways, and navigator around the world with Amelia Earhart, who is a prisoner of the Emperor of Japan"? Would a psychiatrist or nurse in a mental hospital believe a patient who talked like that? Or would they administer therapy and shock treatment year after year after year with professional patience until the poor man himself came to believe his true identity and background were but figments of a sick mind? Could Wilbur Rothar finally be released into the care of a concerned woman, himself convinced at last that he was indeed Wilbur Rothar?

Who was that concerned woman and why was she concerned? Where had she been for twenty-five years? In the 1937 lunacy report, who was the woman referred to as Muriel? The Municipal Lodging House in the Bowery in 1964 referred to a sister named *Doris.* In 1959 the director of Harlem Valley State Hospital had recommended that the man known as Rothar be released into the custody of a sister named *Mary* Rago. What was the real name of the mysterious woman who continued to appear as rescuer for this grievously wronged man?

Was it Amelia Earhart?

The psychiatric report on Wilbur Rothar would appear, with its details of rape and sodomy and cannibalism, to be the ravings of a madman except for two startling things. No less than eight times Dr. Lonnardo recorded the alleged extortionist to have stated, "The Boiler was blown up by ammunition." It probably seemed to the psychiatrist to be a reference to the boiler of Rothar's fictitious gun-running ship. But to Gervais and me it seemed more likely that "the Boiler" referred to by Rothar was the same one referred to in a letter from Philip L. Juergens, public relations director of Lockheed Aircraft Corporation, on December 23, 1964.

"Nicknamed 'The Boiler,' the XC-35 made its first flight May 7, 1937," Juergens wrote in response to a query from Gervais about the type of aircraft we believed Amelia Earhart to have been actually flying instead of her own when she photographed the Japanese naval base under construction on Truk. The ammunition which blew it up would be Japanese ammunition from fighter planes launched from the Imperial aircraft carrier *Akagi* on its intercept mission near Hull Island, accurately mapped and positioned by Rothar as what the psychiatrist understood him to pronounce as "Harl Island."

Dr. Robert Townsley of Oakland in 1968 located an XC-35 (or UC-35, as he has a habit of referring to the plane we ourselves identify as the U-1), which survived the prototype shot down at Hull Island on July 2, 1937. Townsley found the one delivered to the Army Air Corps in August, 1937, under reconstruction in an out-of-the-way warehouse of the Smithsonian Institution in Washington. Townsley, researcher of the disappearance of Amelia Earhart, fed great quantities of meticulously gathered information about the Lockheed 10E and the aviatrix's flying habits into a computer at Stanford Research Institute, seeking an answer to the mystery. Perhaps not so scientifically, he also obtained from her sister Muriel Morrissey a bed jacket that had belonged to Amelia Earhart. Jacqueline Cochran helped him get the bed jacket, which Townsley then submitted to various seers and mediums at ESP sessions and seances in an effort to make the dead reveal in person what had happened to them.

Others have been looking for Amelia Earhart. A group headed by Don Kothera of Cleveland, Ohio, made a couple of expeditions to Saipan and, like Fred Goerner, returned with a bag of burned bones and a few pieces of airplane metal. Dr. J. B. Davidson, a Canton, Ohio, veterinarian, both wrote and published the "findings" of this group in a privately printed 1969 volume called *Amelia Earhart Returns from Saipan*. In it, Raymond S. Baby, D.Sc., curator of archaeology for the Ohio Historical Society, and his associate, Martha A. Potter, concluded that the 188 small fragments which were "ninety-eight percent . . . completely burnt" were the cremated remains "of a female, probably white individual between the anatomical ages of 40–42 years."

"A gold bridge between the first permanent pre-molar (Pml) and the first permanent molar(M1) to replace an extracted permanent second pre-molar(Pm2)" and an amalgam filling were of a small size "within range of a female individual," according to Dr. Baby.

Russell E. Belous, curator of Western History at the Los Angeles County Museum of Natural History, commented on the technique for identifying human remains, a subject in which he majored at UCLA. "The most interesting thing about Dr. Baby's report is that scientifically it is largely incorrect," Belous said. "The sex of an individual cannot be determined by bits of burned bones nor by the size of teeth or dental work. Many women have large bones and teeth. Many men have small bones and teeth."

Dr. Sheila Brooks, an eminent anthropologist at Nevada State University who is one of the nation's leading authorities on the study of human remains, was disturbed that Kothera's bag of bone bits was not submitted to any of the anthropologists who specialize in that science. "Prior to the Second World War the Japanese imitated the United States widely in two things," she commented. "They imitated our eyeglasses and our dental work. Oriental and South Pacific native bones, of course, are most often smaller than those of Western man."

In 1962 when Fred Goerner had brought back a similar bag of bones, it took an anthropologist only twenty-four hours to prove they did not belong to Amelia Earhart. At that time, Goerner received an unsolicited letter from the last dentist known to have looked into her mouth.

"On the day before Amelia Earhart (Mrs. Putnam) started on this flight I removed an upper right third molar for her . . . . I do remember . . . that she had a full complement of teeth from the upper left cuspid to upper right third molar, and I am sure from my recollection that she had a full complement of teeth from the lower left cuspid to the lower right second molar. The third molar was missing," reported Dr. Horace L. Cartee, D.D.S., F.A.C.D., of Miami, Florida.

The bridgework brought back in the Kothera expedition's bag of burnt bones simply did not match Amelia Earhart's teeth as described by her oral surgeon.

Goerner himself still occasionally demands a Congressional investigation into the Earhart disappearance, although not so loudly insisting that her bones lie deposited along with Fred Noonan's in the National Archives at Washington.

Ann H. Pellegreno, who in 1967 in a Lockheed 10E just like Amelia Earhart's retraced the flight around the world to "prove" that the flyers simply missed Howland Island in 1937 and crashed at sea, has since contacted us regarding the Saipan survival reports. In the book she is writing she will apparently not be so certain of the crash-at-sea theory, which after all was only a theory from the very beginning.

Elmer H. Dimity, Amelia Earhart's close friend and advisor in Oakland, has sought on several occasions to mount expeditions into the Pacific to look for his old friend, whom he never believed to have died at all.

There may be as many books about what happened to Amelia Earhart as there are about Custer's Last Stand, where no witnesses survived. But there will never be another investigation like Operation Earhart.

It was Joe Gervais who climbed a mountain in California to find the wreckage of a plane supposed to be at the bottom of the Pacific Ocean. It was Gervais who brought Mrs. Guy Bolam out of seclusion long enough to take her photograph for an orthopedic surgeon, Dr. Martin W. Payne, to study. And it was Gervais who broke the code which made the name Guy Bolam reveal in degrees and minutes the exact location of a beach on Hull Island.

From time to time, Bob Dinger lent moral support, and I helped him a little with research, but Gervais is the man who fell in love with a "dead" woman and pursued her ghost until it came alive.

Those of us who dashingly call our efforts "Operation Earhart" have learned a lot about the world of the thirties, and in so doing accumulated considerable knowledge of today's world ... for it is much the same world. And we entered a nether world of subterranean adventure and intrigue to learn a great deal about who really runs the world for good or for bad. But there are some things we never learned.

How do you make a woman, or any other private citizen, talk unless she chooses to do so?

How do you check a person's identity when there are no legal documents or fingerprints?

Perhaps the press of the world, armed with the information and evidence uncovered by Operation Earhart, may accomplish what remains to be accomplished to erase the last vestige of doubt about what happened to our lady of mystery. But meanwhile, we agree with the most elusive Mrs. Guy Bolam that "Amelia Earhart has not passed away completely so long as there is one person alive who still remembers her."

That one person called me again in the middle of the other night.

"I've got a new phone number," Gervais reported excitedly as I rubbed the sleep from my eyes.

"What new number?"

"Our lady of mystery . . . I've found her again — and this time she may talk."

Perhaps. But only one thing is as certain as the sun:

Joe Gervais is on your trail, Amelia. There's no use trying to die, for he'll follow you wherever you go, and as long as he shall live, you shall live.